RURAL DEVELOPMENT:
WORLD FRONTIERS

RURAL DEVELOPMENT: WORLD FRONTIERS

Laurence Isley Hewes

VISITING FELLOW
CENTER FOR THE STUDY OF DEMOCRATIC INSTITUTIONS

THE IOWA STATE UNIVERSITY PRESS / AMES, IOWA

1 9 7 4

LAURENCE HEWES, recognized authority on rural development, has had a distinguished career as agricultural economist on regional, national, and international levels for the United States Department of Agriculture, Farm Security Administration, Allied Occupation of Japan, United States Agency for International Development, Planning and Development Collaborative International, World Bank, United Nations Development Programme, and the Food and Agriculture Organization of the United Nations. He holds the B.Sc. degree from Dartmouth College, the M.P.A. degree from Harvard University, and the Ph.D. degree from George Washington University. His publications include books, pamphlets, and journal articles on such subjects as land reform programs in Japan, natural resources allocation for outdoor recreation, land tenure, and rural development. He is presently serving as Visiting Fellow for the Center for the Study of Democratic Institutions.

© 1974 The Iowa State University Press
Ames, Iowa 50010. All rights reserved

Composed and printed by
The Iowa State University Press

First edition, 1974

Library of Congress Cataloging in Publication Data
Hewes, Laurence Ilsley, 1902–
    Rural development: world frontiers.

    "Several chapters of this book are heavily dependent on papers prepared for a Conference on Expanding World Needs for Food and Fiber and the Protection of the Ecosystem at the Center for the Study of Democratic Institutions (CSDI), Santa Barbara, California, August 9–13, 1971."
    Bibliography: p.
    1. Underdeveloped areas—Agriculture. 2. International economic integration. 3. Rehabilitation, Rural. I. Conference on Expanding World Needs for Food and Fiber and the Protection of the Ecosystem, Center for the Study of Democratic Institutions, 1971. II. Title.
HD1417.H47   338.1'09172'4   74-5199
ISBN 0-8138-1480-4

TO REX TUGWELL

CONTENTS

ACKNOWLEDGEMENTS	ix
INTRODUCTION	xi
Chapter I: FOOD AND THE ENVIRONMENT	3
Soils	8
Water	13
Nitrogen	20
Chapter II: THE GREEN REVOLUTION	22
The New Genetics	25
Fertilizer Requirements	27
Pesticides and Herbicides	30
Research Requirements	31
Effects on Environment	32
Chapter III: SOCIAL CHANGE AND THE NEW TECHNOLOGY	34
Traditional Rural System	34
Problems	38
Modernization of Agriculture	43
Effects of the Green Revolution	45
Second-Generation Problems	47
Objective	50
Impact on Environment	54
Chapter IV: POLITICAL AND ADMINISTRATIVE ASPECTS OF RURAL DEVELOPMENT	58
Role of Political Leaders	63
Administrative Arrangements	65
Functional Dispersion of Government Services	67
Quality of Administrative Personnel	68
Allocation of Resources	71
Political Systems	75
Latin America	75

East Africa	76
India	78
Chapter V: INTEGRATION OF RURAL AND URBAN PLANNING	82
Rural Character of Emerging Nations	82
Integrated Rural Development	84
Traditional Approach	84
The New Model	87
Regional Approach	89
Strategic Aspects	92
Chapter VI: INTERNATIONAL DEVELOPMENT ASSISTANCE	94
Resource Transfer to LDC Agriculture	95
Financial Aid to Agriculture	97
Efficiency of Assistance	100
Question of Reform	103
Assistance Institutions and Rural Manpower	106
Assistance and International Trade	110
Chapter VII: INTERNATIONAL STRUCTURE FOR RURAL DEVELOPMENT	113
Trade Concessions	115
Prospects for Reorientation of Agricultural Export Products	117
Efforts to Promote Regional Economic Integration	119
Latin America	120
Asia	122
Africa	124
Evaluation of Efforts toward Regional Integration	127
Chapter VIII: AN ALTERNATE PROPOSAL FOR REGIONAL INTEGRATION	130
Lower Mekong Basin	133
Amazon Basin	138
Congo Basin	141
Chapter IX: ROLE OF ENERGY IN LDCs	144
Energy Needs for Rural Development	145
On-Farm Energy Utilization	148
Energy and Water in Agriculture	152
Rice Production	155
Arid Regions	157
Prospects	162
NOTES	165
BIBLIOGRAPHY	173
INDEX	181

ACKNOWLEDGEMENTS

SEVERAL CHAPTERS OF THIS BOOK are heavily dependent on papers prepared for a conference on Expanding World Needs for Food and Fiber and the Protection of the Ecosystem at the Center for the Study of Democratic Institutions (CSDI), Santa Barbara, California, August 9–13, 1971. These conferees were:

MARTIN E. ABEL, Professor, Department of Agriculture and Applied Economics, University of Minnesota.

LESTER R. BROWN, Senior Fellow, Overseas Development Council, Washington, D.C.

JONATHON GARST (dec.), Author, Berkeley, Calif.; former agricultural consultant to the U.S., the U.S.S.R., Romania, Poland, and India.

NORTON GINSBURG, Dean, CSDI, Professor of Geography and Associate Dean for Social Science, University of Chicago.

CHARLES HARDIN, Professor of Political Science, University of California at Davis.

EARL O. HEADY, Curtiss Distinguished Professor and Director, Center for Agricultural and Economic Development, Iowa State University.

LAURENCE HEWES, Visiting Fellow, CSDI.

JIMMYE S. HILLMAN, Head, Department of Agricultural Economics, University of Arizona; former President, American Agricultural Economics Association.

W. DAVID HOPPER, President, Canadian International Development Center, Ottawa.

D. GALE JOHNSON, Dean, Department of Economics, University of Chicago.

CHARLES E. KELLOGG, Deputy Administrator, Soil Conservation Service, U.S. Department of Agriculture.

EMIL MRAK, Chancellor Emeritus, University of California at Davis.

DEAN F. PETERSON, Dean, College of Engineering, Utah State University.

LORD RITCHIE-CALDER, M.P., Senior Fellow, CSDI.

THEODORE W. SCHULTZ, Professor Emeritus of Economics, University of Chicago.

PERRY R. STOUT, Professor of Soils and Plant Nutrition, University of California at Davis.

REXFORD G. TUGWELL, Senior Fellow, CSDI; former Undersecretary of Agriculture; former Governor of Puerto Rico.

Planning for this conference began in the fall of 1970 under the general guidance of Rexford G. Tugwell; Charles Hardin developed the conference outline and served as conference chairman.

I wish to thank Planning and Development Collaborative International (Padco) of Washington, D.C., for permission to use material on the integration of rural and urban planning (Chapter 5) originally prepared by me for the Third Annual Padco Seminar, Washington, D.C., September, 1969. The Center for the Study of Democratic Institutions has given me permission to use material on rural uses of energy (Chapter 9) originally prepared for its Conference on Energy Policies and the International System held at Santa Barbara, California, December 4–7, 1973; my thanks particularly for this permission to Elisabeth Mann Borgese.

INTRODUCTION

THE PROSPECTS FOR MEETING INcreased food and fiber needs of a mounting world population divides into two main subtopics: (1) capacity of the environment to bear increased pressures of an intensified agriculture, (2) human capacity to increase agricultural output within environmental limitations. Our argument identifies critical problems as located principally in the less developed and largely rural regions of Asia, Africa, and South America—the so-called Third World.

Evidence supports the conclusion that physical resources of solar energy, land, water, atmosphere, and climate—when properly managed—provide favorable prospects for the foreseeable future. However, important obstacles to be overcome involve the human condition: lack of initiative, ill health, malnutrition, ignorance, and an exploitive distribution system. We suggest an attack on these obstacles should be accompanied by efforts at regional economic integration and international cooperative effort directed toward development of large natural resources regions.

Our discussion does not claim to be research, nor is it essentially analytical. Our point of departure was the conference at the Center for the Study of Democratic Institutions, Santa Barbara, California, in August 1971, to discuss the combined subjects of world population growth, expanding world needs for food and fiber, and environmental consequences. In some ways the conference was unique; it was not a debate among opposing points of view but rather a prolonged conversation among knowledgeable people with similar points of view. Participants, in addition to the Center Fellowship, were fifteen specialists in agriculture and rural conditions, all of whom had spent time in the less developed countries (LDCs). The disciplines included soil science, water, chemistry, political science, agricultural economics, rural development, and international trade.

Substantial portions of the ensuing presentation are based on material from that conference. Other portions, particularly the last five chapters, reflect this writer's views and biases, modified and altered by the views of others.

The people of Asia, Africa, and South America make up a majority of the world population. They are predominantly rural and very poor. Their birth rates are high and their productivity is low. They are plagued by massive and increasing unemployment. By all prevailing standards their diet and clothing are inadequate. Low caloric and protein-poor food results in low energy, malnutrition, susceptibility to disease, high infant mortality, and short life expectancy. At the same time the population growth is rapid. Thus the LDC human condition, taking into account low levels of welfare among large portions of the world population, leaves much to be desired. The human brotherhood across the global expanse exists neither comfortably nor happily. There is also an appalling contrast in material welfare between opulent and poor regions.

Improvement in this condition requires concerted action on a very large scale. An initial point of attack is to raise levels of agricultural production among these poorer countries. This will also involve efforts at rural development aimed at improving the quality of rural living. The challenge is not only to achieve higher input-output ratios but also to maintain these at levels increasingly above the rate of population growth.

It is our contention—perhaps our bias—that obstacles to LDC rural development are primarily man-made; they are not inherent in the environment. The behavior of these rural people arises out of their condition. Lack of access to resources, uneven distribution of product, economic stagnation, high birth rates, unemployment, and lack of purchasing power are the results of socioeconomic structures and institutions. A corollary of this belief is that sustained LDC rural development is incompatible with extremes of economic, political, and social inequity. This view does not deny existence of physical constraints to increased agricultural output but holds that, so far, science and technology have not been able to overcome these constraints, and there is the further prospect that scientific and technical inputs will be reduced. Failure to fully exploit innovative potentials arises more often in a socioeconomic context than from any deficiency in natural resources. The ills that beset LDC rural populations are results, not causes.

One might conclude (and of course some do) that these conditions exist because LDC rural people do not know any better or are unaware of their misfortunes. On the contrary, our bias suggests that these disadvantaged people know very well where they stand. In the past this state of awareness might have been less prevalent; today these folks know about our luxuries, comforts, and amenities, and they have avid appetites for a better existence. Out of this discontent political leaders fashion revolutionary appeals on the right and on the left. A sense of deprivation and injury probably lies close to the core of much LDC politics, and inherent in such appeals is sharp-edged hostility toward more developed nations.

Westerners are sometimes puzzled about their unpopularity in the Third World, but they should not be surprised when their goodwill and benevolent intentions seem misjudged. They should realize that today few people anywhere do not know about Cadillacs, air-conditioning, television, fine apparel, and pleasant living. What many in the West do not seem to grasp is the significance of the welfare gap separating the two worlds. They do not comprehend the impact on LDC rural masses of charismatic leaders and wielders of power whose dialectic argues that western influence is based on LDC deprivation, past and present.

Offsetting this propensity is a belief—possibly only another bias—that despite occasional outbursts of mass hysteria, individual human behavior in everyday affairs is essentially rational. And this holds for rural people in Asia, Africa, and South America. Of course ignorance sometimes drastically affects the outcome of decisions, but this occurs too among better-informed people. More particularly, however, competent observers have long held that LDC farmers deal efficiently with such factual knowledge as they possess.

Today we must reckon with a post–World War II spread of sophistication and knowledge about the artifacts of the affluent societies reaching to the farthest LDC village. These villagers are aware of what they are missing, and they do not like it. Henceforth their aspirations will include achievement of a chance to share these benefits. Next year there will be more of these discontented people. While in small ways some of these aspirations will be satisfied, these gains will only whet appetites for more and this insistence will be harder to allay.

The first phase of this aspirational process will be reflected in demands that can be met by greater outputs of food and fiber. But there will be an accompanying demand for better quality of product. Some observers have contemplated these prospective LDC demands with misgivings. They ask questions about the adequacy of physical resources to bear the increased pressure, about the adequacy of agricultural technology, and about potential environmental damage from more advanced technology. It is also pointed out that recent experience with agricultural innovation and its diffusion among rural people in the LDCs has had some negative repercussions. Perhaps these questions should be interpreted to mean only that the task is big, complex, and difficult—not that it should not be ventured.

It is unfortunate that so much of our technology for agriculture and rural improvement is oriented toward existing problems. It is an ex post technology; problems have to exist before they are attacked. Very little technology if any is devoted to the solution of problems before they occur. Thus problems are not visualized in all their implications but rather bit by bit. Each solution is partial and can become the parent of new difficulties, and too often solutions are discovered for problems already passing into a different phase. Attention is needed now to reveal potential technological solutions for the tide of rising aspirations among the vast rural populations of the poorer regions.

The LDCs have an estimated aggregate current population of about 2.5 billion in a world population of 3.5 billion. The world's arable land area is estimated at 3.5 billion acres; pasture and grazing lands probably amount to another 7 billion acres. However, double-cropping, reclamation, irrigation, and technological advances combined set very elastic limits to available land resources. Some estimates go as high as the equivalent of 17 billion acres available within fifty years.

By the year 2000 LDC populations may exceed 5 billion if the current annual growth rate is maintained at 2.5 percent. In contrast, developed region population growth may be declining. Some projections are for a year 2000 world population between 6 and 7 billion, of which 4–5 billion would be in the LDCs; with estimates based on undiminished LDC population growth, these regions could have a population of 7 billion or more by 2030.

Contemplation of these population estimates has caused predictions of mass starvation. A happier view suggests that modern history is not a record to justify approaching secular starvation. Catastrophic famines have occurred in Asia on several occasions, and a similar tragedy threatened India for several years beginning in 1965. But these disasters followed crop failures due to drought. They were not the result of excessive population but of inadequate rainfall. Suffering would have occurred in these regions regardless of the size of the resident population. The "rivers of sorrow" around the world, with their recurrent devastating floods, have contributed their share of human misery as torrential rainfall flooded millions of acres of cropland. But these floods were not caused by population; population merely stood in the path of disaster.

A phenomenon associated with drought and flood is an almost universal failure to accept the moral of the seven full years and the seven lean years. Perhaps our belief in the human propensity for rational decision-making must be qualified by man's limited memory span and inability to take full account of potential natural disaster. Otherwise, how can we account for the American custom of locating industrial, commercial, and residential structures on floodplains of rivers and waterways of proven hydrologic instability? It seems that famine from both forms of climatic disaster—flood and drought—results from inadequate measures taken to avert it. In Asia there has been inadequate infrastructure to mobilize surplus harvest for carry-over to lean years as well as inadequate measures to provide protection against frequent monsoon floods. Neither case provides evidence to support a thesis of an inevitable human *Götterdämmerung*.

Nevertheless, we should take these gloomy predictions into account. We should guard against a tendency to base action on ex post considerations, and we should regard seriously man's propensity for perverse collective decisions.

The central issue is still to upgrade production levels of LDC agriculture. Prevailing levels are low and cannot achieve the 3.9 percent annual food demand increase projections of the FAO Indicative World Plan (IWP) without a quantum jump. Thus higher producer input levels are needed along with increased ability to absorb innovative technology. If achieved, these will be the result of farmer decisions; their calculations will be influenced by the incentive of greater payoff. And prospective payoffs must seem achievable within constraints of risk, energy, and availability of inputs. It is important too that the additional output be socially useful. It should not consist exclusively of traditional high-starch, protein-poor subsistence crops. Moreover, the crop increment should be marketable; this implies a marketing infrastructure now absent or deficient in many LDCs. Transition on a large scale must take place as farmers gradually move out of subsistence-oriented agriculture into market- and cash-oriented production where increased volume is of higher quality. More specifically, the IWP focus is on increased output of cereal crops with high protein content—principally rice and wheat. While the LDCs produce a number of fiber crops, the principal concentration there will be on cotton. Increases in the volume of production of animal protein may involve some feed grains which only emphasizes the critical importance of grain crops. Such considerations have already been incorporated in the agricultural production strategy of a number of the LDCs.

One need not be a committed environmentalist or a follower of the Club of Rome philosophy to perceive that expanding agricultural output puts pressure on the ecosystem. More and more catalysts will have to be employed to more efficiently utilize solar energy, including chemical fertilizers and pesticides. More land will be irrigated, and land will be cultivated more extensively. In some areas new lands will come under cultivation and grazing. As successively higher output levels are reached, so will the original environment be progressively altered.

All these changes involve costs—not only perceptible input costs but less apparent costs of environmental drains which should be offset. A principal long-range problem is how to maximize energy-transforming agricultural procedures without degrading the environment through improper use and accumulation of nondegradable waste. One solution that suggests itself is advance-planning calculations to determine at successive levels of output the corresponding environmental costs of maintaining those levels. Such an exercise would facilitate estimates of probable carrying capacity of natural resources at specified states of technology and use intensity. These estimates could lead to preparation in advance of steps needed for adequate environmental controls. From the standpoint of its agricultural capacity the environmental system consists of interacting components of solar energy, soil, water, climate, and chemical cycles of the atmosphere. In this view, farming is a process for using the environmental system. But the secret of successful farming is to identify in operational use the appropriate interaction of these components integrated through photosynthesis.

It follows that a great deal of knowledge is required about each of the environmental components and how they interact in given situations. Thus accumulation and spread of knowledge about soil, water, and climate and their interaction become key factors not only in increasing LDC agricultural production but also in maintaining stability of the ecosystem. The costs involved in assembling and spreading this knowledge are chargeable to increased agricultural output distributed between environmental preservation and direct production activities.

These considerations have sometimes been neglected, and the omission has been serious. Improper resource management has already resulted in some dramatic failures. Too often western agricultural specialists have introduced new technology without due allowance for unique environmental conditions in the LDCs. Unfortunately the end of such dismal experiences may not be in sight. New technology with great initial promise is rapidly being introduced. Yet as these advances succeed each other, they tend to form interlocking systems of great power—a case of the whole being greater than the sum of its parts. Moreover, the full dimensions of this technological power complex are not completely known. One possible hazard may be booby traps in the form of negative side effects. Another negative possibility of this evolving technology is irreversibility.

In such circumstances available solutions require more, not less, technology. Changes in agricultural technology effect environmental modifications. These cumulatively create what amounts to an altered environment with different characteristics and dynamics—successive innovational waves create successive ecosystems. Two centuries ago much of the Indus Plain in the Indian subcontinent was a desert with a corresponding ecosystem. Today that plain is a great expanse of irrigated agriculture with greatly altered geographic features. It possesses a new microbiology, a new system of insect life; its soils have been altered as has its drainage system; and it supports many millions more people on an entirely different pattern of vegetation. The people involved had little choice; they had to convert the plain to irrigated agriculture to support the population whose expanding numbers could only be supported by bringing ever more desert under water. So it is that the pressure of necessity denies the LDCs the choice of foregoing innovation; they have to take the risks. The caveat is that the risks be as well defined as possible and to some extent forestalled.

Whatever subsequent risks may prove to be, it seems clear that the LDCs could not and should not have averted the impact of the Green Revolution. On the one hand, they were probably unable to judge its long-range negative potentials; on the other, they had urgent need for the immediate increase in grain yields the new technology promised. So they must endure any deferred long-range environmental costs or somehow deal with them. But for now the Green Revolution represents a massive breakthrough. In these regions farming has moved in one leap from traditional—sometimes primitive—cultural practices into the mainstream of modern agriculture. This new system is dynamic and provides its own parameters. It must be sustained by a continuing stream of innovative technology or the process may regress. Consequently LDC farmers must adjust to ever changing methods and combinations. Expenditures for new inputs and equipment will be increasingly larger over time; farmer efforts must be supported by well-organized research and by a properly trained field extension staff; LDC governments will need to step up their agricultural inputs well above any previous levels.

The Green Revolution may have significant economic and social effects among the LDCs. These effects in the long run may be even more significant than the technological impact. Thus this particular innovation may illustrate the general effect of innovation on the patterns of LDC rural life. Beyond this are further implications for LDC national development policy as well as for their foreign trade and need for overseas assistance.

How very little anyone really knows about the harassed lives of the millions who make up the populations of Asia, Africa, and South America! With rare exception the LDCs themselves possess little real knowledge about their enormous rural constituency. Foreigners have even less insight, and this includes a good many westerners who have lived among people of the LDCs. The stock of knowledge conducive to understanding the beating heart of human existence in the poorer regions of the earth is slender, and such knowledge as exists is often inaccurate and misleading.

Many of us have seen the farmers of these lands. We have watched while they strained to guide clumsy wooden plows across meager fields. We have seen them, clad in cotton drawers or breech clouts, thigh deep in paddy field mud, painstakingly tending young rice plants. Our arms and bodies have ached in sympathy as we observed the laborious efforts to break heavy clods with primitive hand tools. Perhaps some of us have wished we could somehow penetrate the minds that direct these bent, straining, fragile bodies through endless steaming days of toil. But unfortunately our efforts at understanding place us somewhere between guess and conjecture as we return to our desks—our papers and endless reports to satisfy those who understand less than we. As we observe what looks like a changeless pattern of village life, who can say that what we perceive is stability and security or hopeless stagnation? Yet when we endow these peopled scenes with our intuitive bias of rationality in decisions and self-awareness, we may entertain the possibility of underlying organic and dynamic qualities inherent in the LDC rural system.

INTRODUCTION

Once we grant the possibility of these endowments, explanations become possible if not provable. In any event, we can begin with rejection of notions that conceive LDC rural systems as simple. Even at relatively primitive levels the components and linkages that make up rural systems present a formidable complexity. In these systems custom and tradition have significant effects on shaping individual behavior. But customs and traditions preserve for the villagers important illusions of solidarity and security. These institutions and their sanctions may persist long after utility has vanished and so inhibit change. Or, expressed as power structures, they may facilitate exploitation of many by few.

When we understand the extreme degree of their exposure and vulnerability, we may realize that among many LDC rural people the dominant individual motivation is defensive; the primary goal is immediate survival in a complex, danger-fraught universe. So farmers continue to produce principally those protein-poor but dependable and familiar crops along with a minimum of commercial crops. Their energy is limited, so they husband it with low-yielding, energy-conserving practices. Large families and numerous births are designed to insure against infant mortality and to provide old-age assistance. Lack of personal power and extreme dependence on access to land causes acceptance by many LDC farmers of inequitable land tenure and land-rationing institutions. Many of them lack means for acquiring improved seed or fertilizer. They know from experience that landlords or moneylenders would somehow manage to capture any yield increase. Tradition demands profligate expenditures for ceremonial occasions such as marriages and deaths, so many of these farmers are hopelessly debt ridden. The orbit of their lives is circumscribed by the demands of hierarchical superiors, landlords, and moneylenders.

It is against this kind of background that agricultural innovation takes place, and such were the conditions for introduction of high-yielding grain varieties. It is not surprising in these circumstances that the resulting incidence of costs and benefits was quite uneven. Substantial profits accrued to relatively few who were able to grasp and exploit the new opportunity, but ensuing social costs and disability were borne by many. Displacement of farm labor by machinery has been reflected in large and growing rural unemployment. Landlords with machinery found it profitable to dismiss tenants who then became farm laborers or joined the ranks of the unemployed. Thus innovation has increased crop production while widening the gap between those better off and those worse off. Moreover, any other external costs such as potential or actual environmental damage have been passed on to the public in general and the rural population in particular.

Against these negative conclusions is the belief of some observers that innovation, through its disequilibrating effects, brings more sharply into focus the need for reform of the traditional rural system. These observers contend that rural people are quick to appreciate their changed condition and equally quick to resent imposition of the costs of innovations. Their conclusion is that without reforms to alleviate tenant insecurity and unemployment, development may be offset or impeded by rural discontent, disorder, and political tension. Thus reforms may become easier to implement in the changing economic, social, and political climate of innovation; the issues attract more attention and discussion; the public does not wish to see the promise of substantial gain dissipated as a result of landowner intransigence.

The Green Revolution has provided a big increase in LDC food. Probably this increase will continue and may be enlarged. It seems likely that in the next 30 years LDC grain production will stay ahead of population increases. For those with a cash income (industrial workers, workers in service and commercial sectors, government employees, and urban residents generally) food may be available at lower prices. Some LDCs may even accumulate an export surplus.

So far, so good, for those able to purchase food with money. Unhappily, increasing numbers of rural unemployed and low-paid rural workers are broke. Without cash they are not good prospects as consumers of the new grains. Some of them may migrate to cities and there may benefit from government food subsidies. In the long run, however, it seems more likely that the rural sector, with its dominant share of the population, will not be able to absorb a corresponding amount of the new grain increases simply because they do not have the money to buy it. Thus the LDCs (at any rate some of them) may have to contend with aggravated grain surpluses and lowered prices to producers. But it will not be the physical environment that creates the principal problems: the chief cause will be social forms and organization.

What may be definitive among the LDCs in assessing the impact of innovation is the manner of rationing access to natural resources, particularly land and water, along with institutions governing distribution of products and support of producers. Without the incentive of rising incomes, the number of small subsistence farmers might increase, while fewer of them might participate in a market-oriented system. Thus larger farmers would be producing for a relatively restricted, artificially supported market amidst masses of penniless unemployed rural people and subsistence farmers on the edge of existence. It is against this prospect that efforts for economic and political reform should be directed, and these efforts should be built into the policies that further technological innovation in agriculture.

Innovative agricultural technology and improved rural conditions should not be approved separately; a view that contemplates overall rural transformation is needed. Rural development undertakings should be integrated not only in the rural sector but as part of a total planning strategy. There is in reality no separation between urban and rural sectors; the reality is a rural-urban continuum, and the overall strategy is that of urbanizing rurality.

So far, little attention has been paid to development of such a planning strategy. Some plans for LDC rural development discuss infrastructural components such as communications or markets, but these discussions do not make clear that such infrastructural components are significant principally because they provide closer dialogues between urban centers and rural hinterlands. These urban centers and their rural hinterlands constitute regions, and the overall development policy thus becomes regional development. From this standpoint the quality of living involves uniform conditions of employment, production, consumption, and health over a broad socioeconomic landscape.

A better outcome will certainly require better national policies and programs for rural development than now exist. Political leaders should give higher priority to rural development policies and programs. They should envisage, more clearly than they have, their principal role as governing rural constituencies. They should accept as a fact of LDC political life that a healthy and progressive rural sector is essential to national prosperity and stability.

Such a view would call for elevating rural development to first rank in the affairs of state, a position it does not occupy today in many LDCs. As a result, agriculture is a junior government service—inferior to military affairs, international trade, foreign exchange, fiscal policy, commerce, industry, and transportation. Rural government service does not attract abler and brighter recruits; it does not afford a prestigious career.

Neither in developed nor in less developed countries do governments assign high official rank to agriculture, natural resource administration, or rural development. An exception to this is the high rank and confidence accorded the engineering profession. Enormous financial outlays for design and construction of irrigation works and river control systems are entrusted to engineers, alongside neglect of the technology of irrigated farming. Engineers do not deal with farmers; that task is assigned to an inferior service. This shortsighted arrangement has been responsible for the relative inefficiency and failure of some irrigation projects.

Another unfortunate aspect of this inferior rank of agriculture and natural resources is the evolution of a substrata of political and economic alliances among these lesser officials, larger farmers, and regional vested interests. In time this entente becomes a controlling factor in rural society, tending to pursue its unreviewed and unchecked course independent of national policy and official oversight. Occasionally one aspect or another of these lower-rank matters may attract short-lived, top-level attention—such as when an important political ploy requires a *quid pro quo* involving an important dam site, control of large appropriations for natural resources, or the location of an important fertilizer plant. Generally these decisions are made without regard for the technical views of the services involved and thus further serve to emphasize their inferior status. It is not remarkable then that these services often reflect neither high morale nor professional pride. A specific result has been neglect of good on-farm irrigation drainage practices and adequate irrigation advisory services for farmers in newly irrigated areas. Another aspect is sheer neglect of responsibility.

It has been suggested that many LDC political leaders cannot afford to become preoccupied with the long, slow process of rural development. Particularly in the newer countries, these leaders are primarily concerned with maintaining and extending their charisma. They need to be associated with glamorous, prestigious undertakings. Slower-paced, even tedious rural and agricultural affairs seldom afford much glamor. In fairness it is a primary responsibility for many of these leaders to create national political integration. And, like politicians everywhere, their planning horizon is circumscribed by oncoming elections. At the same time, and for somewhat the same reasons, LDC governments are reluctant to establish and impose citizen obligations. Consequently citizenship may not imply responsibility under law. In these circumstances government lacks power and appears weak and inefficient. Gunnar Myrdal in his *Asian Drama* used the term "soft state" to describe the condition among Asian countries seeking to evoke voluntary and cooperative citizen behavior as a substitute for legal and enforceable obligations. Unfortunately this situation is particularly noticeable in the rural sector.

INTRODUCTION   xxiii

Rural development, lying at the center of LDC progress, is singularly dependent on the capacity of government for effective planning and administration; but many of the Third World nations are incapable of mobilizing resources to implement appropriate rural policies even if these were formulated. Since there is no stick, policy becomes a carrot of misplaced subsidies, inappropriate taxation, unsound price policies, poorly designed foreign trade policies, and inequitable income distribution. Other failures include inability to formulate and administer effective tax policy, promote domestic savings (particularly rural savings), and control inflation.

Most critical of all, however, is the failure of LDC government to establish an equitable land tenure system. Without such a system there is little hope in many of the LDCs for the emergence of a prosperous agriculture. In spite of this clear challenge, LDC political leadership has been unable or unwilling to undertake any land reform measures at all or has backed away from vigorous enforcement of such measures as may have been enacted. The entire post–World War II period in many of the LDCs has been a record of inaction or half-hearted and partial evasion of enacted land reform legislation. The result has been to yield increasing power to large landowners, landlords, usurers, and traditional rural elites. In all too many of the LDCs these rural elites rule social and geographic landscapes as self-constituted surrogates of government, including the judicial process. Given this condition, impeding of development remains unaltered; innovation may provide short-run profits for the elites, but rural standards of life do not improve. In South America inequities in land tenures have blocked access to land resources for millions of rural people. Both India and Pakistan have failed to follow through on their initial land reform momentum: they have been faced down by resolute landowner opposition, judicial obfuscation, and long-tolerated evasion. Ethiopian efforts have become obscured in technical detail, landlord intransigence, and political embroilment despite the Emperor's clear land reform mandate. In Central America large tracts are held by nonresident foreigners and retained in an undeveloped condition as purely speculative ventures.

Rural development efforts by the LDCs have been supplemented by transfers of resources by loans and grants from developed countries and from international agencies including the World Bank. Private investor transfers of $6 billion of the 1969 total of $13.5 billion were mainly for petrochemical and mineral development; some $7.5 billion represented official transfers from national and international agencies. It is only in recent years that these official transfers have emphasized rural and agricultural development. The largest official contributors have been the World Bank and the U.S. Agency for International Development (USAID). In the aggregate these overseas transfers have represented about 20 percent of the total LDC development investment. However, overseas transfers may have had greater weight than this percentage indicates, because they increased substantially LDC access to scarce foreign exchange. This is highly significant because it is the means by which the LDCs obtain the instruments and technology of innovation and development.

A number of criticisms have been made in the course of two decades of operation of these official overseas assistance programs. (1) Binational donor programs are geared to specific foreign policy of the donor country, and recipients sometimes feel they are being used as pawns in cold war strategy. (2) Donors sometimes "tie" their advances, restricting purchases of equipment, machinery, and other merchandise to donor country manufacturers; this raises costs to recipients. In such cases recipients feel that resulting donor country profits and employment are at their expense. (3) A substantial amount of overseas assistance from both binational and international agencies is represented by personal services of high-salaried foreign technicians who receive other emoluments well above domestic standards. This has been the cause of jealousy, particularly in instances where foreign professional or technician attitudes are incompatible with those of the host country. (4) These expatriates often do not stay long enough to obtain a real insight into the country or its needs, and some of them are not very competent.

Overseas assistance programs have been extensively reviewed in the Pearson, Jackson, and Peterson reports (named after the principal official responsible for the report: Lester Pearson of Canada, Sir Robert Jackson of the United Kingdom, and Rudolph Peterson of the United States). These reports say that (1) the UN system is hampered in its assistance efforts by inadequate support from the "have" nations and this support is declining; (2) LDCs face increasing difficulties in meeting loan repayments and from high interest rates, partly because their need is for longer-term "soft" loans at low interest rates and grants and partly because of barriers to the exports on which they are dependent for foreign exchange; (3) the efficiency of UN assistance programs, particularly the Development Programme, is not very high; and (4) U.S. civil assistance programs should be completely divorced from military assistance operations, and more dependence should be placed on the international agencies.

None of these three panels undertook to discuss LDC institutions and power structures which inhibit development and reduce the worth of foreign assistance. In the absence of this kind of discussion the thrust of the reports is that LDC development is mainly a question of efficient technical assistance and larger transfers on easier terms. Yet, for reasons indicated above, it is possible to argue that these advances—unless accompanied by appropriate social, political, and economic change from within the LDCs—may actually inhibit rural development.

United States assistance missions have been reluctant to support land reform in spite of favorable experience in Japan, Taiwan, and South Korea. Persistent American emphasis on free enterprise and the merits of private business ventures as viable instruments of development does not show much appreciation for or understanding of the working of rural power structures. Fortunately the World Bank and the three regional banks of Asia, Africa, and Latin America seem to be aware of need for equitable land tenure as a basis for increased agricultural output. They also do not hesitate to discuss with potential recipients the need for increased capacity for mobilizing resources, including rural savings. Perhaps as these institutions grow in prestige and the volume of their transactions increases, they may become more influential in helping to create a climate more favorable to rural development.

All foreign assistance agencies should become acutely aware that LDC rural progress depends almost as much on *removal* of man-made obstacles to rural progress as on *increased* input flows. They need to pay attention to burning issues of reform. Neglect of these issues will frustrate rural progress throughout the Third World. Conventional forms of assistance without change in the underlying conditions will not do the job. Nor will answers come from undue concentration on urban and industrial development. These sectors are dependent on increased food and fiber from indigenous production and on supplies purchased with foreign exchange earnings earned largely by exported agricultural products. More importantly, industrial and commercial development depends on vigorous rural demand.

The LDCs must increase their foreign trade. It is foreign trade that provides an essential component for a stable agriculture, the foundation of rural development. In the long run, cumulative advances from overseas lenders must be paid in hard currencies, and these have to be earned through exports. Foreign lenders, whether in capitalist or socialist blocs, do not relish, any more than the LDCs, the propsect of having to maintain a permanent financial dependency. Down the road somewhere there has to be a cutoff of further loans.

And grants alone will never fill the development gap. Moreover, if the World Bank and the three regional banks become the dominant official sources of development investment, they will need to sell an increasing number of their bonds in world markets. It is essential that their credit standing remain high as evidenced by a good collection record.

Some of the LDCs will be able to shift foreign exchange earnings from mineral sources to rural development; others do not have this option. In any event, most exports from these countries tend to be low-priced raw materials; imports are higher-priced finished goods; the inherent price differential spells a chronic unfavorable balance of trade. Another drawback to export trade in agricultural commodities originating under a preceding colonial system is that today's producers of these commodities may find the shifts from colonial to independent political status have not altered their economic prospects or the condition of their lives. Thus continued national dependence on this mode of production may tend to maintain rural conditions inconsistent with freedom and equity.

Treading the intricate pathways of international trade is an endless, laborious task for the responsible officials of the poorer countries. They realize that what they have to sell abroad—often duplicated by other poor countries—is subject to wide, uncontrollable, often disastrous price fluctuations (such as those affecting coffee, sisal, and jute in recent years). These sharp swings can disrupt national plans and policies, and there is little room for preventing or offsetting them. Some LDCs benefit from bilateral trade preferences from former colonial parents such as members of the British Commonwealth or the French Community. An extension of this relationship conveys a sort of fringe association with the European Common Market. But such foreign trade symbolizes a frustrating degree of dependence—a poor substitute for historical colonial status.

These constraints on LDC rural development are not likely to be relaxed. In general LDCs may face a long-term decline in overseas demand for their agricultural products, caused partly by a long-range decrease in population growth of the importing regions. Moreover, these regions may become increasingly self-sufficient either by producing more commodities themselves or by the introduction of synthetic substitutes. Also, demand for food is relatively inelastic; per capita consumption of tea, coffee, cocoa, and tobacco will not change very much even though incomes rise in affluent regions.

It has been proposed that the affluent nations establish a deliberate policy of favoring LDC imports and that this concessional trade be distributed in some sort of planned fashion among importers and exporters. This would enable LDCs to count on a minimum level of foreign exchange earnings, perhaps enough to ease some of their debt service problems on their overseas obligations. Unfortunately this would more or less institutionalize LDC dependent status. On the other hand, importing nations would have to walk a fine line, balancing between foreign imports and competitive domestic production.

The LDCs must somehow break entirely new ground. If they were bold enough they might create an entirely new international trade configuration within and between the three LDC continents. Out of such a configuration it is conceivable that existing economic dependency could be reduced. Simultaneously the principle of comparative advantage might work to produce entirely new patterns of regional specialization.

Regional economic integration is not a new idea. It has been developed and expounded by the UN regional economic commissions but somehow has never caught fire. Results so far have been discouraging. In Southeast Asia regional trade groups have been formed but more or less as satellites of Japanese foreign trade. The Latin American Free Trade Association has an unimpressive record; the experience of the Central American Common Market is slightly more encouraging. African progress has been slow and uncertain. For a while the East African Community organization of Kenya, Uganda, and Tanzania seemed promising until tensions arose between Uganda and Tanzania. No progress has been made toward establishing intercontinental economic integration, although such arrangements as the International Coffee Agreement may be a useful preliminary to more definitive cooperation.

Undoubtedly there will be protracted stubborn opposition to efforts at regional economic integration, both within and between the countries of the three continents. Extremely sensitive national pride as well as ideological differences and aspirations will have to be taken into account. So far, principal stumbling blocks have been (1) vested interests of trading and commercial groups unwilling to modify existing preferences and protections, (2) reluctance of stronger nations to share domestic markets with smaller and weaker neighbors, (3) the ingrained distrust by smaller and weaker nations of larger, more advanced countries, (4) uneven grades and standards of products and uneven stages of production and marketing efficiency among LDC nations, and (5) lack of any institutional structure to perform the necessary functions. Some countries seek to increase their share of conventional export trade by price manipulation and export subsidies which can result in sharp declines in world prices with overall loss exceeding any gains. The very lack of order in LDC trade relations may provide an opportunity to develop interregional economic integration.

Little attention has been paid to another great opportunity for LDC economic integration—creation of regional authorities to develop major natural resources, among them several great river basins. In each of the three continents great areas of unexploited resources serve only as physical barriers. These great geographical systems have an inherent natural unity; they do not respect political boundaries. Their promise is international in scope. Such systems include the Congo, the Amazon, and the Brahmaputra. They should be planned and developed as complete units. Development plans along political lines would greatly diminish their potential benefits while entailing enormous costs and possibly irreversible damage. One example is the long train of crises and astronomical capital costs following the division of Indus Basin water and lands between India and Pakistan along the Partition lines. In contrast, a more hopeful potential for large parts of Southeast Asia is the plan for integrated development of the Lower Mekong.

In all these situations, human decisions and actions determine the outcome and thus the volume and distribution of the product of the natural environment.

RURAL DEVELOPMENT:
WORLD FRONTIERS

I

Food and the Environment

FARMING IS A PROCEDURE FOR trapping the energy of the environment, primarily solar energy, and transforming it into food and fiber. Soil, moisture, the atmosphere, microbiological populations, and climate have important complementary functions in this process. Photosynthesis, operating through solar energy, combines a number of chemical elements into living plant tissue and plants which feed mankind.

Thus projections of mankind's food and fiber needs become specifications for increasing pressure on the environment roughly proportional to the dimensions of the population. The problem of human survival is to continually expand food production without impairing the capacity of the environment.

By the year 2000 the world population may nearly double, and the projected 7 billion world population should be eating over 14 billion kilocalories and about 435,000 metric tons of protein per day.[1] This would double the 1965 world caloric intake rate and more than double the 1965 protein intake. To meet these anticipated nutrition levels, the production of wheat will have to increase 134 percent, rice 120 percent, and other cereals about 100 percent. The needed annual output by 2000 in millions of metric tons would be: wheat 430, rice 521, and other cereals 285.[2] These increases will largely arise among people in the less developed countries (LDCs). Pressing food problems exist and will continue in Asia, Africa, and Latin America where nutrition levels are low and population growth rapid.

The projected increase in food needs is a principal reason for maintaining a relatively stable and peaceful world over the next three decades. Failure to achieve these levels means that large segments of the world's population will be undernourished and unable to do the work of development. Moreover, gaps between rich and poor countries will widen perhaps to such an extent that they cannot be bridged by any conventional strategies.

> The prevention of malnutrition throughout the world through the provision of adequate diets for a rapidly expanding population is a task of staggering proportions. Solution of this problem is perhaps the greatest challenge facing nations of the world today. In the less developed countries, it was estimated in the Third World Food Survey of FAO that at least 20 percent of the population was undernourished (received too few calories) and about 60 percent received diets inadequate in nutritional quality. Protein-calorie malnutrition which affects preschool children primarily is the most widespread nutritional deficiency. Malnutrition causes retardation of physical growth and development, and recent evidence strongly suggests that mental development may be impaired also. For the malnourished child, mortality and morbidity are extremely high and the common infectious diseases are catastrophic.
>
> Nutrition has a vital role in the health of adults as well as children and profoundly influences socio-economic and cultural development. Malnutrition leads to deterioration of physical fitness and mental efficiency, to emotional and personality disturbances, and to reduction in the capacity to perform work.
>
> The most urgent needs in less developed countries are an increased supply of calories and good quality protein. In some areas specific vitamin and mineral deficiencies are prevalent and foods furnishing these nutrients must be made available. Anemias, endemic goiter (iodine deficiency) and xerophthalmia (vitamin A deficiency) are frequently encountered while beri-beri (thiamine deficiency) and aribo-flavinosis are observed in some countries.[3]

The world food problem is not new. It has long been a subject for study and discussion. Action, however, has been something else. Twenty-five years ago Lord Boyd-Orr, first Director General of FAO, complained, "The people are crying out for bread and we are going to give them pamphlets." His disciple, Lord Ritchie-Calder, equally frustrated with the gap between knowledge and implementation, declares:

> We know a great deal more about proteins, even their molecular structure. We know a great deal more about amino acids and about intermediate metabolism. We know a great deal more about the fatty acids, cholesterol, bile acids, fat soluble vitamins,

hormones and carcinogens. We know a great deal more about enzymes. We have audited the calorie requirements, like accountants trying to balance the books. But one does not need even those insights to know that when people are starving they need food and when people are malnourished, they need better food. . . .

Alarmingly we know a great deal more about the numbers who need to be fed. Twenty years ago when I was speaking or broadcasting on the population increase I used to say "Every time the clock ticks there is another mouth to be fed." Today I say, "For every two beats of your pulse there are five more mouths to be fed." The estimated population today is 3,600,000,000. The daily increase is about 180,000. Imagine that we are being invaded from another planet and that a daily task force of twenty divisions is arriving without K-rations. Most of the increase is in the countries we call under-developed. By 1980 three quarters of all the people on earth will be in those countries. By the year 2000, unless there is a man-made cataclysm, like a nuclear war, the population will be at least 7,000,000,000, of whom four-fifths will be in the developing countries.[4]

Food supplies are rationed inequitably among populations within countries and regions as well as between developed and less developed countries. In India the gap between the rural poor of parts of Central India and of Uttar Pradesh contrasts dramatically with more affluent regions of the Punjab and Nadu Tamil. Thus aggregate figures for diet and nutrition can be quite misleading.

In the interpretation of averages it should be emphasized that they do not reflect distribution of food to individuals nor do they indicate the percentage or segments of the population receiving inadequate diets and suffering from malnutrition.[5]

Farm skills combine to form strategies for efficient use of energy. Farmers try to induce the ecosystem to yield more through various means—more work, chemical fertilizer, tillage, crop rotation. However, all schemes for increasing man's food must finally conform to the rhythms and limits of the environmental system.

The problem of world food production and the population explosion is one of system design. How do we develop a network of food chains with as much stability as those which evolved earlier in some natural systems or in some of man's more primitive agricultural regimes now being displaced by war, competition, and over-population? How are the new energies, now available to man's civilization, to be best introduced? Which of the various kinds of possible new designs for systems of food production and consumption will lead to the survival of man in affluence, stability and justice?

In recent years, studies of the energetics of ecological systems have provided points of view and means of dealing with complex food networks that combined the basic laws of physics and chemistry with the complex aspects of living systems such as self-maintenance, self-design, self-control, self-switching, self-reproduction and other properties that characterize forests, seas, and anthropological systems, and modern societies. An energy network language is used to organize quantitative data on the parts and their exchanges with each other. Just as the parts of a radio are related to each other and to the whole system in a circuit diagram showing the flow of electric current, so an energy diagram can be constructed that illustrates the flow of energy among the populations using symbols for each component that are mathematically defined and have numerically measured magnitudes. Because energy is a common denominator for all processes, all forces and influences in the world system of food flows can be drawn and measured. When an energy network diagram is prepared, it can be simulated with electronic computing devices so that the consequences of one design feature or one external feature may be tested before some action program is attempted with the nation's food reserves.

When the relationships of world food production, consumption, and internation transfer are clarified with simple diagrams, some principles of system analysis long known in biological, electrical, or chemical systems are found to be at the heart of the present world problems of food and population. Some action programs of food giveaway, for example, turn out to be competitive to closed-loop reward flows that are required for stability. Understanding the world's food production system is essentially the same problem for the whole biosphere as understanding the natural systems that formerly predominated on the earth. Although the study of man's system in this way is new and the details worked out in only a few cases, let us consider from energy flow and analysis what kinds of limitations there are on man and his programs of feeding the world.[6]

Recognition of the systemic character of food production leads to questions of the capacity of that system to support human life. It is not infinite. If finite, what are its limits? Somehow such queries have not received much attention until recently. Yet they have critical import.

> In wildlife management, one sometimes uses the phrase "carrying capacity" to describe the ability of grassland range to support a population of animals or birds. The carrying capacity is that population level which is compatible with the entire net-

> work of supporting plants, the mineral cycles, and especially the maintenance of the essential elements for effective support such as soil, water levels, diversity, and reserves that protect all parts against fluctuations. It is a population level for long-range survival.
>
> The essence of the problem of food production for the world is in the question: "What is the carrying capacity of the earth's surface for man?" The same question arises in the discussions of man in space. What is the area of plant surface necessary to support man on solar energy? How much area is needed when solar energy is supplemented by some fuel energy from earth? The biosphere is really an overgrown space capsule and the questions about carrying capacity are similar. For projected levels of energy supplement from coal, oil, and nuclear power, what is the carrying capacity of the earth?[7]

Thus long-range carrying capacity of food systems, established by man, is at a population level compatible with the network of supporting plants; levels of soil, water, and other essential elements; diversity; and protective reserves against fluctuations. Such a system, using only unsubsidized energy (i.e., only solar energy), is about one individual per acre. It is implicit in this definition that more intense use of the ecosystem beyond such limits could create instability and deterioration. Introduction of energy supplements, of chemical expediters, of cultural practices, or even of water may disturb an essential equilibrium. A principal means for adverse alteration of ecosystems has been the introduction to them by man of the wastes accumulated in the production process.

> There has been little or no conscious concern for minimizing the waste materials discharged into the environment or for minimizing the consumption of physical material and auxiliary energy resources. The designs are based literally on a concept of the environment as an infinite source and as an infinite sink. The overall system that has thus evolved is basically a "once-through" system with the material wastes from the industrial, agricultural, and human sectors discharged into the atmosphere or the hydrosphere at the nearest point where they become inputs to the natural ecosystem.[8]

The spread of farming technology involving introduction of increasing amounts of waste is in effect a double burden on the ecosystem. There is first the expedited call-up of resources needed for intensified production and the subsequent burden of waste disposal. Some ecologists think there is a point in the process when waste burdens may exceed environmental capacity to handle them. Theoretically, when this point is reached, an environment would no longer be as capable of supporting human life.[9]

> One of the most important trends of recent years however is the developing recognition that the environment is in fact a single entity, a gigantic system. It includes radiation and tidal influences arriving from the outside, the solid earth, the envelope of air and water, and life itself and must be described in terms of its relationships and interactions as well as its individual components.[10]

The components of this system directly related to farm operations are soil and water. Within limits these are subject to human control and manipulation. However, the highly important atmospheric cycles and climate remain largely outside human control.

Soils

Soils are a basic environmental component in farming systems. Agricultural soils are those upper portions of the earth's mantle that support the vegetation consumed as food. These soils possess two principal characteristics:

1. They present the surface which receives solar energy in the form of sunshine.
2. They provide the complex nutrients which exist, or are introduced artificially as fertilizers, necessary for plant growth.

Global distribution of soils, their inherent nutrient capabilities, and their exposure to sunlight largely determine the location of the world food supply and consequently of the distribution of human population.

> Soils are the basic resource for farm production. Thus, it seems reasonable to begin with the soils of the world, and how they respond to management, to assess what farm production is biologically and physically possible with at least moderately efficient use. In any such assessment we must recognize the vital need for those combinations of private and public institutions that meet the requirements for efficient sustained production and fit the genius of the many peoples in the 95 less developed countries.[11]

Knowledge about soils is fundamental to improving crop yields. While this has been more or less intuitively recognized for a long time, systematic appraisal of soils and their potentials is quite recent. Indeed, one of the handicaps of farmers in the LDCs is the incomplete knowledge about soils and their management.

Kellogg and Orvedal show that soils are not static; they change. Changes can occur as a result of cultivation or from natural accidents such as earthquake, fire, or flood. Change can occur relatively suddenly; soils formed under original moisture conditions, as in the Sahara, later become part of an arid system. Tropical soils in the Congo Basin, although originally acid, are modified by dust deposited by winds from deserts and mountains. In South America unmodified tropical soils are infertile. Soils have important specific local and regional characteristics.

Practices of cultivators can drastically modify soils. Thus it is critically important to understand the interrelation of soils and the resident population. "For each kind of soil, and the associated climate and length of day, standards can be designed for the combinations of characteristics that an arable soil should have for the most rewarding results."[12]

A great deal of work on soils has been undertaken among the LDCs in the years since World War II. A substantial number of LDC personnel have been trained overseas; more have been trained at home through newly established agricultural institutions. Soil surveys have been undertaken, and soil testing facilities and laboratories are functioning in selected areas in Asia, Africa, and South America.

Nevertheless, the need for work on soils is much greater and more pressing than any likelihood of meeting it. Probably no form of agronomic knowledge can be so promptly and directly effective in improving farm practices. Since knowledge about soils leads to a consideration of more important variables affecting plant growth, each additional soil map and its interpretation represents a solid technological advance bringing definite improvement to food production.

Those who work with an understanding of soils quickly learn what has been called by soil professionals "the principle of interactions." Through soil knowledge they gain an insight into the system of which the soil is a part.

> The most important single principle for guiding improved farming and agricultural development is the principle of inter-

actions: Each practice or each program within a system affects all other components of the system, so that a proper combination gives a far greater result than the sum of the several components considered singly (Kellogg, 1962a). The principle of interactions has been cryptically defined as a peculiar kind of mathematics from which the whole is much greater than the sum of its parts.

In technical assistance for agricultural development this principle guides the process at several levels: (1) reliable interpretations of the responses of a soil to alternative management systems from field study of its characteristics; (2) working out the most effective combination of practices for a system of managing each specific local kind of soil by people of known skills and with the facilities to give optimum production on a sustained basis; (3) fitting together a management scheme for a whole farm or group of holdings having unlike kinds of soil and different enterprises; (4) an effective balance of services needed for an existing or potential farming community to be successful; (5) organizing common services for two or more resource uses in the economic development of a large area or region; and (6) a balance of emphasis between the many aspects of a national plan or system for economic and agricultural progress, considering the skills of citizens, patterns of resources, sources of revenue, transport facilities, and the like.[13]

Sometimes farmers seem almost intuitively aware of the nature of their soil heritage; at other times their practices seem almost deliberately designed for destruction. As a plus, consider how century-old mixed cropping practices of southern Kerala in India have circumvented problems of a lateritic subsoil. If this subsoil had been turned up, destructive effects of a concreted soil would have been irreversible. Again, in heavy rainfall areas of northern Honshu of Japan the author recalls clean cultivation with furrows straight up slopes of 25–35 degrees without any sign of erosion. Somehow these farmers know that these soils absorb moisture fast enough to prevent erosive surface runoff. In the beautiful terraced rice fields of Shiga Prefecture in southern Honshu and similar terraces in the Philippines and Assam, India, we find other examples of sound indigenous soil management predating formal soil science. On the other hand, the savage erosion of Ethiopia's highlands testifies to an unsuitable farming system.

Disregard of soil information, particularly when new crops or new cultivation methods are introduced, can be disastrous. On more than one occasion engineers have permitted construction of irrigation dams, diversion works, and major components for irrigation delivery and then belatedly demanded that soil scientists provide irrigable land. The author well remembers turning down a job on the Helmand Valley development scheme in Afghanistan when it was learned that major irrigation structures were in place *before* irrigable soils had been identified. The water cart was before the soil horse; the result was a semidisaster. The notorious 3-million-acre Groundnut fiasco in Tanganyika by the British shortly after World War II was partly due to neglect of the soil factor. A review of this resounding debacle stated:

> So imbued in fact was the mission with the magic properties of capital that it completed its work in a little over nine weeks only by recourse to aerial reconnaissance of the many thousands of square miles by air, two thousand miles by road, and one thousand miles by rail. It is significant therefore that before the work was commenced at Kongwa, no time could be spared for satisfactory and substantial primary reconnaissance and survey, for preliminary photographic work or topographic soil conservation and soil maps, for adequate investigation of meteorological information bearing on rainfall or even of adequate examination of the economic aspects of crop yields.[14]

Another commentary:

> Soil surveys must be done carefully if large agricultural enterprises are to be located wisely. In Tanganyika they were done with the aid of a few simple chemicals and with a tea strainer used to produce the mechanical analysis. It was small wonder then that when the choice was to be made between two large areas —Kongwa, served by a railroad inland from Dar-es-Salaam, and a southern area, inland from Mikindani, served by no developed inland route—Kongwa received the greater development effort. For the soil survey had failed to indicate that Kongwa soil had a quartz sand content so high that it rapidly wore out the plows and other implements drawn through it, and that it contained so much iron cement that unless rains softened it the fertilized pistils of the peanut could no more penetrate it than they could penetrate a brick pavement.[15]

Customary land tenure arrangements resulting in extreme fragmentation and dispersion of individual holdings can make rational soil and land management extremely difficult. This condition is frequently encountered in Asia; exploitation of farm tenants by landlords in Asia and South America results in destructive soil mining.

Kellogg and Orvedal say that "every productive hectare of arable soil in the world has at least four basic conditions, appropriately related to one another and to the local kind of soil."[16] These conditions define the essential characteristics of soil in the farm energy transformation system.

1. A balanced supply of plant nutrients.
2. Adequate moisture in the root zone.
3. An environmentally adapted crop variety with genetic response potential to the most favorable arable soil that is practical to develop.
4. Plant protection against disease, insects, weeds, etc.

The world supply of cultivated farmland possesses these characteristics.

The amount of potentially arable land has been estimated at over twice the cultivated area. More than half of this potentially arable area—probably more than 4 billion acres—is largely tropical: 2 billion acres in and adjacent to the Congo and Amazon basins and substantial areas in temperate North America and Australia. However, the potential for extending arable areas of Asia, Europe, and the Soviet Union is small.[17]

The bulk of the potentially arable lands is in thinly settled humid and subhumid tropics, not in densely populated areas.

> Human migrations within different countries will almost certainly be required in the crowded agricultural lands of Asia. The marginal productivity of agricultural labor is approaching zero in these countries. It will be quite difficult to apply modern technology to raise agricultural production without moving large numbers of people off the land into the cities. For this, as well as other reasons, agricultural development must be accompanied by general economic improvement and particularly by large-scale urbanization.
>
> The present technology for agricultural production is inadequate for the humid tropics and for most of the sub-humid tropics. New plant varieties must be developed and new methods of fertilization, pest control, soil conditioning, and water management must be found. Even the basic data on soil properties and climatic conditions are scanty or lacking for most of this region. Hence, major emphasis should be given to research and development of agricultural technology.
>
> The need to develop the agricultural potential of the humid and sub-humid tropics is a long-range need. This suggests that in this problem we should concentrate on the development of research and teaching insitutions. It will also be important to increase communication and coordination between different workers and to attempt to recapture what was learned from previous experience.[18]

WATER

Farming requires water as well as soil. Soil with no moisture is sterile and unproductive; too much water drowns out crops. Both conditions occur in different forms throughout the world but are frequent in the LDCs. Water in proper amounts is the solvent that carries nutrients to the plant root system and forms part of the plant structure. In arid regions chemical fertilizers can be introduced into the soil where sufficient moisture is available through irrigation to dissolve the fertilizer and present it in nutrient form in soil moisture.

> Wherever there is arable land which experiences periods during the growing season in which evapotranspiration exceeds precipitation by an amount greater than soil moisture storage, the opportunity to increase production by irrigation exists. Irrigation may be applied to the desert, where rainfall is totally inadequate for any agriculture, as in Egypt or Southern Iraq; it may replace or supplement rainfall agriculture as in the dry farming regions of the United States; it may make possible multiple-cropping in areas where only single-cropping is possible because of wet and dry seasons as in Bengal; or it may serve as insurance against damaging, short-time sporadic droughts, as in eastern United States.[19]

Excessive water in or on soils requires drainage. In either case—insufficient or excess water—man must undertake specific action in order to realize farming potentials.

Dean Peterson has emphasized the effect of water control (drainage and irrigation) on the 7.85 billion acres of arable land in the world.[20] Four billion acres are in tropical regions with limited productivity over 75 percent of the area due to deficient natural moisture. Of the total world arable land resource 850 million acres require irrigation to produce even one crop, the remaining 7 billion acres can produce at least one crop without irrigation, and extensive areas are susceptible to multiple-cropping. With water control in the form of surface drainage the effective world arable area approaches 10 billion acres. If irrigation could be extended to all moisture-deficient arable lands, and if these in turn were multiple-cropped up to their capacity limits, the effective gross world arable area would be over 16 billion acres.

Irrigation and drainage facilitate control of soil moisture and thus improvement of the efficiency of the energy transformation system. Intensification of system output through irrigation provides an opportunity for efficient integrated crop production technology. Intensification of farm operations on existing lands rather than extension of the cropped area to new lands is initially more likely because greater returns are more certain and farmers already know how to go about it. However, as the general level of irrigated farm skills is raised, increasing amounts of land will be irrigated.

According to the Indicative World Plan, irrigation will play a central role in intensified farming in developing countries projecting an increase of 72 million acres between 1965 and 1985.[21] The IWP proposals include new developments and improvements to existing irrigation systems capable of supporting modern intensive agriculture. The plan calls for distribution and drainage systems down to individual farm units along with on-farm land improvements and other services to support a modern agricultural production system.

One might question whether this forecast is realistic. The history of government-sponsored irrigation schemes has not always been successful in the United States where water is traditionally priced well below cost because water users have been either unable or unwilling to pay the full costs of water development. Numerous federal irrigation projects have undergone successive financial reorganizations, and each reorganization has resulted in lower user rates. The result has been that few if any of these projects have repaid the original capital outlay. Moreover, the development of new irrigation undertakings is a slow process and has sometimes involved individual and group failures to manage water properly or to undertake the associated management and cultural tasks—partly because of ignorance, partly because supporting services were not provided at the right time, and partly because anticipated returns were grossly overestimated. Expectancies have too often been above realizable levels.

As in the case of soils, the principle of interactions of a large number of variables determines the outcome of irrigated farming. Control of these variables becomes critical; failure to meet higher levels of operating precision results in disappointing yields. Irrigation water and fertilizer have a distinct complementarity—neither may work well without the other, properly proportioned and timed. For the farmer the difference in his operations between irrigated and traditional nonirrigated farming is revolutionary. Even under more advanced U.S. agriculture the shakedown time from the start of a new irrigation project may be as much as ten years after the first water delivery. It is not an easy adjustment.

Irrigation development costs a lot of money. Land development, irrigation, and drainage works not infrequently run $500–600 per acre in projects in the LDCs. When costs of the main dams, diversion structures, and main canals are added, the investment can reach several thousand dollars per acre. Thus financing of major irrigation development schemes may involve substantial allocation and reallocation of resources including skilled manpower. Depending on the type of development, substantial outlays involving heavy carrying charges may precede returns for a number of years. Thus the magnitude of irrigation capital outlays suggests that intensive cropping should be sought in preference to extensive agriculture. Moreover, profitable irrigated farming depends heavily on the availability and efficient use of other factors such as fertilizer, cultivating equipment, seed, and weed and pest controls. In order for farmers to obtain these inputs it is essential that a source of farm credit be provided.[22]

Irrigation development plans must fit the specific needs of irrigated farming. This consideration implies that water transmission and delivery systems be adapted to prevailing size of farm, to the anticipated cropping pattern, and to the cultivation pattern for these crops. Such requirements also extend to the organization and administration of system-wide operation and maintenance routines.

However, even the satisfaction of these conditions will not result in a successful project if farmer incentive is lacking because of low prices for farm produce or inequitable income-sharing between landowners and tenants or sharecroppers. Thus irrigation planners must also consider such factors as marketing institutions, price policy for farm products, and prevailing land tenure arrangements.

Where agriculture has already developed and the essential institutions are present, the appropriate strategy may be to give priority to smaller water projects. Simple, inexpensive systems should be initially exploited. These modest beginnings provide a basis for testing the efficacy of irrigation under more or less controlled conditions and minimal capital outlay, avoiding to some extent the risks of larger systems and outlays.

A somewhat similar strategy applies to larger developments. Where possible, major irrigation undertakings should be scheduled in successive phases in order to obtain early returns, train manpower, and improve institutions. Frequently the great importance of early adaptive crop and fertilizer research is overlooked. The absence of these research findings deprives planners, engineers, and other technicians of guidance in establishing preferred cropping practices, of important information for structural design (e.g., the capacity of canals and distribution systems), and of criteria for formulating operation and maintenance procedures. In the case of the new high-yielding grain varieties with their known response-sensitivity to even moderate variations in soils, moisture, fertility levels, and climate, failure to provide early adaptive research can result in costly errors and ultimate failure to achieve yield potentials of these varieties.

Underlying the array of practical problems of irrigation development and the production and marketing of irrigated farming products is the major question of selection of lands to be irrigated. The clear logic of applying scarce and costly irrigation to only the better land seems almost self-evident. But determination of the irrigation response of different soil bodies is a detailed, technical undertaking. In all too many cases the need for detailed knowledge of the behavior of soils under irrigation is not recognized, is pushed aside, or is deferred until after construction of major structures (including main canals) has reached an advanced stage. Even when knowledge of soil factors has been determined, political considerations may override or substantially modify its applications. In the same vein, irrigation planning frequently omits measures to insure adequate and timely on-farm irrigation and drainage layouts and land development. The result can place a potentially fatal handicap on farmers confronted with the need to devise their own irrigation systems on possibly unsuitable topography and soils. On this point Peterson remarks:

> Perhaps the greatest weakness in irrigation schemes is the failure to include tertiary and farm-level distribution systems and land development as part of the engineered plan. Most developing countries have governmental organizations that can plan and design dams, reservoirs and canals. Some have hydrographic services at some level of acceptability. Few, if any, have organizations capable of doing anything effective about management and conservation of water at the farm level, and this deficiency is probably the most critical organizational one.[23]

Siren visions of vast dams, of large blue man-made lakes, of smooth-flowing miles of beautifully designed canals, and of landscapes of uniform and green irrigated crops have warped technical judgments of irrigation authorities more than once. The reality has all too often been waterlogged lands, man-made alkali flats, and weed-choked canals. Yet the vision persists, enhanced no doubt by the thrill of large-scale undertakings so dear to the heart of engineers and administrators.

Perhaps it has been the chastening effect of failure on a grand scale that has sometimes turned attention to simpler, easier, and more attainable goals of irrigation from groundwater pumped from wells. This source of water has recently come to be recognized as a substantial natural endowment. In the aggregate it is a vast resource; groundwater interwoven with contiguous river systems stored at depths of less than 3,000 feet is 3,000 times as great as that contained in all rivers and 30 times that contained in all freshwater lakes.[24] In addition there is other underground storage. Current withdrawals from all sources for irrigation are estimated at 2 billion acre-feet now and eventually 3.25 billion acre-feet. Perhaps one-third of this amount may be developed from groundwater supplies. Extensive groundwater irrigation development has occurred in Bangladesh and on the Indo-Gangetic plain in India and is increasing.

There are several advantages to irrigation based on pumped groundwater over surface irrigation. While pumping does require a source of energy and an energy distribution system, pumped irrigation is likely to be less costly—more than half as costly in India and much less than that if cost of major structures and surface works are included. Further, individual irrigators are much closer to their source of supply and can learn their new trade more or less at their own gait; neighbors learn from each other. It is not an all-or-nothing situation as in the case of a surface system where the entire area comes under irrigation service simultaneously.

Linked with irrigation problems are drainage problems. Drainage seeks to rid the soil of excess irrigation water or of floodwaters from excessive rainfall. Irrigation literature contains much discussion of associated drainage problems, particularly the hazards of inadequate drain construction and maintenance.

Insufficient provision of drainage of irrigated lands and resultant high water table have been the cause of many perplexing problems in irrigated areas; in some cases these have amounted to costly near disasters. In any event, the damage to land resources lasts for a long time and is often only partly reversible. Rivers also can suffer damage from the continued inflow of saline drainage from upstream irrigation. The quality of water in the downstream reaches of the river progressively deteriorates, and downstream users of irrigation water from the river are increasingly exposed to the hazard of salinization of their lands. Consequently, plans based on the use of water from mainstream diversions should make a great effort to determine the proper balance to be maintained between upstream and downstream users and consider methods for offsetting downstream salinity. In the case of the Indus Basin, measures to decrease river salinity have taken the form of mixing fresh water from underground sources with the more saline river water.

While drainage related to irrigation is extremely important, it is only one aspect of the water-management problem confronting man in his effort to manipulate the environment by agricultural procedures.

> Water management involves not only bringing water to the land and using it there rationally, but also involves action taken to remove surplus water. Flooding, waterlogging and salinity, the three main problems arising from surplus water, are restricting agricultural production on many lands of the world which would otherwise have high productive capacity. Flooding keeps many of the best alluvial soils in extensive grazing as in parts of South America or in crops of low productivity as in the Brahmaputra Basin in Pakistan or the Chao Pya Valley in Thailand. Flooding limits the application of fertilizers, often does not permit the use of modern high yielding varieties, and frequently damages crops or keeps land out of production in the season when moisture is available for plant growth. High groundwater levels in the high rainfall areas restrict cropping to water tolerant crops, and in the dry areas result in salinization. For example, on a large part of the soils in Lower Mesopotamia, and in the Indus plain, salinity has become such a problem that extensive areas went out of production and according to some estimates yields on as much as 50% of the area are adversely affected by high salinity. Provision of sufficient drainage and proper irrigation practices can solve most salinity problems, but the cost involved and the regulatory power required to enforce optimal practices have often held governments back from taking the necessary steps.[25]

Floodwaters periodically dumped by monsoon storms inundate large areas of North India with immediate destruction of crops, livestock, and human life. Some farmland stays under water for an entire crop season; in other cases farmland is engulfed in new flood channels. Aside from these disastrous effects, this periodic hazard sometimes enforces adapted forms of low-yield cultivation such as the "floating rice" varieties found in the lower reaches of the Mekong and in the highly unstable landscape of Bangladesh.

An interesting development in some areas threatened with high water table is the technique of pumping groundwater to be used for irrigation. In effect this is a recycling process. High groundwater levels resulting from deep percolation of irrigation water are reduced by pumping, and within limits pumped water can again be used for irrigation. This has been done with some success in the Indus Basin lands of Pakistan—the result of investigations by Revelle and others. This procedure is a payoff from careful studies of a particular ecosystem and of instituting measures reinforcing that system. Thus intervention in the natural order can succeed when sufficient time and care are taken to comprehend systemic relations.

The caveat, of course, is that institutional arrangements for water development and management for agricultural purposes are too often at odds with ecosystem imperatives. In the United States major water development responsibility is assigned to the U.S. Bureau of Reclamation and the Army Corps of Engineers. Both are engineering organizations. Agricultural policy and practice (including soil technology) are institutionalized in separate professional enclaves: the U.S. Department of Agriculture, the state agricultural experiment stations, and the land-grant college system. The power structure of which these agencies are a part is also separated so that each has its own political clientele. The drive for financial appropriations enforces a continual effort at vigorous promotion of water management undertakings.

It has been claimed that U.S. water development agencies tend to neglect environmental and ecological considerations. Charles McKinley's study, "Uncle Sam in the Pacific Northwest," portrays the political rough-and-tumble between the Corps of Engineers and the Bureau of Reclamation to control development of the Snake-Columbia Basin. Arthur Maass's study, *Muddy Waters,* describes political maneuverings of the Corps of Engineers on the Mississippi.

This power struggle, with its potential adverse impacts on soil and water management and its possible neglect of environmental aspects, is not confined to the United States. A close facsimile is found in some of the LDCs. In several of these countries agriculture and water development functions are in separate ministries, and the jurisdictional precincts are as jealously guarded as in the West.

Thus it may be argued that institutional arrangements for planning and implementing water management schemes around the world are not entirely satisfactory. This is partly because water technicians enjoy a sort of professional monopoly. From this preferred position they are frequently able to influence policy, and their policy orientation has not always included much concern for the ecosystem or research.

An important deficiency in water development planning is the inability of the public to participate effectively in the policy-formulating and decision-making processes. Lacking this public participation, water development agencies tend to become advocates, judges, and juries of the entire process of water management, planning, and implementation. For these reasons the LDCs need to be alert to the institutional basis of the water management profession and of the policy implications of their proposals.

NITROGEN

Although nitrogen is one of several important chemical elements in the energy transformation system of farming, it is so important that a discussion of its role might be surrogate for a more detailed discussion of carbon, oxygen, phosphorus, potassium, and a host of trace elements; all are important in the production of mankind's food and fiber.

> Nitrogen is the cornerstone building-block of protein molecules which in turn are the basic structural and activity centers of any and all living organisms. For these reasons the nitrogen requirements for the ultimate food goal to be achieved can be determined from knowledge of the biological conversion efficiencies as nitrogen proceeds through soil-plant-animal protein pathways—eventually to be consumed as protein-nitrogen in human food.[26]

Nitrogen is present universally as a natural resource in the atmosphere and in the soil mantle. The original nitrogen stock in soils may be reduced by agriculture; at the same time nitrogen is continually reentering the system from the atmosphere through rainfall (particularly thunderstorms), through nitrogen-fixation processes of leguminous plants that occur in many regions of the earth, and through decay of vegetable and animal matter on the land surface.

> The mobilization of America's soil-borne nitrogen reserves—which began as the pioneers' plows broke the fertile plains—is of such dimensions as to stagger the imagination when compared with industrial capabilities which would have been required to match such a flow of naturally provided nitrogen fertilizer. An analysis I attempted resulted in a figure of 800 million tons of native soil-nitrogen removed from the surface foot of America's plowed soils as a result of 100 years under tillage. Similarly, others have estimated a hundred-year total of 1 billion, 500 million tons of soil-borne nitrogen having been released from the top 4 feet of America's cultivated soils. This reduction of native soil-nitrogen is about 100 times the annual production of fertilizer-nitrogen of industry in 1969.[27]

When one considers the much longer periods of soil-nitrogen mobilization in the more ancient rural societies, it is no wonder that recent efforts at agricultural modernization in these regions call for large inputs of nitrogenous fertilizers. However, nitrogen consumption among the LDCs is much smaller because of their lower consumption of animal protein. In 1968 in the United States over 15 million metric tons of nitrogen were converted to animal protein out of a total conversion of slightly over 19 million tons, or about 80 percent, whereas vegetable protein conversion accounted for only .075 percent. However, the nitrogen mobilized from natural processes including rainfall, animal manures, and fixation accounted for almost 10 million metric tons; 6 million metric tons were supplied by industrial nitrogen. The deficit of 3.1 million metric tons was a direct draft on the original soil-nitrogen stock and free-living nitrogen-fixing soil microorganisms.[28]

In contrast, a rough estimate of LDCs with 2.5 billion population, lower nutrition, and greater consumption of vegetable protein might give an annual draft on soil nitrogen of about 5 million metric tons. For a projected population of 6 billion in the year 2000, using current dietary patterns, the annual soil nitrogen draft might be around 25 million metric tons.[29]

Of course this draft would be modified by increased use of industrial nitrogen, by combinations of seed varieties with larger fertilizer inputs, and by higher intakes of protein. The point to be emphasized is the degree of continued dependence on environmental conditions for the essential nitrogen component. Moreover, increased inputs of industrial nitrogen simply rearrange energy transformation processes, because nitrogen manufacture itself represents a substantial energy transformation in the form of heat and electrical energy and in some cases of fossil fuels.

II

The Green Revolution

Man invented agriculture. He learned how to trap solar energy to produce food and fiber plants by utilizing the basic components of soil, water, and the great chemical cycles of the universe. Yet his progress in developing this innovation was halting, spasmodic, and slow. Traditional farm methods persisted with only slight and occasional modification until well into the eighteenth century, and traditional systems tend to prevail even today in most of the Third World.

Scientific farming as we know it today began in the nineteenth century in Europe, where several distinct lines of inquiry specifically influenced development of modern agricultural technology. Chemical fertilizer was studied systematically by Justus von Liebig in 1840. Plant pathology had several originators beginning with the classical work of Benedict Prevost in 1807 on wheat bunt, followed by the 30-year effort of De Bary and his associates on fungi and the preparation of the Bordeaux mixture for use on grape mildew, and continuing with the introduction by P. M. A. Millardet in 1878 of the concept of fungicidal spraying. This pioneering work led to the modern development of pesticides and herbicides and the 1939 discovery of DDT, followed in 1940 by the development of a series of chlorinated hydrocarbons.

Perhaps the most important, certainly one of the most far reaching lines of inquiry, was that of Gregor Mendel who, between 1856 and 1865, set up guidelines for plant genetics in a series of experiments with garden peas. Mendel's original work, elaborated by William Batson in 1906 and followed by T. H. Morgan and others in 1910, culminated in the Watson-Crick formulation of DNA—the molecular basis for genetic material.

These straight lines of inquiry appear to have had little lateral effect on other approaches, such as the original work by Shleiden and Schwann in Germany in 1839 (and their intellectual progeny) on cell theory, or cytology. Soil science had its beginnings in Russia with the work of two great scientists—V. V. Dokuchaiev in 1886 and Konstantin Glinka in 1908. Independently, E. W. Hilgard in the United States developed a somewhat similar soil concept. A synthesis of the Glinka and Hilgard concepts by C. F. Marbut received worldwide recognition in 1927. Thus it was not until 1930 that the central lines of farm technology were developed.

By the end of World War II the developed nations had a substantial array of separate farm technologies at their command. Then abruptly—partly as a result of the advances of nuclear physics—these separate technologies were brought together, enabling fertilizer, soil, and genetic plant characteristics to be practically combined into a whole new organic structure. The old conventional chemical fertilizers, strengthened and reinforced, were made more readily available to farmers by new and efficient production methods. A whole new array of pesticides, herbicides, and insecticides were developed; and "miracle" strains of rice, wheat, millet, and sorghum were produced, ushering in what has been called the "Green Revolution" with a promise of unprecedented yields. A new technological system had been created—an extremely complex, integrated system of great power whose dynamics were only partially understood and whose long-range effects were largely unknown.

The success of the Green Revolution was dependent on the exportation to developing countries of an intricate and complex system of farm inputs and a body of scientific knowledge. The new seeds required an initial research infrastructure to develop high-yielding varieties and, in the case of rice, to adapt to local conditions. For full potential the new seeds were dependent on heavy use of fertilizers, administered in sufficient amounts and at specific points in the growth cycle, and on concurrently controlled water use. Pesticides and herbicides were required to protect new crops against insects and disease. Modern mechanical devices became necessary in order to spray pesticides, spread fertilizer, deliver water, and harvest yields— all within a shorter growth cycle. The new inputs required an administrative network to make them readily available at low cost to farmers and to train farmers in their proper usage. Thus these new high-yield seeds entailed a complete revolution in traditional farming that involved a transformation of man's exploitation of his environment—a change not without hazard.

> Given the steadily advancing demand for food, further intervention in the biosphere for the expansion of the food supply is inevitable. Such intervention, however, can no longer be undertaken by an individual or a nation without consideration of the impact on the biosphere as a whole. The decision by a government to dam a river, by a farmer to use DDT on his crops or by a married couple to have another child, thereby increasing the demand for food, has repercussions for all mankind.
>
> Modern agriculture depends heavily on four technologies: mechanization, irrigation, fertilization and the chemical control of weeds and insects. Each of these technologies has made an important contribution to the earth's increased capacity for sustaining human populations, and each has perturbed the cycles of the biosphere.[1]

The sudden dramatic success of new grain varieties created a wave of confidence along with some expressions of reservation over the possibility of new, only dimly perceived, problems. One hazard is that the immediate impact of the Green Revolution may cause unwarranted optimism and universal feelings of relief that the world food crisis has passed. A more realistic view is that mankind has gained some valuable time to seek a more permanent solution.

> The discussion of the phenomenon tends to cluster around two views. On the one hand, some observers now believe that the race between food and population is over, that the new agricultural technology constitutes a cornucopia for the developing world, and that victory is in sight in the "War on Hunger." Others see this development as opening a Pandora's box; its very success will produce a number of new problems which are far more subtle and difficult than those faced during the development of the new technology. It is important to give careful attention and critical analysis to both interpretations in order to be optimistic about the promise of the Green Revolution where justified, and at the same time to prepare for the problems that are now emerging. The Green Revolution offers an unparalleled opportunity to break the chains of rural poverty in important parts of the world. Success will depend upon how well the opportunity is handled and upon how alert we are to the inherent consequences.[2]

The Indicative World Plan estimate of projected food production required to meet LDC population pressure calls for a production growth rate in the period 1967–85 of 4.3 percent, well above their historical rate of 2.6–2.7 percent. This increase of 1.6 percent, based on both population increase and shifts in the patterns of demand for food, represents a quantum jump that can be met only by broad use of modern technology in regions still functioning along traditional lines. Yet the volume and cost of new inputs to be mobilized by the LDCs represents an enormous drain on the economic resources of these countries.

By 1985 the annual additional cost to farmers in the LDCs for the new inputs (seed, fertilizer, pesticides, and machinery) is estimated to approximate $14 billion.[3] The total value of quality seeds to meet estimated requirements in 1985 will be $900 million, and the cost of fertilizer will rise from $664 million in 1962 to $7.8 billion in 1985. Crop protection costs will be about $2 billion, and accumulated tractor investments to provide 315,000 tractors for Asia and Latin America by 1985 are estimated at $37 billion.[4] The 1985 staff requirements for trained agricultural, advisory, and associated technical personnel are estimated at 770,000 individuals, requiring an annual training output of 64,000 people against a current training capacity of 41,695,[5] at an estimated annual cost of $1.4 billion.[6] While technology exists for elimination of hunger throughout the world, the financial cost of this technology is presently well beyond the resources of developing nations.

The New Genetics

Ability to shuffle genetic characteristics of plants to create a strain that conforms to desired patterns of performance has enormous potentials for human benefit. But it is one thing to conceptualize a procedure for chromosome manipulation, quite another to produce desired results. Many environmental variables have to be brought under control and incorporated in genetic design, such as interplay between specific soil characteristics and climate in given locations. A number of intermediate and time-consuming procedures must be followed, such as training plant breeders, establishing germ-plasm banks, executing many field plot trials, establishing seed multiplication, and distributing infrastructure and programs of knowledge diffusion.

The central problem is to produce plant varieties adapted to specific climatic conditions, length of growing season, sunlight intensity, temperature, and soil composition and responsive to controllable input factors such as fertilizer and water. Once a genetic variation that performs efficiently under specified conditions has been introduced, it is essential that farm practices conform to those conditions. The genetic technology has produced dramatic results, but this alone does not guarantee continued development.

> The recent introduction of genetic technology into several South Asian countries has spawned dramatic changes in their possibilities for increasing agricultural production. New fertilizer-responsive seeds, however, while necessary have not constituted sufficient conditions for agricultural development. . . . The phenomenon currently called the green revolution is not unique to the 1960's. Insights gained from other countries that have experienced technological change in agriculture suggest caution in attributing increases in farm production in South Asia entirely to genetic technology. The improved genotypes currently spreading throughout that area are highly visible, while changes in the use of other farm inputs are not. . . .
> As compared with a 62 percent increase in the production of wheat, the production of rice in India in 1969–70 was only 5.2 percent greater than in 1964–65. While 27 percent of the area sown with wheat is now sown with semi-dwarf varieties, only 10 percent of the area sown with rice is in high-yield varieties.
> The relatively slower progress in the production of rice is related to many factors. Improved varieties of rice are more susceptible to disease. Further, they require stringent water management. Finally, many improved varieties are discounted heavily in the market because of the inferior quality of the grain.[7]

It should be noted that research on wheat breeding began in Mexico in 1944, whereas work on rice at the International Rice Research Institute in the Philippines only commenced in the 60s.

The transformation effect of new genetic varieties is principally expressed in pressures on farmers to conform to conditions imposed by built-in response capabilities of the new varieties. The implication of the Staub-Blase statements is that traditional farming methods in developing countries must be changed. Farmers are now forced to become in effect farm managers, allocating available resources and labor quite precisely among a number of newly learned operations. Transformation of traditional methods in a society based on farming produces corresponding social changes whose outlines are vague. For developing countries introduction of new grains and the entire panoply of technology on which they are dependent means perhaps social dislocation and readjustment—in effect, creation of a new technological society.

In straightforward terms of increased physical output of grain, genetic work done at the International Rice Research Institute in the Philippines and the International Maize and Wheat Improvement Center (and previous work by the Rockefeller Foundation) in Mexico has already had an enormous payoff. Average Indian wheat yields increased 62 percent in 1968 with new dwarf wheats having been planted on only 18 percent of India's wheat acreage. Pakistan, a food-deficit area, is becoming self-sufficient in grain and might become an exporter. Wheat yields in Turkey with new varieties were 52 bushels per acre compared with 22 bushels per acre from indigenous varieties. Ceylon's rice crop increased by 34 percent in two years. Since 1900 the Philippines had been a rice importer; in the three years ending with 1970 there were no rice imports.[8]

While doubts and misgivings persist about long-range effects of the Green Revolution on traditional societies and cultures and on a fragile ecosystem, the short-range gains seem to have been real and tangible:

> No authority has ever suggested that this transition would be a smooth one, for all authorities recognize the serious economic, social, and political imbalances that characterize rural life in the developing world. We are all aware of the economic inequalities, the ancient bitternesses among various social groups, the deep-rooted prejudices, the political injustices, and the religious animosities. And it is an historical fact that the introduction of technological change often has the effect of bringing long-dormant social ills to the surface and forcing them into greater public awareness. However, one cannot, in all fairness, place the blame for these ills on the technological innovation itself.[9]

The Green Revolution, primarily a genetic innovation, does set in motion profound and far-reaching societal and ecological changes. We know very little about the dynamics of this new system and presently have little control over its long-range outcome. Less developed regions will undoubtedly experience the greatest and most direct social and ecological changes; they are also least able to mobilize resources to meet new challenges.

Fertilizer Requirements

A large part of the success of the new "miracle" seeds comes from built-in fertilizer response potentials much greater than those of indigenous strains. Although many indigenous varieties of grain would show marked improvement in yields if treated with liberal application of fertilizer, the much greater response of new strains to fertilizer and a controlled and sufficient water supply has made a strong case for larger expenditures for fertilizer among small farmers. Hence introduction of new varieties has greatly extended knowledge about fertilizer use among developing nations. In addition the single-minded approach that fertilizer usage was the key to agricultural development has given way to views that fertilizer inputs must be considered along with other inputs in the context of a *system* of farming. Ten years ago Jonathan Garst wrote:

> Fertilizer is certainly one of the best ways to aid undeveloped countries. Most of the people and the poorest people are small farmers. Fertilizer gets down to the bottom of the social scale. The foreign aid cannot all end up in the capital city. Experience shows that any farmer quickly learns to use fertilizer. Its use does not require any change in the pattern of farming. It can be placed by hand, if necessary, on any size, any shape, field. The results can be seen in the growth of the crop all season. It shows in size, color and luxuriance. Moreover, with efficient distribution, it is profitable.[10]

Garst contended that the initial farming push in developing nations could start with fertilizer and then farmers, impressed with results of chemical fertilizer, would seek to improve seed quality and methods of cultivation. He urged that fertilizer be made available in large amounts rapidly; small initial quantities and slow increases in availability would be less productive.

Still on the same theme, Garst argued in 1971 that credit should be given to farm chemicals for much of the recent worldwide surge in farm production.[11] He pointed out that the largest increases in production came in developed areas able to make capital outlays necessary for increased production of fertilizer but did not explicitly explain that fertilizer could also be viewed as a part of a whole new farming system—that greatly increased productivity also required a steady and abundant supply of water, new seed varieties with built-in fertilizer response potential, a corps of agricultural personnel to instruct farmers in proper fertilizer usage, an efficient administrative structure to deliver fertilizer to farmers at reasonable prices, a marketing structure to deal with expected surpluses of grain, and a research infrastructure to design fertilizer application techniques for specific grains and specific growing conditions.

After the initial flush of excitement concerning fertilizer and its potentials, observers began to raise questions concerning environmental effects of heavy fertilizer use. It was alleged, for example, that heavy or indiscriminate fertilizer doses resulted in depletion of important trace elements and minerals due to increased plant growth. Also, since chemicals are carried by natural drainage to streams and lakes, both nitrogen and phosphorus used as fertilizers would stimulate undesirable underwater vegetation in shallow ponds and lakes, ultimately damaging their scenic and recreational values as well as impairing the quality of drinking water.

In developing nations where fertilizer inputs on a large scale are relatively recent, it is probable that pollution may not become serious for some years. Yet it is a factor to take into account in long-range planning. Pollution is one inescapable by-product of the new cultural technology, and little thought has been given in developing nations to provision of either early warning sensors or countermeasures to offset long-range adverse effects. Fertilizer advocates point out:

> In ranking fertilizers in order as pollutants, nitrogen comes first and phosphorus second. Both nitrogen and phosphorus have been implicated in the eutrophication of water bodies—particularly shallow lakes. Fixed nitrogen converts to nitrate and moves freely with water percolating through soils. Since nitrogen is the cornerstone element of all living things, the greater the degrees of soil fertility and productivity and the greater the number of human beings that have to be supported by agriculture, the greater are the probabilities for escape of nitrogen into percolating waters and the surrounding environment. These facts have been very disturbing to ecological purists who oppose any changes in environments.
> The underlying problem of "nitrogen pollution" is related however to the number of people being supported. It may be considered axiomatic that for *every additional human being that joins our number, something has to give way in the non-human part of ecological systems.* To the extent that this ecological change is distasteful, the results are credited to pollution. . . . The importance of this presentation is that it clearly relates human food demands to nitrogen fertilizer requirements at the farm site; and makes it equally clear that choices can be made between degrees of nitrate pollution that society wishes to accept versus the kinds of food that members of any given society demand.[12]

Pesticides and Herbicides

Farmers all over the world will continue to use chemical pesticides and herbicides in large volume. Among farmers of developing nations, use of these chemicals will expand along with increased use of other farm inputs. Subsistence farmers have little choice in this regard; their alternatives are to forego benefits of modern agricultural technology or to endure heavy crop losses with the new varieties, and neither alternative is acceptable. Losses currently sustained by farmers in developing regions due to plant disease and pests are enormous, and rapid increase in pesticide use testifies to its value. In India it is reported that use of pesticides increased from treatment of 10,120 hectares in 1946–47 to over 6 million hectares in 1961–62 and over 17 million hectares in 1965–66, the last figure representing over 11 percent of the total crop area.[13] The amount of DDT used in plant protection rose to 2,400 metric tons in 1968–69 from only 600 metric tons four years earlier, and use of chlorinated hydrocarbons increased twelvefold in the same period.

In concrete terms, Indian losses due to insects were 17.7 percent of the total 1967 crop, and for rice the comparable figure was 38.7 percent. In millet and sorghum the loss was 13.7 percent in Asia and 15.4 percent in Africa. For maize South American losses were 25 percent, for Asia 13.7 percent, and for Africa 38.9 percent.[14] For the subsistence farmer these losses directly diminish his food supply. Under commercial production where cash outlay for technical inputs is substantial, such loss rates are intolerable. Consequently, extension into less developed regions of modern agricultural technology is inevitably accompanied by widespread use of chemical poisons. The annual expenditure for pesticides for use in agriculture in the Third World is expected to approach $2 billion by 1985.

Among developed countries continued widespread (and often indiscriminate) use of pesticides and herbicides is raising questions about their environmental impact. While direct evidence of significant harm to human beings is inconclusive, there is some evidence that harmful accumulations of poisons are creeping up the food chain and may present a danger to mankind. It would not be surprising, however, if peoples of developing regions viewed this concern askance. Dr. Martin Kaplan of the World Health Organization is reported as stating:

> In the United States, if you hit an animal with a high dose of a toxic substance and he is affected, we can ban it from human

use. This is a completely unacceptable standard in 98% of the other countries.15

Potential environmental damage, particularly when evidence of impact and even of cause is still sketchy, is probably viewed by LDCs as tolerable risk when compared to tangible evidence of substantial benefits. In addition, insecure national leaders have usually been more concerned with short-run tangible results than with long-range ecological damage. Prudence in advance planning is often neglected for immediate political expediency. Emil Mrak put the problem in the context of developed nations:

> As time went on our society became more affluent, not only because we produced more and better foods at a lower cost, but also because of the production of other consumer goods and luxuries which we consider so important. On the other hand, bringing about these changes as a result of efficient technologies in agriculture and factory production, we also set the stage for lowering our standard of living by contaminating the environment. In the last few years these environmental changes became more and more apparent and of concern to those who had an adequate supply of food at a reasonable cost, and too, the question about the safety of foods arose. . . .
> It is unfortunate that as technological advancements were made in agriculture, the technologists who developed chemicals, methods of application, and so on did not realize how serious the relationships of such advances were to environmental contamination. It was perfectly natural to ignore these problems that had descended on us so suddenly because there was little concern by the general public until quite recently. Today, of course, things are different and so many are prepared to point their fingers at environmental contamination as related to agriculture. We were so busy with our constructive advances that we just overlooked the possibility of destructive ones. Now we find ourselves in a situation that is dangerously near getting out of hand as a result of the pressure of emotions, misguided activists, and even the failure of some bureaucrats to exercise good and considered judgment before pushing the panic button and outlawing this chemical or that.16

Research Requirements

The new man-made environment, created through long sustained farm research efforts, will be dependent on continuing research to maximize production and minimize ecological imbalance. Partnership with science is irreversible in modern farming. New seeds adapted to local growing conditions must be developed by indigenous research personnel. One of the important research objectives is to determine the combination of farm practices most favorable to maintaining yield performance, and the makeup of these combinations will change over time. Thus fertilizer application will cause weeds to flourish, fertilizer requirements will change, and cultural practices will have to be modified to meet shifting patterns of fertilizer and water application. Double- and triple-cropping sequences may have to be shifted. New farm tools will have to be designed and produced.

Established institutions of developed regions cannot supply research needs of developing nations; they can supply knowledge of research methodology, scientific procedures, and outcomes of basic research with universal application. Research for LDCs must be specific to local situations.

> Some who are concerned with the world food problem reason that high-level technology of developed nations can be applied directly in the developing countries. Only in a few cases is this correct. Plant varieties, animal breeds, and farming practices must be developed for each environment.[17]

Along these same lines a noted American research agronomist with extensive overseas experience in plant breeding stated:

> Only a few years ago it was assumed that the agricultural needs of the less developed countries could be solved by a direct transfer of modern technology. Fortunately this misconception is becoming less widely held and the research needs in the tropical areas are being considered with more realism.
> Our present agricultural technology rests upon two sequential developments. First there was the long period of trial and error by individual farmers from which evolved the general guidelines on times and rates of planting, the widely grown crop varieties, and improvements in animal-powered equipment. The second development began shortly after the establishment of the Land-Grant Institutions. Each innovation helped condition the farmer to further changes and improvements. The more progressive farmers are now reluctant to wait for adequate evaluation of new varieties or machines and do much experimentation on their own initiative. In contrast the subsistence farmer tends to be ultra-conservative. He fears that any departure from custom may place the survival of his family and himself in jeopardy.[18]

Effects on Environment

The new Green Revolution technology raises hopes of erasing hunger from the world. In effect, mankind has set in motion a new and rapidly changing worldwide system to supersede traditional farming systems. Yet, in tampering with a natural complex biological environment he only partially understands, man may be substituting a relatively unknown new ecological system. Such a substitution is fraught with difficulties. One aspect may be to create new forms of life while destroying still other forms. That this system is vastly more productive of food and fiber in the short run is evident. What is less clear, however, is man's ability to exercise sufficient controls over the new system, including potential adverse side effects, to insure long-range maintenance of a favorable ecosystem. Man's lack of knowledge on this point is more a matter for concern than isolated cases of environmental damage. Has man set in motion an interplay of forces he does not comprehend? Is he to some extent therefore proceeding in ignorance of the ultimate consequences of an unguided dynamic of vast potential for blocking the functioning of the energy system—of expediting entropy and disorganization? This more profound inquiry should attract attention rather than more superficial debates over use in particular situations of particular chemical pesticides, or fertilizers, or new methods of water diversion and usage.

The new technology offers enormous potentials in terms of production, but it is not costless in terms of either the resources of the developing nations or potential environmental displacement.

III

Social Change and the New Technology

THE OUTSTANDING CHARACTERISTIC of the less developed countries is their dominant rurality. The United Nations Food and Agriculture Organization estimates the proportion of the population engaged in agriculture at 82 percent in Africa south of the Sahara, 70 percent in Asia and the Far East, 65 percent in the Near East and northwestern Africa, and 44 percent in Latin America.[1] In contrast to the large widely dispersed rural population residing in small villages and towns is the concentration of the relatively small urban population in large metropolitan agglomerations such as Calcutta, Rio de Janeiro, Saigon, Manila, Rangoon, and Karachi.

In 1968 agriculture (including forestry, hunting, and fishing) accounted for at least half of the Gross Domestic Product of India, Nigeria, the Sudan, Tanzania, and Uganda and 30–40 percent of the GDP of fourteen other countries of Africa, Asia, and Latin America.[2] Farming provides food and fiber to support the LDCs and is the source of much of their export volume. Farming and associated trades and crafts provide principal employment outlets for the LDC population.

Traditional Rural System

Rural social organization and the farm production and distribution process make up rural systems of components and linkages. The principal components are soil, water, farmers and their families, products, tools, traders, moneylenders, animals, natural vegetation, pathways, storage facilities, transport facilities, money, cooperatives, and so on. The linkages of rural systems are functions involving interpersonal and intergroup relations, production, distribution, consumption, exchange, and community obligation. Even a relatively simple rural social organization turns out to be complex. When such components as teachers, technicians, research establishments, marketing centers, and irrigation systems are added, the pattern becomes even more intricate. When communication assists such a system to interact with other systems, a complex of systems results; this in turn may be expressed as a hierarchy of rural systems with resulting specialization of function.

Rural systems are in a continuous process of adjustment to environmental change—changes arising within the system and changes caused by outside factors. Theodore Schultz asserts that efforts to adjust to change are directed toward achieving equilibrium by taking advantage of new opportunities and by offsetting adversities.

> Analytically the equilibrium approach is applicable to firms and households as producers and consumers and to alternative economic systems, whether they are predominantly capitalistic or socialistic including the soviet variety.[3]

The effect of these efforts may be a spiral process of adjustment or a repetitive cycling in the same orbit.

In their rural development efforts, LDC governments confront shifting combinations of population and environment, and development requires a strategy for bringing about change in rural systems. New components such as research institutions and technical personnel may be introduced in the process. These components establish new functional linkages and thus modify the system.

Agro-rural systems exist in a context of land, water, climate, and states of knowledge about farming. Landholding and other institutions ration access to resources needed for farming and thus determine individual income levels. For example, the social hierarchy of Indian villages predetermines to some extent income distributions among richer and poorer farmers. The prewar Japanese landlord-tenant system gave landlords power to determine the amount of land tenants could cultivate, the amount of rent they paid, and thus their income level. A similar situation prevails in the rice-growing areas of Southeast Asia. In parts of India the right to use irrigation water is determined in some cases by government and in others by customary arrangements within and between villages. Land rationing to farmer-users by landowners is widespread throughout Latin America. Before World War II cotton farming in the southern and southeastern United States was done very largely by black sharecroppers for white landowners in a rigid rural system.

Land quality varies widely, and extreme fragmentation and wide dispersion of individual farm holdings in separate tracts in many LDCs is partly a result of efforts to equalize holdings. However, the resulting fragmentation and dispersion complicates farming and inhibits introduction of new technology. Similar adjustments are made to compensate for or take advantage of location, varying degrees of climatic exposure, prevailing winds, low elevation, flooding, sunlight intensity, and natural drainage. Land use and farming configurations of rural villages are thus the expression of farmer efforts to adjust the environmental endowments within institutional frameworks. They represent a compromise between ecological and social imperatives.

In soil-water-human relations the starting point is where the people are. Thus rural development plans need to consider not what a more desirable distribution of rural population might be but what it is. Account must be taken of relative population density and of available natural resources. Plans must fit the densely populated regions of Lake Tanganyika and Kilimanjaro in Tanzania along with the sparser population of its Masai Steppe. Very small scale grain farming in the northern highlands of Ethiopia contrasts with the wide expanses of relatively sparsely populated southern rangelands. The almost grotesquely overcrowded lush farmlands of Kerala in southern India contrast with the drier interior regions of Madya Pradesh. Northern Honshu and Hokkaido in northern Japan with less hospitable climate have larger farms in contrast to the tiny holdings of the warmer regions of southern Honshu, Kyushu, and Shikoku; enormous population density in the lower Nile Valley with its intensive agriculture contrasts with the nomadic culture south of Khartoum.

There are no standard sets of rural characteristics of LDCs; the LDCs as well as their rural sectors differ widely. Some share one or more characteristics in common, but differences often overshadow similarities. In southeastern Asia one common farm characteristic is wet-field rice production. There are also millions of acres of wet-rice fields in India; South America also produces rice, and each system is different. In order to draw meaningful generalizations about the characteristics associated with a specific crop, several countries would have to be analyzed and compared in detail. Even in a phenomenon of such seeming uniformity as energy flows in agriculture, Odum's treatment contrasted the agricultural-livestock complex of a section of Uganda, Indian rice-cattle production, and complex natural rain forest systems in the Congo and Amazon basins.[4] Hayami and Ruttan in discussing induced innovation include comparative analysis of data from many countries and regions including western, southern, and southeastern Asia; Japan; South Korea; Taiwan; India; and others.[5]

These references to specific countries, typical of the literature of farming development in LDCs, indicate the location-specific character of each and consequently the difficulty of drawing general conclusions. Still another aspect is the egocentric predicament of observers, most of whom come trailing hard-to-discard prior conditioning.

Observations by even more self-critical westerners about Asia or Africa remain western observations. Even statistical and data categories westerners customarily use as analytical tools entail specific cultural bias. Peter Dorner points out that the principal rural development problem among poorer nations is an interacting combination of poverty, employment, production, and distribution. Yet in western thought each category tends to be analyzed separately.

> On some problems our theories and professional economic analyses are serving reasonably well in the United States and in other industrialized countries. The relevant questions are being asked and the data needed for analyses are being generated. But the categories in our census and other statistical series are not accidental. They too are products of the policy issues and the theoretical formulations developed through the interaction of problems and ideas.
> On other important policy questions, however, present theories provide little insight even on U.S. issues: environmental quality, poverty, race relations, a more acceptable distribution of economic and political power, congested cities, rural development, automation, and basic changes in the structure of resource ownership. Present theories do not seem to encompass these issues; they do not help us to formulate the right questions; hence, appropriate data are not available, and fundamental policy questions tend to fall outside the boundaries of traditional academic disciplines.[6]

In western terms development often means increased physical production. But when increased output is accompanied by intensification of poverty, loss of income, unemployment, and increased insecurity for large numbers of rural people, a different analytical model

TABLE 3.1. AGRICULTURAL HOLDINGS

Country	Year	Number	Area (hectares)	Average Size (hectares)
Colombia	1960	1,209,672	27,337,827	22.59
Peru	1961	869,945	17,722,044	20.37
Iran	1960	1,877,299	11,356,254	6.04
Turkey	1963	3,409,846	17,142,777	5.02
Morocco[a]	1961	1,106,765	5,117,000	4.62
Philippines	1960	2,166,216	7,772,485	3.58
Thailand	1963	3,214,405	11,149,190	3.46
Uganda	1963/64	1,170,921	3,856,196	3.29
Togo[a]	1961/62	217,127	569,830[c]	2.62
India[a]	1960	48,882,000	123,047,000	2.51
Korea, Rep. of	1961	2,331,874	4,815,471	2.06
Ceylon	1962	1,169,801	1,888,461	1.61
U.A.R.	1960/61	1,642,160	2,614,111	1.59
Vietnam, Rep. of	1960	1,892,789	2,511,783	1.32
Taiwan	1960/61	808,267	1,029,503	1.27
Indonesia[b]	1963	12,236,470	12,883,868	1.05
Madagascar	1961/62	882,000	917,000[d]	1.03

Adapted from: United Nations, FAO, *Production Yearbook*, 1969, 23:11, 12.
a. Provisional results.
b. Farm households only.
c. Arable area.
d. Cultivated area.

is needed. Investment in western terms usually connotes material capital, not primarily increased worker consumption. But at the low nutrition and energy levels of rural people in the poor regions, expenditures for food with resultant higher energy output provide a relatively high investment return.

Problems

It is often noted that farms in the LDCs are very small in contrast to their western counterparts. In South Vietnam 48 percent of the rice farms were 3 hectares and under. In Taiwan the cultivated land per farm averaged 1.27 hectares. Table 3.1 indicates the average size of land holdings for selected countries.

The small size of farms forces farmers to choose carefully between subsistence and commercial production. When farms are very small, it is natural for farmers to think in terms of immediate food needs for themselves and their families. Only after subsistence production is secure can they contemplate production for market. These decisions are important for economic development in predominantly rural developing countries, for marketed farm output feeds the urban-industrial population and provides savings for investment in expanded farm operations and industry.

Sustained increases in LDC agricultural output must come from farmers able to purchase additional farming inputs with money obtained from sale of their products. Thus in several East African countries farming contributes the larger part of the Gross Domestic Product, and about half this contribution is subsistence products consumed by the farmer on the farm. This part of farm production never reaches the marketplace.

Subsistence farm production is generally associated with traditional farm practices without technical inputs and tends to increase at the rate of rural population growth. It is that portion of resources utilized for nonsubsistence or commercial farming that produces a surplus. Hence the strategy for rural development includes inducement of shifts from subsistence to commercial farming and beyond that to achieve increased commercial output per farm worker. This involves motivating farmers (1) to shift part of their output to commercial crops and (2) to intensify commercial crop operations.

Shifting farm operations in the direction of a larger proportion of marketed crops means that some farmers are able to acquire additional fertilizers, better seeds, perhaps more water, and insecticides. The dimensions of the shift over time depend on farm income, and most LDC farmers are dirt poor; many millions of them exist on annual incomes under $100. As indicated in Table 3.2, this poverty condition corresponds to a low per capita contribution to the agri-

TABLE 3.2. AGRICULTURAL GROSS DOMESTIC PRODUCT IN SELECTED COUNTRIES, 1965

Country	Million Dollars	Dollars per Capita
Colombia	1,511	168
Iran	1,631	134
Turkey	2,890	127
Peru	697	121
Taiwan	692	118
Ceylon	647	116
U.A.R.	1,417	87
Morocco	633	87
Philippines	1,528	82
Korea, Rep. of	1,136	73
India	21,223	62
Togo	81	62
Uganda	369	54
Thailand	1,251	52
Vietnam, Rep. of	545	50

Adapted from: United Nations, FAO, *Production Yearbook*, 1969, 23:228–57.

cultural portion of the Gross Domestic Product in a number of countries.

Not only are farm incomes low in the LDCs, but income distribution is badly skewed. Opportunity for poorer farmers to increase production is narrow because of structural disadvantage.

> As agricultural development becomes based more on technology and less on the use of traditional resources, there occurs a growing need for the development of institutions which will permit the exploitation of the new technology and distribute its benefits in ways which result in a tolerable distribution of income, minimize social and political tensions, and permit a reasonably orderly process of development. This will not be easy to do in most cases because of inherent social and economic inequities of long standing. These inequities inevitably get highlighted by rapid change based on new technology.[7]

Income skewness is a counterpart of marked skewness in distribution of agricultural land. Unfortunately per capita averages of land holdings do not reveal the very large numbers of below-average holdings or aggregate land resources in large holdings. Tenurial status is another aspect of structural deficiencies of land distribution. In some LDCs more than half the farmers are tenants-at-will of landowners who impose burdensome rentals, provide a minimum contribution towards operating costs, and afford no tenure security. In this situation large numbers of farmers live and plan only for the immediate future. Their inferior economic situation is frequently reinforced by inferior social status. In their perspective any change is likely to make them worse off. Consequently their motivation is protective and conservative; they are slow to change from traditional farming to more modern practices.

In a number of LDCs these people form a majority of rural inhabitants and of total population. It is their child-bearing patterns, therefore, that tend to be reflected in LDC population characteristics. Schultz sees child-bearing and child-rearing motivation among LDC rural population as rational, given their circumstances:

> Most of the people of the world are very poor and children are in a very real sense the poor man's capital on which parents are dependent for shelter and food when they can no longer provide for themselves. But whether they are poor or rich, the social and economic characteristics of the community of which they are members systematically affect the costs and benefits of having children. The subjective and pecuniary costs encompass (1) the

opportunity cost of the woman's time, (2) the value of child labor, (3) family income, (4) education, (5) institutions, and (6) contraception information and techniques. The demand of parents for children both with respect to numbers and quality (e.g. investment in the child's health and schooling, etc.) is clear and cogent from recent studies of the micro-economics of the household.[8]

Therefore, one might predict that the preponderance of population increases anticipated for the LDCs will originate among poorer, less secure, and more numerous rural people. The production pattern will tend to reflect an effort to offset potential adversity of individual poor families.

Widespread unemployment, another characteristic of LDC rural people, is closely related to their large numbers and small-scale farming operations. Poverty, population, farm size, and unemployment are so interwoven that consideration of any one aspect involves the others. These considerations have important policy implications.

> Policies that emphasize modernization and increased production from the commercial farm sector without explicit attention to the creation of employment opportunities will yield increased output of certain farm commodities and growing labor productivity for a part of the farm labor force. But they tend to widen the income disparities and throw the burden of adjustment on the disadvantaged who join the ranks of the landless, become migrant seasonal workers, continue to crowd into existing small farm areas, move out to rapidly shrinking frontiers, or join the underemployed in the cities. There is no evidence that the increased volume of commodities moving through commercial channels as a result of increased production creates sufficient jobs for workers displaced by modernization or for the continuing new additions to the rural labor force.[9]

The cycle connecting poverty, unemployment, insecure tenure, and small-scale farming is aggravated by dietary deficiency (Chapter 1). The result is apathy: malnourished bodies cannot mobilize sufficient energy to do a full day's work; unemployment is mixed with resting time enforced by lack of energy; and inertia becomes part of a pattern of life in which innovation is unwelcome. Energy outputs are minimized, and leisure has a relatively high marginal utility.

This LDC rural characteristic sometimes frustrates efforts of agricultural technicians and policy makers. The author recalls the impatience of such an official in Tonga District of Tanzania after his persistent efforts to develop a farmer cooperative had failed, or the barely concealed contempt of officials in Uttar Pradesh at the lackadaisical behavior of rural laborers on a public works project. And the widely held stereotype of lazy Mexican peons has been a standard U.S. explanation for the backwardness of Mexican farmers—an attitude sometimes shared by better-off Mexican haciendados.

If prevailing land ownership and tenure institutions work against the security and incentive of smaller-scale LDC farmers, one might inquire about institutions that might assist them. The absence or inefficiency of such institutions often helps make LDC rural development difficult, partly due to lack of resources for better institutional support and partly because available resources are not properly mobilized. One very evident institutional deficiency is inadequate research. Linked with this is inadequate diffusion of information. Farmers cannot be expected to undertake new techniques without knowledge and guidance. Closely related to the disabilities of rural people is lack of institutional arrangements to internalize to beneficiaries costs now externalized. Such costs include (1) tenant insecurity which causes bad soil practices with resultant erosion, (2) welfare costs of unemployed landless rural labor representing the convenience of an available labor pool into which the large landowners can dip at will, (3) large farmer monopoly of government services and facilities, and (4) uncompensated environmental damage. Other institutional deficiencies include lack of credit, inefficient farm supply delivery systems, lack of facilities for storage, and inefficient marketing channels for farm produce. The literature concerning LDC development and agriculture discusses fully these deficiencies, which amount to constraints to participation in development processes. Rural development requires relaxation of these constraints.

> In almost all developing countries, particularly those in Asia, a major consideration is how to enable the small farmer to participate in agricultural development. A companion consideration is how to increase rural employment more rapidly to provide better employment and income opportunities for the landless labor and small landowners who rely on wage labor for part or all of their incomes. Briefly, there are at least three reasons for being concerned about the income and employment opportunities of the small farmers and landless laborers. First, extremely uneven distributions of rural income can result in explosive social and political instability which undermines orderly economic development. Second, the future food and fiber needs of most countries cannot be met unless the small farmers increase their output and productivity. Finally, improving the incomes of small farmers and landless laborers creates a demand for the

products and services of the nonagriculture sector and contributes to the growth of these sectors.[10]

Modernization of Agriculture

Improvement in traditional low-productivity farming of the LDCs involves altering the rural system. This is difficult because such systems tend to be rigid, culturally embedded, and change-resistant. Change involves unfamiliar combinations of inputs and conscious fostering of new interactions. Moreover, modernized farming may entail environmental effects not likely to be perceived in advance. Consequently, caution should be exercised when new technology is introduced. At the same time benefits from increased productivity need to be prompt and substantial.

> *First,* economic development will be slow and benefits probably badly distributed without technological change and an attendant rapid growth in agricultural production. There are some exceptions to this generalization, but in most developing nations without the application of modern technology to agriculture, growth rates and income of people in poverty are likely to be small or nonexistent. *Second,* technological change in agriculture is a biological phenomenon which is almost always certain to alter the biological and physical environment, and to upset the ecological balance. *Third,* currently there appear to be few options to the basic forms or "packages" in which technological change must come in order to increase agricultural production. Where there are conflicts with environment, accommodations usually must be made outside agriculture, but there are choices available within the agricultural sector which gives a country an option to avoid destruction conflicts. *Fourth,* in light of these points, the need is not for extremes of either-or, but for intelligent analyses of long-term social costs and returns of various alternatives, choosing among the alternatives and improving research and education resources to expand the range of alternatives.[11]

The process of introducing innovation requires first the innovation itself and the process by which it is produced. The second step is establishment of institutions and procedures for adapting innovation to conform to specific environments. The final step is the diffusion of knowledge among farmers.

The new high-yielding rice varieties were initially developed in the Philippines. Adaptation of these varieties to Indian conditions involved substantial additional work in Indian research establishments, which meant that India had to mobilize necessary resources to perform the task. It was also necessary to perform preparatory tasks of multiplying seeds and distributing them to farmers. This involved additional tasks of mobilizing and organizing resources and people. Simultaneously a great deal of work by the central government of India and of constituent Indian states was necessary to insure proper diffusion to farmers of knowledge about new varieties and associated farm technologies.

As Hayami and Ruttan point out, these tasks place considerable pressure on trained personnel who have to shoulder responsibility for introducing not only new seed varieties but also knowledge of a complex set of interactions involving tillage, irrigation, fertilizer, and insecticides. In the short run it is difficult to expand LDC scientific and technical cadres, and the process also involves substantial new investment outlays.[12] Even more difficult is deployment of properly trained field staff.

Farmers that adopt innovations do so because they believe they will profit. Thus those farmers capable of absorbing information quickly and obtaining necessary resources tend first to grasp new opportunities. If returns are prompt and substantial, such individuals gain an initial advantage over others. This initial advantage can well result in a permanent and widening gain in wealth and prestige for some but a gradually increasing handicap for those less favorably placed—they will tend to "lose out."

> The opportunity to modernize agriculture is as a rule very unequal within countries. The heterogeneity of the agricultural production possibilities, especially in large countries, sets the stage for area-wise income disparities and for differences in the population pressures among farming areas. What this means is that the modernization of agriculture alters significantly the *comparative advantage* among agricultural areas within the country. Western countries have not been spared on this score. Clearly parts of agriculture in Italy and France have long been depressed. The U.S.S.R., despite her centralized planning and administered economy, is not spared, and the depressed Appalachia is poignant testimony of the very uneven agricultural development in the United States. Among the poor countries Mexico and India illustrate the implications of this development. Mexico, which is now well along into the third decade of successful modernization of parts of her agriculture, faces increasingly serious income disparities among major agricultural areas. Agriculture in north and middle Mexico has progressed and the stagnant south of Mexico has become a major depressed area by comparison. The internal migration implications are profound in terms of redistribution

of the Mexican population. In India, the agricultural comparative advantage of the producing areas is shifting to the northern parts and to the major "rice bowls" of the southern parts as a consequence of modernization. A large triangle in central India is losing out competitively. Scores of millions of people who are dependent upon agriculture reside in this large area. They will be left behind. The new varieties of rice, wheat, corn, millet, etc., that are fertilizer responsive and the larger and cheaper supply of fertilizer are decisively less productive within this large triangle because of the lack of rainfall and of water for irrigation.[13]

Effects of the Green Revolution

Effects of the Green Revolution have been to raise levels of grain production very markedly, and use of the new seeds has spread over wide areas of Asia. India and Pakistan have prospects of being self-sufficient in wheat. Although Indian experience with rice has not been as satisfactory, present difficulties are susceptible of solution. Other Asian grain-producing regions may become self-sufficient, and some may move from rice import to an export position.

The Green Revolution itself results from several factors that have interacted in rural systems to bring about extraordinary changes. A great deal of credit goes to the Ford and Rockefeller scientists who produced main genetic lines of the new grain varieties. These were basic. But these varieties require fertilizer and water. Fortunately world fertilizer supplies have been expanding rapidly in recent years with accompanying sharp price declines. Recent tube well development in the Indus Basin and on the Indo-Gangetic Plain has been successful. This has provided the third element—a satisfactory, controllable water supply to complement new strains and available chemical fertilizer. In other regions similar degrees of success have been enjoyed, but also favorable grain prices to farmers have provided a highly important incentive.

In the initial stages the Green Revolution has provided grounds for an optimistic outlook for the world food supply. Consumers benefit from substantially increased marketings of food grains and increasingly lower prices. For now farmer profits provide an adequate incentive for production. Eventually prices may fall, but in LDCs this will tend to contribute to a consumer surplus. Schultz interprets these changes in terms of economic equilibrium.

> The gains in agricultural productivity that are obtained from the adoption and efficient use of modern agricultural inputs,

under competitive conditions, are in general as equilibrium is approached, transferred to the consumer. These gains are revealed in lower farm-food prices. They are in the language of economics a *consumer surplus*. To the extent that they are distributed among an increasing number of consumers, it is obvious that the surplus per consumer is thereby reduced. Nevertheless, the agricultural and demographic processes underway imply that a substantial part of the increases in per capita income in many poor countries during the next several decades will originate out of gains in agricultural productivity.[14]

If the world grain supply expands in conformity with yield potentials of the "miracle seeds," it seems likely that some LDCs will become food grain exporters. Such exports would then provide a source of badly needed foreign exchange. This would be a neat solution for two pressing LDC economic problems—cheaper domestic food and a source of foreign exchange. Other potential outcomes, however, may be less auspicious.

If existing trade barriers constrain grain exports, resulting domestic surpluses might lower domestic grain prices and discourage producers. According to Gale Johnson, the outlook is unfavorable too if LDC grain prices are held above world market prices.

> One factor not taken into account . . . is the extent to which a number of developing countries have price supports for certain key agricultural products that hold the prices above world market levels. To some degree the price supports above world market levels are offset by overvalued currencies. But even so a number of developing countries have producer prices for grain that must fall substantially before these countries can compete effectively in international markets without the use of export subsidies. In four countries that have had considerable expansion of wheat production due to the introduction of high yielding varieties—Mexico, India, Pakistan and Turkey—the wholesale price in 1969 ranged from a low of $101 per ton in Pakistan to a high of $127 per ton in Mexico. In the same year Australian wheat was landed in the UK at $66 per ton.[15]

The situation is made still less favorable by high domestic grain price policies of the developed countries, particularly the European Common Market countries and Japan. These policies partially or completely foreclose these markets to LDC grain imports. One possibility sometimes mentioned is a shift of food grain into cattle feed. However, this would not be a feasible alternative in southern and southeastern Asia, which do not have a substantial livestock tradition, and it seems doubtful that shipping costs for LDC grain as feed in other LDC cattle areas would be attractive.

There is, however, one definite gain of the Green Revolution: it has provided the model of a successful technique for increasing yields per worker and per acre in the LDCs. The latter is important in most regions with an adverse man-land ratio. Not only have crop yields per acre increased, but also double- and even triple-cropping have become feasible in some areas, equivalent to a substantial increase in cropland endowments of these land-hungry regions.

The outcome of increased worker productivity is less clear, since it depends on the degree of equity in distribution of actual earnings in proportion to increased per capita production. We have already discussed the benefit accruing to producers able to seize an initial advantage from innovation, and this advantage will probably affect distribution of increased productivity earnings among smaller producers.

SECOND-GENERATION PROBLEMS. The real key to long-range Green Revolution potentials is contained in the words *momentum* and *income;* they are related. Will improved consumption levels provide an appetite that demands further innovations? Will appetites for innovation bring about an increase in institutions to support innovations? Will rural systems develop increasingly complex linkages, and will components of systems enlarge and multiply? Will millions of small rural producers who have the dominant role in LDC development shake off lethargy and apathy and respond to opportunity?

These questions may not evolve in concert, and some may not develop at all or may be offset by other developments. But grounds for such questions exist. For example, a principal potential physical barrier to spread of the Green Revolution is dependence on irrigation. The revolution's spread will be defined by the speed with which irrigation can be developed. Such large-scale schemes as development of the Mekong Basin require huge capital investment beyond the capacity of basin countries. A substantial portion of the India-Pakistan increase in irrigation acreage is from pumped groundwater. However, the extent of this resource, its quality, and economic limits of pumping lifts have not been nailed down; nor has adequate emphasis been placed on water management.

In all LDCs marketing, storage, and transport infrastructure is imperfect. Therefore, supplies of improved seed, fertilizer, and insecticides do not flow smoothly or in accord with imperatives of the farm calendar. Marketing and storage facilities in many places are not adequate to meet substantial crop movements. The result is frequent loss to farmers through spoilage and market gluts.

In those countries where wealth and social status are unequally distributed, existing inequities among rural people can be transformed into cumulative economic advantage. Thus, unless institutional reforms accompany technological innovation, gains are limited to elites, and broad economic advance does not occur. Clifton Wharton foresees that in these circumstances the rich will become richer and the gap between them and the rank and file of smaller farmers will increase:

> From all this one may deduce that the "first" or "early" adopters of the new technology will be in regions which are already more advanced, literate, responsive and progressive and which have better soil, better water management, closer access to roads and markets—in sum, the wealthier, more modern farmers. For them, it is easier to adopt the new higher-yield varieties since the financial risk is less and they already have better managerial skills. When they do adopt them, the doubling and trebling of yields mean a corresponding increase in their incomes.
>
> One indication of this is the large number of new private farm-management consultant firms in the Philippines which are advising large landlords on the use of the new seed varieties and making handsome profits out of their share of the increased output.
>
> As a result of different rates in the diffusion of the new technology, the richer farmers will become richer. In fact, it may be possible that the more progressive farmers will capture food markets previously served by the smaller semi-subsistence producer. In India, only 20 percent of the total area planted to wheat in 1967–68 consisted of the new dwarf wheats, but they contributed 34 percent of the total production. Such a development could well lead to a net reduction in the income of the smaller, poorer and less venturesome farmers. This raises massive problems of welfare and equity. If only a small fraction of the rural population moves into the modern century while the bulk remains behind, or perhaps even goes backward, the situation will be highly explosive. For example, Tanjore district in Madras, India, has been one of the prize areas where the new high-yield varieties have been successfully promoted. Yet one day last December, 43 persons were killed in a clash there between the landlords and their landless workers, who felt that they were not receiving their proper share of the increased prosperity brought by the Green Revolution.[16]

If principal Green Revolution benefits are confined to larger and wealthier farmers, the innovational impetus might run its course fairly shortly. Benefits to the economy might be limited to consequences of a partially adopted technology. Increased incomes of a minority might be dissipated in luxury consumption; savings might be invested outside agriculture or even outside the country. Such an income effect would not promote development, and momentum of innovation would gradually decline or be stabilized at less than optimum levels.

Another factor to be considered is social and political unrest which may be engendered by inequitable distribution of Green Revolution benefits. Small farmers can see as well as anyone else the immediate benefits reaped by their more affluent neighbors simply because they are already big and rich, and their response is likely to be expressed in social discontent and political discord not furthering the development process.

Wolf Ladejinsky estimates that 67 percent of the Indian rural population in 1969 operated fewer than 5 acres per family, and over 100 million rural people owned no land at all. These small farmers and landless rural people had annual per capita incomes of about $21.[17] Since larger farmers in India customarily operate with tenants or hired labor, some economists have seen this increase in labor employment as an offset to rural unemployment. Unfortunately motivation to substitute hired labor for tenants may also result in replacing labor with machinery.

As Ladejinsky sees it, the Green Revolution in some parts of India has tended to aggravate the preexisting economic disadvantage of tenants, sharecroppers, and landless farm laborers. Land values in these areas have risen sharply, and landowners have an increasing incentive to maintain full control of their holdings. Inevitably in these circumstances, the rights of tenants become increasingly precarious, and any prospects of land tenure reform recede still further.

Many landowners would probably like to rid themselves of tenants altogether, their only restraint being fear of active tenant revolt. Nevertheless, landowners are in the driver's seat, and the process of tenant disestablishment proceeds inexorably. Through the leverage of increased rents combined with usury, tenants become sharecroppers and sharecroppers become wageworkers.

In some of the Green Revolution areas in India farm labor is apparently more fully employed and wages may be higher. Temporarily at least, the Green Revolution is labor-intensive partly due to increased double-cropping. In part this gain is illusory as employers shift from payment of wages in kind, which insured a minimum food supply, to the uncertainties of the local retail market. The longer-run prospect for farm labor in these areas is not very good because of the increasing substitution of labor-saving farm machinery for wage labor. The spectacle of a few rich beneficiaries of the Green Revolution surrounded by increasing masses of impoverished partially unemployed rural laborers is not reassuring for either political stability or rural development.[18]

In terms of income criteria for innovational agricultural progress, Ladejinsky's analysis indicates that the institutional situation in India would tend to reduce income for a majority of those affected by the Green Revolution. Moreover, the scope, intensity, and volume of the innovation would be reduced. In some regions of Latin America where land ownership is a status symbol for urban elites, there might be small incentive to undertake innovation at all since the objective is not primarily economic.

Another factor to be taken into account in assessing momentum of the push from traditional to scientific farming is the response of public-supported research; maintenance of momentum requires a proliferation of the national research network. As Hayami and Ruttan have indicated, research investment is evoked by public demand; since such research has to be location-specific, the demand has to be fairly universal in such locations.[19] Public support would probably not be strong if gains were limited to a few while disabilities increased for many.

> More serious is the possibility of widening income disparity among farmers. The income position of farmers who have no access to new technology, due, for example, to the lack of irrigation facilities, will become relatively worse as the aggregate supply schedule shifts to the right. Declining prices and widening income disparity among farm producers may cause significant social tension and disruption in rural areas and major political instability at the national level.[20]

It seems probable that the necessary innovational transformation of LDC farming cannot be realized without simultaneous institutional transformation insuring wide participation in the process and sharing of its benefits.

Objective

The objective of development is to enlarge the rural system by increasing the size of existing components, strengthening existing linkages, introducing new components, and establishing new linkages so the new larger system functions symmetrically at higher dynamic levels. In this concept imbalances represent eccentric socioeconomic forces which increase orbital distortion and generate centrifugal pulls endangering the entire system. Hayami and Ruttan voice a similar view in contrasting U.S. and Japanese agricultural development through what they term "dialectic interaction" among components of "farmers, public institutions and private farm supply firms: which achieved a highly developed mechanical technology in U.S. agriculture and a highly developed biological technology in Japanese agriculture," consistent with resource endowments of the two countries.[21]

Some take the view that an agricultural system will eventually make adjustments to offset temporary imbalances and that these adjustments move the economy toward equilibrium. Consequently Green Revolution social and political repercussions are only part of the adjustment process—a consequence of technical innovation—and steps taken to reform rural institutions would follow rather than precede scientific innovation. This view might be acceptable if there were sure knowledge of a satisfactory outcome, but there is no such assurance.

Indeed it could be argued that dissension feeds on itself. In this vein, the adjustment process might be a long-run proposition with intervening stages of violence, economic disruption, and material destruction. Or the innovative process might just dry up. Except for a small group of economic beneficiaries, the rural scene would sink into apathy, indifference, and inertia. Such negative potentials would indicate that institutional reform should be an ex ante, not an ex post, condition of scientific innovation in agriculture. Unfortunately this kind of forward-sensing behavior seems to run counter to the ordinary course of human affairs. Perhaps the best that can be hoped for is sufficient awareness of the certainty that technical innovation always has disequilibrating effects, and these effects should be taken into account alongside innovation.

> It follows from these now generally accepted points that while science and technology will represent the "engine for change" in the process of agricultural development in the poor countries, translating it into a real force for economic development will require drastic social, political and institutional changes. New technologies of the biological and chemical type (seed and fertilizer) generally are in themselves neutral with respect to scale. However, where these technologies are highly productive and profitable they will (a) highlight inherent inequities of long standing in social and political structures and (b) simul-

taneously create the demand for a large variety of changes. With advances such as the new high-yielding varieties of cereals, farmers, particularly the smaller ones, will demand improvements in water resources because water is now a more productive input; they will demand more credit because purchased inputs are essential for the production of the new varieties; they will want access to the new inputs; and they more than ever will desire a tenurial status under which the legal system in fact treats them as equals and with which they can participate equally in factor and product markets and in the institutions which collectively manage provision of inputs and the disposal of outputs.[22]

Lest there be doubt as to the practicality of undertaking institutional reforms, it is well to state again that long-run practicality lies in widespread participation in the new technology by all farmers. Without this participation, full output levels would not be achieved, partly because small farmer incomes would continue to be so small that the farmers could not acquire new technical inputs. Hence this large group would be unable to use the new technology.

It certainly is not in the national interest of the LDCs to increase numbers of landless farm laborers where rural unemployment already exists. It is unsound to aggravate insecurity of tenants by continuance of a system of large ownership alongside a system of tiny, fragmented holdings. Nor is it in the national interest for LDCs, with limited land resources, to encourage or tacitly approve absentee land ownership, particularly when part of the motivation for such ownership is social status and prestige.

It is necessary to increase security of tenants by specifying minimum terms of occupancy, to increase the size of overly small ownerships by redistributing holdings of land above maximum ceilings, and to restrict absentee ownership. The noted Indian economist, M. L. Dantwala, considers that effective institutional reform is unlikely in a traditional system. But where a technological breakthrough such as the Green Revolution provides new incentive horizons, policies for economic and institutional change are needed to prevent monopoly of technological gains.[23]

Adjustment of land tenure institutions is a step toward widespread adoption of innovative farming. But it is also essential to bulwark such structural changes with appropriate prices. These are the direct incentives for increased production. In addition, smaller farmers must have access to credit. Their savings margins are not adequate to cover the additional cash outlay of innovation. However, neither credit nor pricing policy should encourage capital-intensive methods at the cost of labor displacement.

Martin Abel feels that in the soil and water domain, three areas are of great importance:

> The first is more information about and a better understanding of the technical (physical) relationships involved. The second is a better understanding of the type of technological innovations which can help to solve some of the problems and possibly also deal with some aspects of the externalities involved. Finally, and in the long run possibly most important of all, is the creation of institutions which will permit collective action in dealing with these externalities. These institutions could (a) be regulatory in nature such as controlling the density of tubewells in an area or the intensity of grazing; (b) facilitate cooperative management of resources such as water-users associations for the collective management of canal irrigation systems; or (c) facilitate the implementation of economic policies such as pricing of resources, taxes, and subsidies which would narrow or eliminate differences between private and social benefits. Considerable improvement will have to take place in information, research, and training systems to provide a basis for rationally bringing about improvements in each of the above areas.[24]

The ability to handle innovation implies that large numbers of farmers and their families emerge from the cocoon of tradition and undertake self-conscious planning and management. This entails an extension of margins of knowledge not only of farming and its technology but, even more significantly, of the whole farm household. This is a neglected area of study and research.

> My concern is about the neglected area of knowledge, the part that is not on the agenda of our research-oriented universities, research institutes and thinking centers. As a consequence there are all too few advances in knowledge that would serve the family, i.e., the household in its nonmarket activities in the choices that are made among purchased goods and in the use of the time of its members in acquiring additional satisfactions for themselves from consumptions, from the way they live, and . . . from the number and quality of children. . . . Let us put aside the all-too-popular game of projecting massive population aggregates. What we need instead are advances in knowledge that may be had by concentrating on the microbehavior of families (households) with a view of providing them with new and better opportunities and information that will increase their sources of satisfactions.[25]

Thus innovational process within LDCs produces other results perhaps as significant in the long run as greatly increased productivity. One of these results is the substantial political consequences of increased self-knowledge among impoverished rural masses as they come to realize the extent of their disabilities. Another result likely to occur is in the range of ecological consequences of the new technology. Very little thought has been given to this latter aspect.

Impact on Environment

Innovative farm technology inevitably affects the surrounding environment. The developed countries, where basic features of this technology originate, are becoming aware of environmental impacts of this technology on their ecosystems. We have already discussed (Chapter 2) effects of chemical fertilizers and pesticides on water and air resources and on plant and animal biota. We cannot escape the conclusion of analogous impacts as these components are introduced into LDCs. However, there is a difference. Developed countries have some choices as to tolerable degrees of environmental damage. Food and fiber supplies relative to foreseeable demand and to environmental impact are relatively ample and secure. Starvation or even hunger and malnutrition on a wide scale are not serious threats in the developed world regardless of alternates selected. Of course this is aside from isolated pockets of inexcusable poverty, misery, and malnutrition and from obvious instances of unnecessary pollution tolerated simply because of lower priorities we accord them.

In the LDCs hunger and malnutrition are often widespread, and the specter of starvation may be a chronic threat. They need more food and fiber, and they need them now; greatly increased future needs are discernible. They have not, therefore, been greatly concerned about environmental impact of western technology. As "have not" regions, it is easy for them to discount western concern with environmental deterioration as "a rich man's disease."

One can sympathize with this view. Water management is of little concern to one dying of thirst! Still, failure to fully comprehend environmental phenomena can have serious short-run effects. Hydrologic considerations in the form of stream-flow data become a vital part of plans for major water retention structures. Scanty or inaccurate stream-flow data can lead to serious and costly mistakes; dams built in wrong locations can never fulfill expectations and may cause serious damage. This kind of environmental miscalculation can be very hard on LDC developmental undertakings. Siltation of reservoirs due to deforestation and grazing of upstream areas shortens the period of reservoir usefulness both for power generation and for irrigation. Deforestation, overgrazing, and cultivation of steep slopes can cause destructive erosion. In poor countries trade-off considerations between immediate survival pressures and longer-range conservation alternates have to yield to survival. Still, intrusion into the ecosystem without full knowledge of the chain of adverse events set in motion is hazardous.

The reaction of LDCs to environmental concerns of developed countries implies that to poor regions costs of ecosystem protection is beyond their means. But when institutional and structural conformations are as badly skewed in their distributive effects as they are in some LDCs, benefits accrue to the more powerful groups and costs often are passed on to the weaker many. Some responsibility also may rest with the exporters of technology who fail to take into account environmental impacts of technology on regions that cannot afford to recoup costs of potential damage.

> Notable among the type of schemes which should come under scrutiny are those which would extend land areas under cultivation. These include all the possibilities where large scale capital investments are necessary: conquering equatorial lands, irrigating the deserts, valley development, resettlement or colonization of people on farmland, and various land reform schemes. All such schemes result in environmental change, some more than others. . . . From all the evidence, more attention has been given to the productivity quotient in rural structural development than the pollution quotient. Plan after plan in the LDC's have calculated the most minute details on cost-benefit analysis but few have attempted to incorporate the environmental cost of the projects. However, how can we in the U.S. expect such when it has been only in the last few years that our own Bureau of Reclamation and U.S. Army Corps of Engineers have done so, and with great reluctance.
>
> Little yet, so far as I can determine, has been attempted to internalize the social costs of environmental deterioration in developing countries. Again, how can we expect farmers in traditional agricultural countries to pick up the costs for such things as conservation and other practices when we still pay several hundred millions of dollars for these practices, the major benefits of which are clearly specific to the firm.[26]

As LDCs increasingly import agricultural technology from developed regions, they move from what Earl Heady describes as a "closed system" to an "open system."[27] The closed system of traditional agriculture is one in which the inputs to production are all part of the farm system itself. These inputs consist largely of land and labor;

fertilizer comes from livestock manure and seed is simply saved from preceding harvests. Advanced technology has the effect of reducing the amount of land required for various levels of output and the system becomes "open." Technological inputs purchased off-farm include chemicals, seeds, machinery, and feed additives.

In the United States, work of developing these new inputs originally included little if any study of environmental repercussions. That came later, as evidence of damage accumulated from a variety of sources. For example, nitrate and phosphate accumulated in drainage water, enormously increased cattle populations in feedlots concentrated animal waste and constituted a sewage problem, drift of airborne chemical insecticides and pesticides used on one crop destroyed insect and plant populations elsewhere, irrigation water used unwisely (because of unsound water price policy) produced salinization and waterlogging of good land. Added to this was continuing destruction of the typical American rural countryside with its homes, villages, and towns and the accompanying rural way of life. It is claimed that part of the trade-off for this was abundant food supplies at lower prices. But along with lower prices for farm products came a farm-price subsidy to protect farmers from unfavorable economic consequences of their intensive use of technology. This included a program of withdrawing land from cultivation while production mounted on remaining acres.

In developed countries effects of farm technology have been costly to the environment, and efforts to contain these costs have been only partially successful. Heady suggests a trade-off by reducing amounts of fertilizer application and calling into production some of the national acreage reserve, perhaps at no increased cost to consumers or losses to farmers in the long run.[28]

As the LDCs move increasingly from "closed" to "open" systems by importing western farm technology, the risks of environmental damage increase. When this probability is recognized by technology exporters and importers alike, it may lead to exporters extending their research and development work to include greater environmental concern. Importers will have an opportunity to consider economic trade-off policies to direct innovation along Hillman's "path of least disturbing innovations."[29]

These considerations should include a review of food price policies encompassing *all* costs of production, and these policies should seek to internalize environmental costs to the production process rather than to permit such costs to continue as externalities at general expense or as misallocations borne by groups and individuals unable to pass them on.

For good or for ill, changes wrought by agricultural innovation may prove irreversible, and traditional rural systems are particularly vulnerable. Once Green Revolutions are set in motion, rural systems will have to make the required, successive stages of adjustment. The social cost of the Industrial Revolution in ruined lives, death, and misery was paid immediately by those who suffered—not by those who benefited; ameliorative adjustments came after the technology was well entrenched.

If any lesson has been learned, it is that technological change is always disturbing to sociopolitical systems; the greater the change, the greater the disturbance. In the LDCs the advent of the Green Revolution combines potentials for great change and great disturbance. The challenge is to facilitate adjustment, extend benefits widely, and distribute costs equitably within the rural system.

IV

Political and Administrative Aspects of Rural Development

Rural development signifies a great deal more than increased farm output. Farming may be conceived as a series of activities carried on by individuals on a particular piece of land to achieve a material objective; rural development not only includes increased farm production but also connotes a continuous social and political process among rural people ceaselessly reaching out toward a better life. It is possible to increase farm production without improving rural society. Thus in the United States vast increases in farm output were achieved at the same time rural progress ceased because American rural society ceased to exist.

The situation in the LDCs is very different from that in America; there are large metropolitan regions, but none of these is presently able to engulf a large portion of rural society. Instead LDCs continue to confront the need to increase farm production and achieve rural development. However, for the most part these rural people have not been able to improve the quality of their own society nor to participate in the political life of the country.

In the Latin-American democracies the rural political power structure is largely a matter of status, and since most rural people have little or no status they are largely disenfranchised. In the newer countries of Africa and Asia numerically small political elites rule because there is no one else to do the job. Thus political life in the LDCs tends to evolve as an oligarchic process. Political action in some of these governments is limited to infighting among members of the elite, and resulting coups d'etat sometimes become a means for effecting meaningless changes in personnel.

Apparently Latin-Americans have never been able to solve the political dilemma posed by the conflict between democratic political forms and an extremely status-conscious, prestige-oriented social order. The problem of overcoming the political limitations imposed by a colonial past still persists among the newly independent countries of Asia and Africa. In the latter case the changing of the guard was negotiated primarily between elites on both sides. Then, faced with the staggering task of governing a newly independent country, the new leaders depended on an incumbent bureaucracy to keep the country going while they sought to consolidate and expand their leadership. But this effort did not create a broader political power base; it simply organized, more efficiently perhaps, those already in positions of power. In the rural areas these were larger landholders, religious leaders, and merchants who by one means or another maintained political and economic control of the rural masses. In any event the traditional hierarchical controls of caste and tribe went largely unchanged, and the bureaucracy went on functioning in the colonial tradition—the only way it knew.

There were occasional improvements. In some places and at some times some rural people in some LDCs enjoyed some material benefits from improved farming. But it is not apparent that rural people as a whole have participated more fully in policy decisions affecting them. It is questionable whether LDC rural development connoting continuous forward movement of the rural masses has made any significant gains.

In the LDC capitals the terminology of government and political affairs is speciously modern and the component parts of up-to-date government seem to be in place. In this congenial atmosphere it is quite easy for an observer to be lulled into believing that all is done that can be done. The verbiage and the terminology one hears are similar to what one has been trained to accept. Although perhaps only superficially, many of the LDCs are organized along proper democratic and parliamentary lines, and tables of organization have a familiar appearance. In some respects several of the LDCs seem even more politically progressive than their European or American prototypes. At least formally, these countries are committed to planning as a central tool of government, whereas the United States prefers the opaque profundity of annual Presidential messages on the state of the union and the national budget, and somehow Britons find solace in backward-looking reports of Chancellors of the Exchequer and Chairmen of the Board of Trade.

Most of the LDCs accept the need to use the powers of government to direct, control, and guide national economic affairs. At least their intentions in this respect seem clear, and this is much to their credit despite substantial lags in performance. On the surface then, one might conceive that the LDCs are in pretty fair political shape if their adherence to democratic forms, their acceptance of the use of planning, and their adoption of an interventionist role of government in economic affairs are accepted at face value.

Unfortunately all this applies only in the capital at the center of government and not at all or only to a very limited extent in rural areas among rural people. It is not that these governments have not tried to reach rural people; they have. In India and Pakistan real effort was put into the systems of Panchayat Raj and Basic Democracy designed to achieve grass roots political expression. But neither of these has yet demonstrated ability to deal effectively with the traditional centers of rural power, and the same may be true of the Ujamaa Village program of Tanzania. Many LDCs find it nearly impossible to deploy an adequate field staff to carry out their policies. Moreover, in a number of these countries, despite lip service, many of the elite are hesitant to unleash the latent political power of rural people. The result has been few organs and routines for effectively mobilizing and expressing rural political judgments. A political chasm exists, with leaders and bureaucrats on one side and a vast voiceless rural population on the other.

This is particularly true of the planning process, accepted and endorsed by most LDCs as essential to the conduct of their affairs. Despite the trappings and apparatus of planning, LDC governments have not inherited or created the means for effectively involving rural people in the process. At best the plans of LDCs are prepared and reviewed by technicians (often expatriate technicians), so whatever satisfaction LDC elites may obtain from plan preparation and promulgation should be muted by realization that these documents are not plans in any real sense. Since they do not represent a political consensus, there is no certainty that they will or can be implemented. They remain simply recorded exercises in economic, statistical, and financial projections and extrapolations representing possibilities, not probabilities.

The architects of LDC government are in a predicament. They have opted for policies dependent on wide political involvement but have been unable to create the institutions linking the center to rural communities. To put it another way, LDC leaders have not yet found a way to decentralize political power. They have attempted to find a substitute by sending large numbers of government people into the rural area to tell people of their good intentions. However, the task of training such cadres has proved time-consuming and costly, and it is doubtful that these government newcomers have been accepted by the people. More likely these agents are taken into camp by the existing power structure and never achieve significant liaison with the people. Although the LDC authorities genuinely desire rural political participation, they have not been able to reconcile themselves to use tactics of political agitation and organization somewhat along the lines used by trade unions and perhaps similar to methods used in China.

Those arrangements for working with rural people that have been attempted have not resulted in strengthening the governments of the Third World. Indeed the continuing turmoil testifies rather to basic political weakness. Since the bulk of those populations is rural, this weakness reflects a serious lack of solidarity among rural people and between them and the nation. While the weakness of fledgling nations is comprehensible, less reassuring is the persistence of attitudes and policies sustaining elites but reinforcing political weakness and inhibiting development. The time may have come for the LDCs to recognize the political strength accruing to the nation from forthrightly yielding to the rural constituency powers, enabling them to participate effectively in formation and execution of development programs.

This commentary is not original; 137 years have passed since Alexis de Tocqueville described what he conceived to be the political dynamics of rural New England. Whether he was correct in his interpretation of the New England scene is less important than his success in demonstrating how a vigorous political unit composed of free individuals could contribute to national strength and solidarity. In today's terms Tocqueville's description is a political model.

Examination of the mechanics of LDC government operations reveals the lack of availability of functions presented in Tocqueville's model. Instead, a small political leadership and an imperfectly functioning central bureaucracy seek to run the entire country, although they lack local support and cannot depend on responsible citizen performance in the rural hinterland. Unfortunately neither the history nor the traditions of many of these nations provided for free local political expression. Being unaware of this gap, the new leaders did not perceive the need to create these political precincts. Instead they tinkered with existing local power structures and the inherited administrative units in the hope that somehow these could be cobbled into a semblance of valid political institutions. But these local power structures represented not equality and free association but the exact opposite. Too often they were instruments of petty despotism operating on the custom-sanctioned ethic that the weak existed for exploitation. Indeed the entire rural landscape in many regions came close to constituting a mosaic of political fiefdoms ruled by men strongly opposed to the very democratic principles promulgated by the elites and stated as the foundations of new national constitutions.

While Tocqueville's model may never have existed in real life (and, if it did, is nowhere significant in today's American political life), his concept or something close to it may be apropos of the transformation of LDC rural institutions to further the ends of rural development.

One of the aspects of the New England village emphasized by Tocqueville was the broad assignment of public duties among the citizens. These included almost the entire spectrum of local government—taxes, police, records, finance, public instruction, the poor, roads, weights and measures, and parish committees. Administrative authority, vested in elected selectmen, was strictly limited by the requirement for referral to village meetings of any changes or proposals for additional undertakings. Another aspect was the ease of making new proposals whenever small groups in the community wanted to make them. The system provided a broad distribution of power; the right of public participation in review and proposal was important, but more important was the wide opportunity to participate in managing community affairs. The result was to elicit maximum citizen interest and wide distribution of power, and at the heart of this structure was universal personal freedom and equality.[1]

In contrast, Myrdal and others indicate that in many LDC rural communities authority and the use of power are restricted to a small group attaining its prerogatives through birth, caste, tribal affiliation, or wealth. Central government tends to deal with this group; its representatives ally themselves with this leadership and so become a part of the traditional establishment. As a result, community undertakings are involuntary for most of the participants and have the features of forced and therefore unwilling contributions. Most of the community generate nothing of public significance on their own initiative. Instead each family draws into itself, seeking to avoid as much as possible any contact with authority.[2]

Role of Political Leaders

So far, our discussion of the political and administrative impediments to rural development has emphasized relations between rural people and government. Other impediments flow from specific attitudes of LDC political leaders and government officials toward agriculture, natural resources, and the environment. These attitudes influence decisions in rural development; their effects are emphasized by Stefan Robock who, in his discussion of natural resource development in the northeastern Brazil SUDENE program, points to the political aspects of large natural resource undertakings, particularly among top echelon political leaders.[3] In order for major development to start at all, strong support must be provided by national leadership. However, this support evolves through political negotiation possibly calling for sacrifices of technical principles and even of some objectives. Thus the SUDENE program as finally implemented represented important compromises. Robock concedes that a later evaluation of the program may support its wisdom, but he suggests that the intervening political struggle was very costly. It seems likely that, in the political bargaining, hopes for rapid development were encouraged; in order to satisfy these, important longer-range benefits had to be subordinated.

Political leaders can be tough bargainers; they also seek at times to avoid issues involving direct confrontation. When the opposition is strong and well organized and proponents are not, political common sense dictates that issues be soft-pedaled even though basic principles of social equity are sacrificed. Politicians with records of supporting lost causes do not stay long in office. Probably such considerations are responsible for long delays in changing existing LDC land tenure arrangements and instituting broad agrarian reform. While these changes and reforms are generally recognized as essential to rural modernization and progress in many of the LDCs, exploitation is most extreme where landed interests are strongest and best organized and small farmers and tenants are poorly organized and led. The oppressed do not constitute a viable base for enlisting leadership support. So, short of revolution, the land tenure and agrarian reform issue is not likely to emerge as a major issue at the national level. If it does, it is very likely to be subjected to crippling compromise.

The urban-industrial populations in LDCs are probably confused or uninformed about agrarian reform and the associated rural political issues, so these issues have not become clear-cut national issues. There is no national climate for rural reform, and political leaders have not displayed the statesmanship necessary to raise the issue to its real national significance. As Hiram Phillips sees it, the need is for a sense of national direction.[4] The least that conscientious political leadership could do is to evaluate the strength—overt and latent—of opposing interests and determine those aspects susceptible of remedy. Such leaders could support widespread study and debate of this pressing national issue, and from such activity more able leadership might arise. However, new LDC political leaders have not been willing to incur even the minimal risks of such encouragement.

When LDC political leadership is willing to sacrifice major long-term development goals for less important short-term advantage and is further unwilling to incur even minimal risks for important reforms, what can be said of its real objectives? One interpretation is that the entire universe of rural development, natural resource management, agriculture, and the environment has no priority in the panorama of the LDC political elite. The most generous interpretation of this perspective is that the foremost LDC political concern has to be immediate national survival. This paramount responsibility focuses attention on political management and enforces a short-term pragmatic view. The immediate demands of today and tomorrow must take precedence over potentials of next season, next year, or the next five or ten years. Unfortunately the time span of cyclical movements of natural events—seed time and harvest, plant and arboreal growth, farming, environmental transition, and rural development—correspond to "God's time," not to man's.

It can also be noted that politicians are seldom held accountable for natural disasters or environmental damage, even if these events could have been prevented or mitigated. No one seems to be answerable when schistosomiasis appears on Lake Nasser and in the canals below the Aswan Dam. No heads roll when lands in the Indus Basin and northern India are gradually lost to salinity because of bad irrigation practices. In the Soviet Union dissident writers may go to jail, but there are no reprisals when enormous areas of improperly used lands increasingly become "dust bowls." Soil damage causes abandonment of farmland in Asia, the Middle East, North Africa, and Central America because of inadequate safeguards; but the unhappy farmers seek no political sacrifices. Since there are no penalties, problems of population growth and food supply are reflected in vastly complex environmental consequences.[5]

Related to their pragmatic concern for immediate problems is the preoccupation of LDC leaders with nation building. This preoccupation is probably due to the recent arrival of these nations at independent statehood or because their administrations rest on very recent coups d'etat. In the view of the new leadership, their challenge is not development but rapid accomplishment of vertical political integration. W. David Hopper, long a close student of the development aspects of newly emergent states, says:

> The problem of creating a state out of a colony and molding its people into a nation is a problem which is uppermost and foremost. . . . The rationale of locating steel plants or the rationale of bringing in reforms or not bringing in reforms, as the case may be, is a rationale within the framework of a political structure. . . . The issue that faces the political elites as a paramount issue is not only the retention of their own power, but the retention of their own power is very much dependent upon creating a vertical integration of the nation, of breaking out the disassociated units, the villages, the rather independent separate groups, of breaking these and combining them into a nation.[6]

In Hopper's terms, politically important developments in the LDCs are those with fast payoff in national prestige and leadership credit. The Green Revolution might have been long delayed had not its promise coincided with the Indian drought of the mid-60s and the accompanying threat of starvation. Thus political motivation concentrates leadership attention on the trappings of power and partly accounts for the initial emphasis on large-scale industrial plants and monumental public works rather than on rural development.

Administrative Arrangements

In the organizational structure of LDC government administration functions, rural development, farming, natural resources, and environmental matters are placed in junior-grade ministries. This administrative pattern is not unique with the LDCs; it is more or less universal. The ranking government services are those concerned with foreign affairs, national defense, fiscal affairs, economic policy, commerce, and industry. For example, in the United States farming, forestry, fisheries, and land and water use are responsibilities delegated to administrative echelons at least one step below cabinet level. This is also the case for rural development, rural social problems, and rural education.

Among the richer nations this governmental pecking order may not be immediately critical, but in the case of the LDCs the junior rank accorded services responsible for rural development reinforces their inferior political role. And this is not the end of the matter;

these less glamorous services, standing apart from the trappings of central power, may then develop their own separate power structures in combination with rural political and economic interests, and these interests will likely be selfish and very conservative. In time this semisyndical relationship flourishing in semiobscurity develops its own objectives and priorities. It becomes exclusive, monopolistic, and difficult to penetrate or evaluate.

The professional staffs of these particularistic government structures are in a strategic position. They have been trained in narrow specialized fields; since the sole professional outlet for this training is in these governmental institutions, these officials come to have a dominant role in the conduct and content of the training institutions. Ultimately, professional recognition in these fields depends on service in and for the specialized structure. Since there are very few career opportunities outside these services, the institutions have a monopoly of skills in these fields. So it becomes increasingly difficult to establish any objective informed insight or oversight of the work performed by these bodies or for any informed criticism of their operations or policy to arise.

Organizational discipline within these specialized services is made more severe because of the lack of outside employment opportunities. It is extremely difficult to transfer to higher-ranking ministries; the kind of people who become foresters, soil scientists, and agronomists very seldom aspire to become cabinet ministers or members of Parliament. What may be important to such individuals is security, followed by improved professional status and recognition within the institution. However, these rewards are determined not entirely by professional excellence but probably more by conformance to the conventions of the syndical power enclave. One of these conventions requires avoidance of conflict or controversy with syndical allies. Another requires that any differences that may arise be settled "within the family"; thus there may be a tendency to reveal very little of the inner workings of the enclave to the public and to closely guard and closely edit public utterances. Indeed this diffidence applies not only to the public and the communications media but also to other ministries and the Parliament.

An inevitable consequence of this organizational discipline is to defeat and frustrate independent professional judgment while encouraging a protective and conservative service morale. At the same time that these services become less capable of perceiving the general public interest they tend more and more to become the instruments of the special political and economic interests of the syndicate. In these circumstances the objective of these services is not the welfare of of the great mass of the rural people but the overriding desires of the syndical allies.

Functional Dispersion of Government Services

Complicating the effects on rural development of low political and administrative rank are those arising from inappropriate separation of government functions. Here we encounter administrative patterns, in developed as well as developing nations, defying any system of logical arrangement but receiving almost universal acceptance. Everyone accepts the concept of an integrated environment, but everywhere the government services for environmental problems are so badly dispersed and fractionalized that a major effort has to be mounted to achieve coordinated action.

The LDCs had the opportunity of avoiding the illogical functional arrangements of developed nations with respect to development, use, and control of natural resources and the environment, but many of them repeated the schizoid pattern. Now very commonly one finds among the LDCs that irrigation is a responsibility of one ministry and agricultural development of another. In some countries not only are agriculture and irrigation administratively separated, but also rural development is divorced from agricultural cooperatives. In Panama an agricultural component at the National University performs some agricultural research functions quite separate and apart from similar research functions of the Ministry of Agriculture also administering agricultural training institutions. Ethiopia has a Ministry of Land Reform separate from the Ministry of Agriculture; a Ministry of Community Development conducts rural community development projects; irrigation is still another administrative entity. India and Pakistan place irrigation development in one ministry and agriculture in another. In a number of LDCs the functions of farm credit are separate from those of agricultural development.

Not only does this atomization of function make for administrative problems, it is also very expensive. Seemingly these administrative disfunctional arrangements would call out for reorganization in the name of efficiency, but this does not happen readily. However, very wisely India did merge its separate ministries of Cooperative and Community Development with its Ministry of Agriculture some years ago. One suspects that more of these reorganizations are not effected because of political considerations, particularly the resulting reduction in attractive patronage opportunities or the embarrassment of forcing some incumbent politician out of a comfortable post. Then too, the alliances these specialized units may have formed represent forces able to cause considerable political disturbance. Certainly in the United States considerations such as these have set at naught for nearly half a century efforts to reorganize into more efficient patterns those administrative units of the federal government responsible for administration of natural resources.

Among the LDCs the situation is aggravated by bureaucratic jealousy and competition among UN affiliates such as between the Food and Agriculture Oragnization and the International Labour Organization. Thus in one country the ILO may attempt to promote its concepts of rural cooperatives under the aegis of Community Development in one ministry at the same time that FAO pushes a similar operation as a function of the Ministry of Agriculture. This is not fun and games for the target country, for the effect is to confuse the development effort and to intensify wasteful and inefficient deployment of scarce LDC resources.

Quality of Administrative Personnel

The quality of personnel in the government services of the LDCs and their attitude toward that service greatly affects the performance of government functions. In turn, the quality of personnel attracted to these services is affected by the career opportunities they afford. It is only natural then that the secondary rank of government ministries concerned with rural development and the administration of natural resources does not make these services attractive to abler people. More ambitious, brighter, and better-trained young people seek careers in the higher-ranking services. Moreover, placement in these services usually means that one will work in the capital city with all its comforts and amenities while enjoying the status conveyed by high-ranking service, and among the LDCs these are extraordinarily important considerations.

In a number of LDCs the process of career selection begins at an early age. In order to qualify for entrance to the higher-ranking services one must have attended the prestigious universities at Calcutta, Bombay, Manila, Montevideo, Addis Ababa, or their equivalents. But only the select can afford to attend these institutions. Thus to many young people the agricultural colleges and other institutions training for careers in rural areas represent second choices. Those who fail to meet the higher academic requirements of the prestige institutions or who cannot afford them turn to these less prestigious schools. These candidates may not be as interested in farming, in rural people, or in the natural environment as in achieving a degree of status attached to higher education and ultimately the security of a government job—albeit one of secondary rank. Thus it frequently happens that individuals who begin this kind of career are not from rural areas and have no previous connection with farming or farm people. And so the system works as a selection process, automatically routing to professional work in the junior ministries many who accept such careers not out of preference or interest but out of necessity or lack of alternative.

Reinforcing this process is the general low esteem for the rural sector and its affairs by the elites of these countries. While land ownership—particularly abstentee ownership of large estates—may convey prestige, farming itself is considered to be a distinctly inelegant occupation. Hence those who work with farm people may suffer humiliation; their social status suffers and so does their self-esteem. In these circumstances many individuals devote much energy to wrangling transfers from posts in rural areas to the seat of government.

In the end the government workers in rural development services are not highly motivated toward their work. Many of them are serving time waiting for retirement or a possible but unlikely transfer out of rural areas to a larger city and a desk job. Their own status preoccupation inhibits sympathy for their clients and the desire to understand rural people. These officials tend not to be innovative but rather to reduce the scope of their activities to routine tasks requiring neither initiative nor energy. In the field they receive little support or communication from upper echelons, so they lead an isolated existence. As newcomers to the village scene they find it difficult to achieve acceptance among their rural clientele and are frustrated in efforts to initiate meaningful relations enabling them to demonstrate new agricultural techniques or to make helpful suggestions for improvement of farming practices. Sometimes they are denied materials essential to performance of their duties, such as new tires for bicycles or replacement of worn-out batteries for radio receiving sets. Sometimes funds enabling them to travel to higher headquarters are lacking so they cannot even report their needs. Their own youth and inexperience put them at a disadvantage in rural societies where age is equated with wisdom. Eventually these representatives of the central government lapse into indifference and inertia.

This kind of arrangement lacks valid local institutions for the formulation and expression of local will. It was precisely this vital element of local expression plus the native genius for organization that made the Japanese Land Reform Program of 1946-51 an outstanding success—a success due almost entirely to the vigor and enterprise of locally elected Village Land Commissions vested with full responsibility for decision and action. With this impetus their work and sense of responsibility succeeded in transforming in a few short years a centuries-old feudal land tenure system into a new egalitarian system dominated by small independent landowners. The role of the central government and its agents was advisory and informative. No one at the time thought much about it, but the commissions—both in the manner of their formation as freely elected bodies and in the distribution of their responsibilities—seem in retrospect to have followed very closely the Tocqueville pattern. What followed was a tremendous release of energy directed toward realization of local objectives. Of course this analogy is subject to the reservation that Japan was not an underdeveloped nation. Yet, given the circumstances prevailing nationwide at the end of the war involving dislocation, wide devastation, and disruption plus the universal acceptance of feudal principles and traditional organization, the situation was much closer to today's LDCs than to the developed countries.

The revolutionary change in Japanese rural society consisted in endowing local communities with an instrument for full self-expression with an equal opportunity for every individual, regardless of economic or social status, to have a hand in formulating community decisions. In this system government people appear in a new role. Their advice and assistance gain authority by endorsement of these local bodies. Thus officials do not appear as an arm of the central power. In the Japanese experience their work had meaningful content; what they had to contribute was something everyone wanted, and they became identified with the community.[7] Community motivation became their motivation; their progress and recognition was the result of their success in meeting self-determined village needs and in helping to solve village problems.

As the rural sector achieves success, political power accrues to it, with a corresponding accretion of prestige and rank. In this process the agricultural and rural institutions become politically powerful and influence national policy. As the rural sector gains power and prestige, the careers of rural civil servants become more attractive and abler people seek to enter the service. Moreover, these recruits increasingly come from a rural background and share the aspirations of rural people. This is the process to be set in motion by LDCs in their efforts toward rural development.

Allocation of Resources

Many LDCs have adopted central planning for achieving development and growth and for allocating national resources. Whether LDCs use central planning or more occult procedures, all of them in common with universal practice make some kind of estimate of the amount of central resources to be deployed for development purposes. In all these forward projections governments reveal their intentions toward the rural sector. At this point decisions are made about the extent of steps to redress the inadequacy of rural infrastructure and amounts of central resources intended for feeder roads, rural electrification, irrigation works, schools, storage facilities, regulated markets, extension services, manpower training, and research. It is also at this point that qualities of vision and imagination of the administration personnel are most important and the need to upgrade the quality of the administrative services is most keenly felt. At a recent joint OECD Development Center/World Bank seminar on rural development, several participants expressed the view that before improvement in rural development procedures could be effective the entire status of rural affairs would have to be improved.[8]

At the outset of the planning process the effect of lower rural rank-order would mean lower allocations to rural development items. This was the case in India, at least through its third Five-Year Plan (1960–65). I noted this trend in 1964 in a study for USAID outlining a strategy for long-range assistance for rural India. Observing that under the third Five-Year Plan the proportionate share of resources proposed for Agriculture and Rural Community Development was 14 percent compared to 24 percent for Industries and Minerals, 22 percent for Irrigation and Power, and 20 percent for Transport and Communications, I commented:

> India's very substantial efforts to achieve planned and balanced economic development have probably been less effective in the agricultural sector. From First Plan to Third and looming over Fourth Plan formulation and perspective planning through 1976 is the largely unresolved problem of adequately quantifying agriculture's base, potentials, and proper role in the nation's sustained economic growth. Inability to organize an economical sound approach to sectoral development of agriculture inevitably weakens economic planning and perspective for all other sectors.[9]

Even if the overall amounts allocated for rural development among the LDCs were adequate, there would remain the equally important function of programming and scheduling the investment flow to rural development. It is in the performance of funding functions that heavy demands on skill and training are imposed. Even if these are present, they have to be organized properly in an effective administrative structure, and here too weakness is encountered. Thus neglect of the rural development role in government places a double handicap of less-qualified personnel and poorly articulated organization on the planning function. It was the latter handicap that attracted comments from participants in the 1972 OECD/IBRD seminar:

> It seemed to many of the participants that the *existing organization* of the administration in many countries was a major obstacle to adopting an *integrated approach* and the evidence provided by Mr. Mule from Kenya on this point was of particular interest. A large measure of agreement was also reached on the need to devise organizational arrangements which would enable *decision-making* to be really *decentralized*. (Emphasis added)[10]

Those familiar with the planning function understand the heavy demand it imposes: it takes acute, detailed, and intensive effort sustained over long periods to fit together in proper sequence the components of a balanced scheme for rural development. When these burdens are placed on inadequately trained staff, the result may be sloppy planning and poor implementation. This performance is not so much the fault of those engaged in the task but rather in the bias resulting in establishing a second-rank standing for government work in rural development. As time passes and these workers gain experience, performance may progressively improve. Still the lag is expensive for the nations and for their rural constituencies.

In our concern with planning we should not lose sight of the need to link plans closely to implementation. Thus planning for rural development and the execution of these plans are a continuous process. Plans, to be effective, must comprehend an awareness of the capacity of the executing agencies to carry them out. Moreover, no plan is so good that it does not have to be modified continuously during implementation stages. On the other hand, if implementation is laggard or careless, no plan can succeed.

> Past experience has shown that even the most well-conceived and well-designed schemes flop at the implementation level. Sev-

eral reasons are adduced for this: lack of enthusiasm on the part of top political and administrative leadership and/or its inability to transmit the same to middle and local level of leadership; redtape, archaic administrative procedures and general ineptitude and inefficiency of the administrative machinery at lower levels; economic and political vested interests which are indifferent to the schemes which are of no direct benefit to them. Numerous cases have been noted in which funds allocated to such schemes are diverted to schemes which benefit the better-off.[11]

It was such a combination of sloppy planning and indifferent execution that resulted in a failure of Ethiopia's second Five-Year Plan (1963–68) to meet its agricultural objectives when government capital expenditures for agriculture were only 42 percent of planned objectives.[12] The explanation seems to be that planners overestimated the performance capacity of the Ministry of Agriculture and possibly also the availability of resources. One specific shortfall was a three-and-a-half-year delay in establishing the important Agricultural Research Institute with a subsequent failure to implement research programs. More generally those departments of the Ministry of Agriculture responsible for extension services, agronomy, education, training, statistics, river surveys, and the Cadastral land survey were unable to meet planned goals because of insufficient funds. Recurrent expenditures (used for the payment of salaries) for the ministry as a whole were only two-thirds of planned levels.

Several factors probably worked in combination to create this unhappy record. One is the likelihood that funds, originally allocated to the Ministry of Agriculture, were diverted to higher-ranking ministries. Another possibility is that personnel to staff the several programs were unavailable; some regular staff may have transferred to other ministries and recruits in the process of in-service training went to other jobs. The overall cause of the poor performance was the low ranking of the Ministry of Agriculture plus bad planning practices. In any event, the end result was a deplorable shortfall in the progress of rural development.

Sometimes conscientious planners may be misled by inaccurate or erroneous data. This in turn may be the result of neglect of rural statistical reporting services. Also the newer LDCs may not have been in business long enough to accumulate sufficient time series data to justify using them as a base for extrapolations. This deficiency may be aggravated by the bias inherent in syndical loyalties (referred to above) taking the form of overstating organization performance capacity in the interest of making one department or bureau "look good." When these distortions get cranked into a plan there is bound to be a breakdown, because the plan simply cannot work.

Something like this happened in the case of Tanzania's first Five-Year Plan ending in 1969. Almost from the outset it became apparent that the departments concerned with rural development could not carry out their assignments.[13] A second cause of near failure was a substantial underestimate of national population and rate of population growth. This error led to further miscalculations of per capita income, saving, and capital formation. As if this were not enough, progress was further impeded by an acute shortage of trained manpower for the rural program and a major overestimate of foreign exchange flows. However, what distinguishes the Tanzania situation was the careful supervision enabling the government to detect these errors and the resiliency of the leadership in making the necessary difficult midstream adjustments to offset what otherwise could have been a real disaster.

A further critical element in planning for rural development is the degree of understanding of the process of rural development possessed by planners. This quality of perception is manifested in the overall development strategy and in the priorities and emphases of the accorded plan components. From this standpoint it is not so much whether rural planners are right or wrong in selecting components for rural development but rather how they conceive the total development process as evidenced by the choices they make in allocating resources. Do they see that process as systemic unity where all components are related? If they do not perceive this unity, it is likely that the flow of development investment will be atomized in such a fashion that there is no coherent integration of development. John P. Lewis, who was familiar with Indian planning procedures, called attention to the blithe disregard by planners of demographic concentrations in the Indian rural landscape in contrast to what he conceived to be the critical importance for development of planning of these clusterings because they provided a central focus for administrative, political, and economic activity.[14]

In more specific terms, neglect of the systemic aspects of rural development tends to permit uncoordinated programs for the location of processing plants, warehouses, supply depots, marketing points, fertilizer mixing plants, and feeder roads. If these components are located without respect to other components, the paramount advantage of maximizing development complementaries is lost, as is the opportunity to break through the isolation and stagnation of small villages. According to E. A. J. Johnson, this lack of coordinated planning effort is due to poor training of planners aggravated by political incentives to dole out projects in a political pork-barrel fashion.[15]

If the central plan for rural development becomes a collection of separate undertakings, the corresponding investment flow will be irrational. Thus installations constructed "out of phase" with the development process or located inappropriately will be underutilized or completely unused. Whereas Lewis and Johnson view these planning miscues as a result of poor training, ignorance, indifference, or political expedience, our thesis inclines toward the view that these shortcomings have their origin in the low ranking of rural affairs among LDC governments.

Political Systems

LATIN AMERICA. Throughout Latin America, by one means or another, programs of land reform have frequently been initiated and usually stifled or sidetracked through the political maneuverings of large landowners and their allies. Yet it is generally agreed that the existing farm tenancy system is largely responsible for low productivity, rural misery, and a technically backward agriculture. There have been some exceptions to this in Bolivia's insurrectionist land seizures by tenants, and to some extent colonization in Venezuela has provided a partial answer to the problem of land reform. Chile's long-stalled land reform program might have stood a chance of resuscitation under the Allende regime. But Brazil's situation is characterized as limited to a few small-scale projects and half measures. The general outlook in Latin America is a frustration of the necessary reforms to provide dynamic change from the present rural stagnation.[16]

Backward agricultural development in Colombia affects the national economy and is related to the preponderance of rural people among the nation's poor.[17] One observer related this situation to deficient leadership not competent to support rural development planning and operations. While more than 100 separate agencies are engaged in rural development activities, rural stagnation and decline are universal. Also apparent is a completely inadequate system of rural education. Since only about 3 percent of those entering first grade in rural areas will later register for the fifth and final grade, there is an almost complete absence of rural students among those receiving professional agricultural training. This means that the staffs of agricultural agencies are made up mostly of people who have had no personal familiarity with farming or rural life. Consequently an almost complete vacuum of interest and concern exists between those who farm and those who seek to improve farming technology and rural development. The technical and official group seems primarily to have been recruited among lawyers, economists, and engineers.[18] A further conclusion is that Colombian taxpayers are unwilling to support rural education, preferring to support urban public education. Because taxpayers are usually an elite group, it has been conjectured that those who financially support government are unwilling to support measures that would give poor people an opportunity to compete with the young of the powerful elites.[19]

EAST AFRICA. In Ethiopia agriculture and rural development suffer the consequences of an old feudal system. Grants of land to those serving the imperial establishment have preempted large areas. Many of the cultivators in the northern and central highland regions are tenants with insecure tenurial rights. In the late 1960s Emperor Haile Selassie undertook several measures designed to reform this system; he established a Ministry of Land Reform and appointed as Minister one of his abler administrators. Unfortunately, very little has been accomplished since these beginnings except for the creation of a sizable bureaucracy. It appears that while the Emperor lent his personal support and prestige to the reform, the vested power of both his hereditary nobility and the Amharic Christian Church had sufficient power to obfuscate and inhibit action. Parliamentary delays and maneuvers prevented passage of basic legislation, disregarding repeated imperial insistence on enactment. These powerful interests were also instrumental in securing the removal of an able Minister of Land Reform and the appointment of a more amenable replacement.

Among younger Ethiopians, particularly among university students, land reform has become one of a number of burning political issues which have aroused their opposition to the Establishment. Up to the present time this opposition has not achieved significant expression. On the other hand, there have been rumors of strong repressive police action serving to increase tensions and anti-Establishment sentiment. However, this unrest is probably an urban phenomenon confined largely to Addis Ababa and its environs. Little is known about farmer reaction, perhaps because of the substantial amount of unsettled land in the southern part of the country. There is some evidence of a gradual southward migration out of northerly regions, which may have been hastened by large tenant displacement as a result of increasing mechanization.

Agricultural development in Ethiopia is impeded by the primitive level of farming and lack of means to improve productivity. Technical assistance to farmers through the extension work of the Ministry of Agriculture is impeded by the low ranking of that ministry. Extension field workers are poorly paid and poorly trained. Moreover, the ministry is handicapped both by budgetary limitations and by the manner in which budgeted funds are disbursed and is also plagued by competition from and conflicts with more powerful units of government having peripheral and tangential responsibility for both rural development and farming.

In contrast to other countries of the Third World, Ethiopia seems to neither fear nor distrust foreign assistance or investment. Under the prompting of overseas assistance agencies several promising and forward-looking agricultural projects are under way. Large-scale and successful foreign-owned agricultural enterprises have been developed; and Ethiopia has not been unresponsive to suggestions for improvement in agricultural administration, organization, training, and research. The major uncertainty relating to the widespread implementation of these initial steps is with respect to the highly conservative and very powerful elite group whose basic entrenchment in control of land resources will sooner or later have to be challenged. To what extent, if any, this confrontation would involve the development role of foreign entrepreneurs is a matter of speculation.

Socialist Tanzania, under the leadership of Julius Nyerere, has adopted a unique administrative and political approach to agricultural and rural development based on the principle of rural villages conceived as communal organizations. Nyerere, as leader of the TANU party,[20] visualizes rural development primarily along political lines. In rural areas agricultural technicians work to assist the political arm of government, the Ministry of Rural Development, in its efforts to create Ujamaa villages—a form of communal social organization based on the concept of the indigenous extended family. One might conjecture that this concept is not unrelated to the rural communes of the Peoples Republic of China and the philosophy of Mao Tse-tung.

These concepts are in the process of implementation within a process of nation building and rapid transition from previous colonial status. Thus the Ujamaa principle is making its way among Tanzanian farmers who are mostly small holders. These farmers will receive government assistance encouraging them toward collectivism in farming operations.

Land reform in its distributive aspect is absent because the Tanzanian land tenure system is apparently not characterized by landlordism or typical tenancy patterns. Thus the political and administrative aspects of rural development seem to take the form of indoctrination and persuasion. To the extent possible, government exercises its power by helping rural people in such a fashion that they find themselves better off within a Ujamaa context.

Within the bureaucracy this means that everyone conforms to TANU party discipline: TANU sets the major principles for national planning, and ministerial conferences on planning are subject to party dictates. In the field TANU policy is continually manifested to farm advisors and all other government functionaries. Just what effect this may have on technical and professional personnel in the several ministries is difficult to judge, and just how well the Ujamaa principle conforms to the imperatives of agricultural technology is still a matter of conjecture. But what Nyerere does is to instill a sense of nationhood among a population historically tribal in outlook. He also seeks to socialize farming while stimulating it to achieve higher levels of output.

In contrast to other LDCs, although most of the rural people of Tanzania are very poor and ignorant, they are at least not oppressed or exploited. On the other hand, evidence that the Ujamaa principle has or will result in raising levels of production is not apparent. Tanzania has also undertaken several ventures in large-scale state farms. Opinion on the likelihood of success of these ventures is divided. Another aspect of agricultural policy with a doubtful outlook is that of producing food grains at costs above world market prices. Finally, the continued discouragement of small traders of agricultural commodities in some areas without providing alternate marketing outlets was not wise. Thus one is forced to the conclusion that short-run political actions may have doubtful effects, but that in the longer run Ujamaa policy may be dynamic in raising farm production levels and improving rural life-styles. The contrast may be between production as a short-run goal and ultimate integrated rural development.

INDIA. The dominant political party in India since independence is the Congress Party, and all Indian governments since independence have been Congress Party governments; it was the party of Gandhi, Nehru, Shastri, and Indira Gandhi. Whoever controlled the Congress Party ruled India. Consequently Indian agricultural and rural policy has been set by the Congress Party. This party has included a great variety of economic interests; one very important component in terms of establishing rural policy was the farm group, particularly landowners.

The Constitution of India places much power in the hands of the several Indian states, including administrative responsibility for agriculture. Because many of the states are predominantly rural and agricultural, it is natural that dominant landowner interests should strongly color state politics. This deployment of political power was decisive in offsetting the original land reform objectives of the central government which visualized as a fundamental political tenet redistribution of agricultural lands to tenants along with rights to secure tenure on lands they might rent.

Initial efforts of reform began and largely ended with abolition of a particular layer of rent receivers, the Zamindari. The Zamindar system was established by the British in the latter part of the eighteenth century.[21] It was conceived that these functionaries would receive rent in perpetuity and forward a stipulated amount as taxes. In time the Zamindari parceled out these rent allocations to others; in some cases there were as many as 15 or 20 layers of rent receivers between the cultivator and the last receiver.[22] Apparently this system did not uniformly cover all Indian states; the relations between Zamindar right and land ownership varied in different localities.

It was relatively easy in the period after independence to abolish the inexcusably exploitive Zamindar system as an example of the malfunctions of the British raj. And that, to all intents and purposes, was the extent of Indian land reform. Some states passed legislation setting ceilings on the amount of land in a single ownership, but from that point on the record is replete with a tangle of land litigation and proceedings of commissions of various kinds. Today both landlordism and tenancy are almost universal throughout India. It is in this setting that the Green Revolution in India has taken place.

It has been difficult for the central government to exert sufficient influence over state policy and administration to achieve a national consistency in implementing its rural objectives because agriculture is a "state matter." Nearly twenty years ago Paul Appleby reported to the government of India on this situation:

> The Centre is without any real powers in almost the entire field of development; its function is the "staff" function rather than the "line" or "action" function, and its method slows greatly, and expedites hardly at all. Land policy is related to development of agriculture, but land policy is exclusively within the field of state responsibilities. Even farm credit, about which the states

can never hope to do anything of consequence, is in their field. And farm credit is important to agricultural development. The influence that is associated with Central financial assistance is so cumbered by an intricate system of multiple reviews both in the states and in the Centre that the Centre often may be said to rescue the states from trouble rather than stimulating the states to bold, big, new action. And responsibility for all this is so diffused that almost no one knows who can be held accountable for what.[23]

In this context the charisma of Indian leaders becomes the principal unifying force in pushing a progressive rural policy. The formal structure, the division of administrative power, and the limited colonial procedures act as impediments to the design and extension of powers. For this reason the maintenance of personal qualities of prestige and elitism become extremely important aspects of leadership. But this also means that the reservoir of leadership power can be drawn upon only for critical issues. This consideration may explain the past unwillingness of leadership to forthrightly challenge entrenched rural land interests. The price for a greatly expanded food production so vital to national well-being apparently has been to permit these landed interests to reap major benefits from the Green Revolution and to risk widespread exploitation of small and weaker cultivators and landless laborers.

The political paradox between an enlightened leadership and a backward electorate was due to the political power of conservative economic interests in local and state politics. Since these interests constituted the dominant power centers, they controlled political machinery up to the state level. Their followers, who gave these local power centers control of political majorities, were the same small farmers, tenants, and landless laborers who needed relief. These oppressed rural people provided the clientele for the wielding of local power, and this political structure was reinforced by the caste system. Exploited rural people provided the numerical support to keep their exploiters in power. Since national and state elections coincided, conservative control of national politics continued, but so did the frustration of the progressive leadership. This political process was also causing erosion of the prestige of the Congress Party and growing social discontent with a mounting threat of violence and revolt. Efforts by the Prime Minister to implement land reform were threatened or brought no response; the response to the government's efforts to enforce a new wealth tax on agricultural property was challenged by several of the ministers and overturned by the Punjab and Haryana high court.[24]

Perhaps no one in India perceived what was going on as well as Mrs. Gandhi or saw better the threats an uncorrected future might imply. She took a calculated risk, first separating state and national elections and then setting the latter in 1971—a full year in advance of the regularly scheduled date. This enabled her wing of the party—now called for purposes of the election the New Congress Party—to go to the rural areas with a specific call for support of liberal and progressive parliamentary candidates while emphasizing the need to correct social injustices, including unemployment and land reform. She won an overwhelming victory.

This important political victory opens the prospect of orderly change in the Indian countryside, but it will still be difficult to achieve in practice the measures advocated by the Prime Minister. The complex state-central administration arrangement will have to be surmounted, and there may be need for amendment of the Constitution—a step hitherto found infeasible. If the central government can win and hold the loyalty of the rural masses, the opposition interests may be forced to a workable compromise.

V

Integration of Rural and Urban Planning

The development planning of emerging nations is frequently formulated in terms of sectors. Most often encountered are separate discussions and plan objectives for agro-rural and urban-industrial sectors. These are aggregative abstractions. Whatever technical convenience may be derived from this dichotomy is more than offset by its lack of reality. If (as we believe) the dichotomy is false, the resulting development plans fail to take into account the most significant feature of the nation—the interplay of component factors through a network of linkages across the entire national socioeconomic landscape.

The effect of imposing this agro-rural and urban-industrial dichotomy may be to produce two or more imperfect plans based on two or more imperfectly conceived and partial systems, whereas there should be only one integrated plan utilizing a total strategy based on the system that actually exisits. Ultimately planning based on such sectoral dichotomy can conceivably result in a misallocation of resources, economic waste, and failure to realize opportunities to develop the rural-urban continuum.

Rural Character of Emerging Nations

The less developed nations are characteristically rural. Agriculture is the principal occupation; most of the nations' people live in small rural communities. The prevailing social milieu is that of a rural village. The national socioeconomic landscape consists of a few primary cities such as Bombay, Nairobi, Singapore, Montevideo, or Santiago and extending out from these a wide horizon of rurality arranged in concentric belts of decreasing population density and organized in tiny agglomerations, which in many instances provide little more than shelter and elementary defense against common dangers. Massive poverty and unemployment exist among these rural people; productivity is low, and farming tends to be at a subsistence level. In many of these countries a very dense rural population presses against the land resource. There is also a persistent out-migration to the slums of the primary cities where rural unemployment becomes urban unemployment.

Hope for development of these nations depends initially on increasing agricultural productivity, since farming is the nearly universal occupation of the people and agriculture is by far the largest component of the GNP. But strangely this self-evident fact seems to have been neglected in the development planning for LDCs in the earlier postwar years. Somehow it was conceived that some kind of a bootstrap operation would permit concentration on rapid development of large-scale industry. Perhaps this was a spillover effect from the postwar reconstruction of the predominantly industrial areas of Europe which was highly successful. But the situation was entirely different in the underdeveloped regions of Asia, Africa, the Near East, and Latin America where no resources could be accumulated for such a massive investment. Responsibility for this false start is widely shared, but the principal error lay in the wholesale transfer of western development models and macroeconomic theory and analysis derived in the context of a mature urban-industrial society to the agro-rural context of emerging nations.

Recognition of the strategic role of agricultural production as the primary economic resource of developing regions began to prevail about 1955; universal acceptance, with major policy changes emphasizing agriculture as the critical factor in GNP projections, took place in the early 60s. The new view recognizes that the institutions and structure of rural society provide the basic cultural endowment of many LDCs. These institutions and structures developed earlier, endured longer, and involve more people. Moreover, the contribution of agriculture provides the nutritional base that supports the national existence; specialty crops provide the bulk of the foreign exchange earnings of the nation. Since national development is dependent on capital accumulation, agricultural production must be looked to for this investment increment.

Development priorities for the LDCs must include removal of

the obstacles to increased agricultural output. These would include mitigation of massive rural poverty, reduction of unemployment, change from a static subsistence-oriented agriculture to a dynamic market-oriented agriculture. These are in fact preconditions for any significant national development.

Integrated Rural Development

The process of transforming the rural socioeconomic context of emerging nations has been defined recently as *integrated rural development,* the objective of which is the evolution of a well-rounded rural-urban continuum. The term *rural development* is used to emphasize the dominant rurality in the LDC socioeconomic context but by no means is intended to signify that development as sectoral. We do not view the sectoral approach as viable. An alternative but awkward term might be the *urbanization of rurality*. In any event, interdependency of urban and rural functions urges an integrated approach in development efforts. Thus the term *integration* defines the comprehensive effects of several disciplines and activities with the objective of national economic growth and social progress, combining measures for increasing agricultural and industrial output, providing infrastructure in rural and urban areas, and improving living standards of rural and urban populations.

Integrated rural development planning involves synchronization of development operations, which in turn requires recognition of the systemic character of rurality. Even at primitive levels there is an organic arrangement through which natural, social, economic, and physical factors are linked in a complex of relationships. Development planning should begin with a specific knowledge of this universe of complexes; rural development must be integrated because the rural system is inherently integrated.

Traditional Approach

Socialist and democratic-capitalist planners alike have tended to focus their concern with rural development on the agricultural production function. This is not to say that no consideration has been given to the need for institutional change in land tenure, land distribution, rural education, and a number of other institutional aspects of the rural context; but usually these have not been specifically tied to efforts to increase agricultural production. To put it in the vernacular, the big shots in agricultural development have been the agricultural technicians, and the main push has been to improve agricultural technology largely in the form of increased and improved inputs to farming.

Some of the results of this activity have been spectacular, as in the case of the Green Revolution resulting from long patient work in the development of high-yielding varieties of food grains. Yet obviously these efforts, albeit successful in themselves, do not constitute an integrated approach to rural development; for this reason it may be that full value of this technical breakthrough is not fully realized. Such efforts sooner or later are confronted with the fact of farmer attitudes; if there is not sufficient motivation to utilize the new technology, the effort falls short. In the confines of the traditional quietude of rural villages where the central purpose of farming is to produce family subsistence, there is little incentive to produce beyond the family needs.

Not all the efforts to improve agricultural production have failed. There has been a considerable increase in the total volume of agricultural production in some of the disadvantaged areas of the world. But this increase has barely kept abreast of rapid population growth and has not provided enough capital accumulation to achieve significant general development. Rural unemployment has not been significantly decreased. While public services in some places have improved, the level is still very low. Some improvement has occurred in the availability of farm supplies and credit but at a low level and then only in certain countries. Technical advisory services to farmers have improved in a number of countries, although the quality of these services leaves much to be desired. Still it is important to note that the value of these services is now rather generally appreciated.

It is particularly in the failure to provide adequate infrastructure that rural areas have suffered general deprivation. Although allocations of funds for electric service, roads, markets, transport, storage, and communications have traditionally favored metropolitan-industrial areas, it is highly probable that the development potential of rural areas is much greater.[1]

Another typical aspect of rural development investment has been large, spectacular construction projects and expensive settlement schemes. Both have absorbed large amounts of foreign exchange and technical personnel. While such undertakings may have some symbolic prestige value, they frequently prove extremely costly. In many cases the anticipated returns have not been realized, nor have such investments paid off in terms of stimulating rural development. In addition to the very large initial capital investment these schemes have large annual operation and maintenance costs. They require a substantial professional administrative organization which must be maintained at a high level of efficiency throughout the life of the installation. In some cases this has been neglected with resulting serious damage to land resources. There is not, in many instances of this type of investment, much reason to be encouraged because of the effect in providing incentive for better production motivation.[2]

One of the results of traditional rural development planning efforts is the tendency to make spotty, unrelated, and sometimes highly specialized investments on a more or less ad hoc basis. In some investments of this type it seems that the planners were not concerned with or were possibly unaware of the potentials of integrated rural development, nor did they consider the systemic character of rurality. A striking omission in the earlier efforts is the failure to develop sophisticated models of place, location, and spatial arrangement including regionalism as tools of planning. More unfortunately the planning unit, selected on what appear to have been intuitional and romanticized grounds, was the existing pattern of village settlement. Thus the objective of systematically filling in a rural-urban continuum to transform the national economic landscape with a newly created hierarchy of urban-commercial-industrial centers has not for most of the period since World War II served as a principal guide to rural development planning. A good deal of rural planning seems to proceed on the assumption that the present punctiform array of tiny villages represents a permanent and satisfactory settlement pattern.

Urban planners, on the other hand, tend to be preoccupied with spatial arrangements and considerations. They are accustomed to dynamic pressures and have to deal with the industrial complex as much as with residential problems. They are used to dealing with all urban aspects of human life and society because each of these has its planning and spatial analogue. Thus the layout of an urban development plan is an expression of many interrelated factors centrally focused in the confines of the metropolitan area. Urban planners, in contrast to rural planners, are professional manipulators of space. Moreover, urban planners have to think in terms of integration in order to provide a single viable urban system.

But these concerns leave small room for thought about the national landscape or regional development planning. By and large, urban planners pay little attention to the impact of their proposals on the rural hinterland. They also seem unaware of the significance for national development of the concept of the rural-urban continuum. Given these limitations, it must still be recognized that in contrast to the simplistic approach of rural planners the urban developers are more technically sophisticated about planning; they have a multifaceted technology including penetrating and sharp analytical procedures. This discipline can be very helpful in working on the planning of integrated rural development as defined above; the caveat is that they must expand their horizons to encompass the rural-urban continuum and learn how to work with the agricultural technologists and the agricultural bureaucracy.

The New Model

Rural development in the LDCs requires a transformation of the existing economic landscape; it is possible that the required effort also involves creation of an economic landscape in areas where the development is slight or nonexistent. Our model is a single large central place surrounded by an extensive rural landscape which, for our purposes, can be geographically featureless—simply a large plain. Scattered throughout this landscape are numerous small villagelike population agglomerations supported primarily by a subsistence agriculture. Each of the villages is primarily self-centered; the extent of the village influence on the landscape is established by prevailing modes of movement, which in many cases may not be more than a five-mile radius. Within this space villagers live, breathe, and have their being. Outside contacts are few and infrequent. Change does not occur, nor is significant development or even innovation likely. Relations between the primary center and the rural hinterland are vague and at more distant points nonexistent.

Required to initiate development in such a model is the introduction of new factors that promote change and open the door to innovation. The inertia characteristic of the existing system must be overcome. This will result in and can be brought about by new and different spatial arrangements and patterns of settlement. The most effective form of change is through the creation of *central markets*. Long ago John R. Commons acclaimed the principle of the extension of markets as a revolutionary influence on human and social development.[3] With the appearance of regulated markets for agricultural produce, the farmer is free of the deadening thralldom enforced by petty village traders who habitually "skin him alive." With markets it becomes possible to break down the apathy and indifference of a static, tradition-bound subsistence agriculture, substituting for it the incentive of profit and commercial exchange of agricultural commodities for previously unknown consumer goods. With the appearance of market centers serving several villages, the traditional routines of rural life are broken and replaced by new ones.

The establishment, operation, and regulation of rural markets should be a function of government. In planning market establishment, government is forced to recognize a very important aspect of rural development: in the LDCs the really critical impediment is the lack of infrastructure. In order for the new markets to function it must be possible for farmers to move their produce, so roads and road improvement become necessary. As the market function develops, the new market becomes a nucleus for a new form of population agglomeration; this is the commencement of a new and different spatial arrangement within the existing rural-urban continuum and, along with this, a change in the linkages and factors that make up the rural system.

At this point we should acknowledge the very real debt rural planners owe to the labors of the late E. A. J. Johnson of Johns Hopkins University in presenting an illuminating study of the effects of regulated public markets in India.[4] Johnson undertook careful diagrammatic analysis to indicate how such markets should be sited. This analysis makes possible the establishment of a matrix combining a number of factors and linkages from which strategy can be derived by observing the clusterings of factors and linkages. Thus the establishment of a market requires prior consideration of a number of factors simultaneously: What is to be marketed? What standards should be required for the commodity? What will the volume be at alternate locations? What storage facilities will be required? What area will the market serve? How will the produce be transported? How many individuals must be accommodated? What roads are planned? What will be the electrical service? What rail and truck transport facilities will be needed, and how will they be provided?

We can perceive that our original model will undergo considerable modification and elaboration as additional regulated market centers are added. The composition of these centers is expanded by the need for auxiliary services with corresponding new employment opportunities for the redundant rural labor supply. There must be places for the farm draft animals to be secured and a supply of fodder for them. There must be eating and hostel facilities for farmers and traders. Offices and clerical staff are needed for the requisite market supervisory services. Farmers will have money to spend as a result of their market operations, and thus there is an opportunity for new retail outlets. All these create the possibility for a new type of community performing multiple functions and with specific functional relevance to adjoining villages and to the primary city.

Johnson has described how Puerto Rico, Yugoslavia, and Israel have systematically planned a proliferation of decentralized light-industry centers in rural areas. These efforts have all been successful to some extent in transforming the rural countryside. In the case of Puerto Rico the development effort met with remarkable success; principal achievement has been a rapid solution to the problem of population pressure and rural unemployment. Another aspect is that these methods have produced more effective procedures for rational combination and allocation of resources. The alternative and unsatisfactory procedure, which has been used in more than one emerging nation, has been to squeeze more and more industrial units into the confines of existing metropolitan areas. It takes real leadership plus incentives and subsidies to site industrial plants in appropriate locations throughout the continuum. Also involved is the formulation of plans utilizing growth-center development theory which is only beginning to be utilized by the LDCs.

As we deploy these new centers at one end of the spectrum in the form of organized and regulated markets and at the other in the form of smaller-scale industrial satellites, we begin to approach the development objective—to redeploy the massive unemployment characteristic of so many LDCs. John Lewis recognized this redeployment as essential to economic progress in India.[5]

Equally important is the fact that agricultural production in developing situations comes to have functional relevance to a system which transcends the village. Previous infrastructural limitations and constraints on agricultural producers are mitigated and some disappear as a result of the broader development. The entire development scheme works because it is an integrated effort. In these circumstances agriculture commences to provide a significant capital accumulation essential to overall economic growth.

Regional Approach

Integrated rural development is most efficiently managed in the regions into which an emerging nation may be divided. In countries with small areas regionalization of development is essential; in nations of larger areas regionalism is indispensable. This is because different regions have different growth potentials and different products and require different methods and because regionalization permits, within national boundaries, exploitation of the differential advantages of specialization. On the physical side, regions have different and sometimes quite distinct problems such as topography, flooding, disease, over- or underpopulation, physical barriers, drought, and so forth. From an administrative point of view a proper division of government along regional lines makes the implementation of a plan more workable and controllable. In the preparation of a development plan, the perception of regional characteristics is essential to the creation of specific applicable measures sensitive to local conditions.

But regional integrated rural development requires a close synchronization with major national planning objectives and with the plans of other regions if regional anarchy is to be avoided. Regions are functional units of the nation. At the same time properly identified regions are at a level permitting assimilation of local and subregional interests. The regional approach facilitates detailed consideration of the applicability of urban and industrial activity in formulating development programs. It also facilitates concentration of attention on the specifics of human resources and institutional development by bringing these into focus in regional application. For example, land tenure and land consolidation problems must be approached very differently in the Mekong Delta from similar problems in the upland areas of Vietnam; land development problems in the drier interior of Ceylon require different methods of social organization from land problems in the wet coastal areas; settlement proposals for nomadic tribes require a totally different approach from those applicable to a more sedentary society.

These examples are all more or less self-evident, but in actual practice the delineation of valid regions is difficult. It is primarily a function of the central government to make these delineations, but this must be done with the consent of the regional residents. Since the national government probably cannot undertake full development operations in all regions simultaneously, it will be necessary to classify regions and then establish criteria for broad development priorities based on analysis of systemic characteristics of factors and linkages. Three types of regions might be selected by national planning authorities for initial action:

1. *Urban-dominated regions.* Such an identification would help to indicate at the outset the main lines of regional develop-

ment planning and operation with particular reference to creating an integrated rural-urban continuum rather quickly: for example, the need for land-use adjustment between urban and rural uses. Also in such a region the whole gamut of transfer, marketing, handling, and processing arrangements for agricultural commodities could be systematically put together, as could projections of regional communication and transport requirements.

2. *Regions with unique characteristics.* These might be regions with high production and growth-center potential; natural resource regions such as river basins; mixed resource regions where agricultural potentials can be complemented by mining, forestry, or fishery development.

3. *Remote, isolated, and backward regions.* These regions must not be excluded from priority consideration for development. Although returns from inputs may be small and long deferred, humanitarian consideration, equity, and indeed political expedience demand that such regions be tackled at the outset of a national development program.

Since development resources are limited, interregional allocation may be accomplished by pairing more and less promising regions up to a cutoff point determined by budget ceilings. However, within regions the selection of development opportunities should be the result of sophisticated study. This may take the form of system analysis. The strategy is based on establishing those factors and linkages in the system that have the greatest spread of influence in the form of interaction with other components and linkages in the system. These are the "hot spots"—corridors for breaking into the existing system with maximum effect. Development strategy depends then (1) on recognizing that a system exists; (2) on accepting the concept of integrated rural development; (3) on recognizing that the solution of the problem of national development takes place in a rural-urban continuum; (4) on acknowledging that within this continuum the basic strategy is a matter of making logical adjustment in and reorganization of space which involves development of market centers, decentralization of industry, absorption of unemployment, and redeployment of population; and (5) on realizing that both planning and administering development must take place along regional lines and that the delineation and classification of regions for development purposes is an intensive and difficult task.

Strategic Aspects

A strategy for integrated rural and urban development is needed (1) at international levels among donor agencies in order to obtain optimum global results from slender resources and (2) among the LDCs in order to allocate limited resources effectively among components and linkages of the rural-urban continuum. At the present time there is no consistent strategy; rural development theory has not been particularly helpful because of its western bias expressed as an aggregative and sectoral approach. This has prevented conceptualization of rurality as unified and systemic. As a result, rural development efforts—particularly those involving foreign assistance—have tended all too frequently to become an array of poorly articulated specialist ventures.

The appropriate strategy seems to be a sequence of planned actions along a critical time path designed to round out the rural-urban continuum. The fundamental agricultural production function is modified or changed as new markets appear and new and stronger linkages are formed among farmers, rural artisans, merchants, processors of agricultural commodities, industrial workers, cooperative workers, credit institutions, and extension workers. The inert rural manpower pool is redeployed into the cadres of industry, trade, and service centers as the continuum matures. This to a considerable extent must involve substantial public investment in training and education (including adult education and functional literacy).

Typical of underdeveloped countries and their regions are the absence of development-fostering institutions (which have to be created) and the presence of development-inhibiting institutions (which need to be modified or abolished). The former include institutions for cooperation and extension, improved forms of local government, encouragement of local public works, and community development agencies. These and all other incentive-encouraging institutions must be fostered; sound institutions are transmission agents of change, incentive, inspiration, and innovation. Among the development-inhibiting institutions are exploitive land tenure systems, status-reinforcing customs (particularly those discriminating against women), caste systems, and those fostering wasteful ceremonial and religious expenditures. The effect of all of these is to destroy initiative and frustrate incentive.

Since the objective of integrated rural development is to improve the quality of life, a precondition of the industrialization effect in rural development is its intention to raise rather than lower regional levels of living. The urbanization process must insure that urban life is appreciably better than the misery and hardships of the village. The transformation of rural employment should not be the cause of industrial unemployment. For this reason the initial technology of industry should be labor- rather than capital-intensive. In this process, however, urbanization is essential to provide the organizational system through which an interplay of infrastructure and social overheads, on a scale adequate for self-sustained progress, can commence.

VI

International Development Assistance

A DISCUSSION OF LDC RURAL DEvelopment necessarily involves consideration of the role of foreign assistance. In that process a number of ideas and concepts have been transferred from the developed countries as well as some specific production procedures and technology and substantial amounts of foreign capital.

Perhaps the most dramatic contribution to LDC rural development has been the high-yielding varieties of rice and wheat resulting from the work of private U.S. foundations. Large-scale river basin development has been undertaken by the World Bank and, in the case of the Aswan Dam, by the Soviet Union. The United States Agency for International Development (USAID) among other activities has financed a number of agricultural colleges, built highways and communications systems, promoted a successful malaria eradication program, and shipped large amounts of foodstuffs (principally grain) on lenient terms. The Food and Agriculture Organization (FAO) of the United Nations has missions in a number of the LDCs and engages in a variety of rural development activities. The UN Development Programme has financed rural development training, cooperative development, research, and many preinvestment surveys and studies. Several countries—among them Canada, the Scandinavian countries, the United Kingdom, France, and West Germany—direct and finance rural development operations in a number of LDCs. Religious and charitable organizations are also active participants in LDC rural development. The private sector usually contributes very little to LDC rural development except in connection with mineral exploration and development.

While the aggregate foreign assistance is an impressive amount, for individual LDCs the outlay is not large. Moreover, foreign assistance outlay usually announced in lump sums is spread over a number of years; the annual amount is sometimes surprisingly small. But more significant than dimension is the question of accomplishment. In the case of rural development this is difficult to assess, particularly since overall goals of development have not always been clearly identified. Another complication is the multiplicity of donors, frequently with little coordination and control among them. Sometimes too, original goals and objectives have been altered in response to LDC political shifts. In still other cases goals and objectives were established in order to obtain funding which might otherwise have gone elsewhere.

Nevertheless, foreign assistance is important to LDC rural development. One of the effects may have been the policy shifts proposed by donor agencies in the interests of aligning LDC policy objectives with donor institutional criteria. There are also the longer-range effects of educating and training thousands of young people abroad and at home in modern agricultural technology. However, the longer-range effects on LDC rural attitudes and behavior are not identifiable in many cases.

For these reasons a review of foreign assistance is pertinent to a discussion of rural development, not only in terms of its dimensions and direct economic impact but also because of its social and political implications.

Resource Transfers to LDC Agriculture

The LDCs themselves finance about 85 percent of their agricultural development out of their own resources. The remaining resources for development are from foreign assistance. This small contribution is highly important to LDCs because it does not disturb their current balance of payments and can be used for long-term investment. Grant assistance provides items that many LDCs find difficult or impossible to provide themselves, and these may be critical to agricultural development. Consequently the amount of foreign assistance transfers as well as the policies and procedures of contributing agencies plays an important role in impeding or expediting increases of food and fiber supplies and in promoting rural development.

Private overseas investors are motivated by profit considerations. Religious bodies and private foundations performing valuable strategic institution-building and scientific research are motivated by opportunities for useful service as defined by their charters. Motivation of bilateral official donors is more complex; one guideline is national foreign policy. Still, particularly among the Scandinavian countries and Canada, there is evidence of genuine altruism as a guideline in selecting areas and amounts of assistance. The multinational official agencies are presumed to be objective in selecting assistance programs. However, this is not always the case; for example, the United States has threatened to withdraw its support of the UN International Labor Organization because of U.S. trade union objections to an appointment from an Iron Curtain country of a senior ILO official. The United States has also objected to some proposed World Bank commitments in Latin America where U.S. corporations have been threatened with expropriation.

In 1969 assistance transfers of goods and services to the less developed world totaled about $13.5 billion. A little over $6 billion was from private investment; the remainder represented grants, loans, and technical assistance from official public assistance agencies. Among these the World Bank and USAID contributed the most. Contributions from the Peoples Republic of China and Iron Curtain countries, not included in these aggregates, were much smaller.[1] The overall magnitude of U.S. participation in the transfer function (AID plus contributions to multilateral institutions) has been over 50 percent of total foreign aid flows since 1956.[2] Other substantial contributors have been the United Kingdom (10 percent) and France (15–20 percent). In recent years the Federal German Republic and Japan have become significant contributors.

Although in earlier years the lion's share of assistance went to industrial and urban development, this situation has recently changed. The World Bank reported 32 loans and credits to agriculture in fiscal 1970, with a combined value of 412.9 million. The cumulative World Bank total for agriculture was $2 billion as of June 30, 1970, out of a grand aggregate of over $17 billion, or 11.5 percent. About 40 percent of the World Bank cumulative agricultural total was advanced after 1967.[3]

It is unlikely that any substantial amount of the $37–$38 billion of private flows through 1969 went to agriculture or rural development,[4] since at that time assistance flows did not favor rural development. Apparently this has now been substantially corrected.

American aid is guided by its Southeast Asia, Soviet, and mainland China political orientation; British and French assistance is colored by political and economic ties to former colonies and Commonwealth countries. Japan's foreign trade orientation is reflected in overseas loans on fairly tight terms, mostly in Asia. Soviet assistance programs are believed to be directed toward foreign policy objectives, as is assistance from mainland China.

The orientation of USAID flows is particularly evident in the comparative amounts of its allocations. In fiscal 1970 South Vietnam, with perhaps 2.5 million farmers and a total population of about 15 million, was allocated $366 million. India, on the other hand, with a population of 600 million and perhaps 75–100 million farmers, received only $244 million. All of Latin America received $254 million.[5]

In terms of the rule-of-thumb target for donor country contributions of 1 percent of their Gross National Product, practically all nations slipped in the 1960s. Since nearly one-half of all transfers originated from the United States, its percentage decline from 2 percent of GNP in the days of the Marshall Aid Plan to 0.75 percent in 1960 and 0.65 percent in 1968 was significant; U.S. *official* flows in 1968 were 0.38 percent of GNP.[6]

The United States transfers science and technology assistance to LDC agriculture along traditional administrative, institutional, and policy lines. These are dominated by the land-grant colleges, the federal-state experiment stations and cooperative extension services, and the U.S. Department of Agriculture. Domestic accomplishments of these institutions in multiplying American agricultural output have been manifold and in some instances spectacular. At the same time their contributions have tended to emphasize physical technology; little attention has been given to welfare. Indeed U.S. agricultural institutions have been identified with the agricultural power structure reflected in the conservative political philosophy of the American Farm Bureau Federation. This philosophy has affected USAID's rural policy and programs.

The other countries extending assistance to the hungry nations have their particular orientations which influence their contributions and may also serve to impede or expedite political measures for efficient utilization of agricultural science and technology.

Financial Aid to Agriculture

The principal overseas contributions to LDC agricultural development are:

1. A supply of technical inputs—principally fertilizers, pesticides, seed, and farm machinery. In some instances irrigation pumps and motors assist development of irrigation from groundwater and large-scale irrigation.

2. Technical advice on establishment of agricultural colleges, agricultural research stations, training institutions for farmers; demonstrations of seed, fertilizers, and irrigation practices; and advising and training field staff.

3. Infrastructure installation such as farm-to-market roads, small water systems, storage facilities, agricultural credit institutions, and marketing systems.

Table 6.1 shows the characteristics of financing of LDC development in 1970–71 by the principal multinational financial institutions and USAID (largest binational development agency). Agricultural loans were 23 percent of all development loans made by these institutions. Concessional credits (low-interest, flexible term credits and grants) to agriculture were about 40 percent of all concessional credits. Overall, agriculture received about 31 percent of all development financing from these institutions.

These figures do not fully reveal the effect of this assistance on overall rural development. For example, World Bank assistance for a high-voltage transmission line in Cambodia may well have some spillover effects in rural areas. The same may be true of an African Development Bank credit to Kenya for roads. It can also be argued that progress in modernizing LDC agriculture is dependent on building infrastructure and that allocations to infrastructure should be counted as agricultural development. The difficulty is that infrastructure also benefits other sectors, so measurement becomes a problem. On the other hand, the 31 percent development finance that does go to agriculture probably requires a substantial infrastructure underpinning.

This review shows that financial assistance to the LDCs has not been particularly generous and has tended to favor conventional and conservative undertakings. Well over half the credits have carried substantial interest rates and can be considered as conventional investments. Only one-third of the assistance flow has been to agriculture— the most important sector of LDC economy. Nearly half the assistance to agriculture is in the "hard loan" category with current interest rates at 7 percent or above. The average charge on *all* hard loans, including those made in previous years, is about 5.5 percent. This rate is very

TABLE 6.1. CHARACTERISTICS OF DEVELOPMENT ASSISTANCE, 1970–71

Institution	1 Loans ($ mill.)	2 Agricultural Loans ($ mill.)	3 Concessional Credits ($ mill.)	4 Concessional Agricultural Credits ($ mill.)	5 Aggregate Development Finance ($ mill.)	6 Agricultural Development Finance ($ mill.)	7 Terms (years)	8 Normal Interest (%)	9 Concessional Interest (%)
World Bank	1896.0	191.0	584.0	228.0	2480.0	419.0	20–25	7.0	2.0 –3.0
USAID	807.0	367.0	1069.7	400.0[a]	1876.7	767.0	23	5.75	2.0 –3.0
Inter-American Development Bank	644.0	236.0	443.0	213.0	1087.0	449.0	12–25	8.0	2.25–4.0
Asian Development Bank	212.0	30.0[a]	34.0	27.0[a]	246.0	57.0	10–20	7.5	2.0 –3.0
African Development Bank	21.0	2.7	...	...	21.0	2.7	25–15	10.0	...
United Nations Development Programme	...	...	230.0	75.0[a]	230.0	75.0	5	...	...
Total	3580.0	826.7	2360.7	943.0	5710.7	1769.7			

Source: Adapted from Annual Reports of the World Bank, International Development Association, USAID, Inter-American Development Bank, Asian Development Bank, African Development Bank, and the United Nations Development Programme.

Note: These figures are only approximately correct partly because of the difficulty encountered in reconciling different reporting periods and reporting categories. The estimates in columns 2 and 4 are based entirely on judgment.

[a] Estimated.

close to the growth rate of LDC agriculture and well above considerable portions of it. Only high-value specialty crops, usually produced on plantations, could provide returns of 7 percent or over charged by the World Bank and the regional development banks.

At least in the hard loan category of assistance to the LDCs the lending agencies have not shown much imagination. Their loans have been made for standard objectives on standard terms of interest and amortization. Unfortunately this policy has also affected the handling of concessional credits and grants, and this kind of credit has been used in conjunction with hard loans to insure adequate security for the latter. It also seems likely that official lending agencies may be forced to utilize some of their soft loan resources to bail out commitments originally made on hard loan terms, or a soft loan could finance some other need with the end result that resources would be released to meet pressing hard loan repayments. The net effect of these financial methods is to channel all overseas financial assistance toward objectives that favor large-scale farming ventures and plantation agriculture. In these circumstances fewer concessional credits would go to smaller farmers and rural social improvement. Thus we begin with a less than proportional share of financial assistance to rural development, and we find that share to be considerably reduced in its effect on small farmers and rural development.

Grant funds for LDC agricultural development often represent salary and subsistence payments to foreign professionals and technicians. Salary and living standards of these expatriates are so much higher than those of indigenous personnel that friction and ill-feeling result. Moreover, high salaries necessary to attract competent expatriates have to be paid as grants, because the LDC would find it politically embarrassing to incorporate these costs in its borrowings.[7] Thus grant assistance to some extent is a means of avoiding unpleasantness due to expatriate compensation discrepancies.

Efficiency of Assistance

Many of the expatriate professionals and technicians have doubtless done good work. However, observers have found serious shortcomings among several UN agency projects. In East Africa nationality clashes were compounded with professional and policy controversy; important posts were unfilled for long periods, and some were never filled.[8] However, the criticisms of United Nation Development Programme operations by Sir Robert Jackson are far more serious.

This leads to a general conclusion about the content of the present programme; there is, in my judgment, about 20 per cent of "deadwood" in the present operation—projects that are not worthwhile if subjected to the acid test: "Is it *essential* for our development?" In a programme costing some US$180 million a year in project costs, they represent an expenditure of roughly US$36 million. Obviously, it will not be easy politically to eliminate these, but it is clearly in the interests both of the developing countries and of the UN development system to do so, in order to get the maximum use from available resources. Even 50 per cent success would permit US$18 million per year to be directed to better use.

The root cause of these deficiencies can be identified by an analysis of the constraints at each of the various phases of the programme:

(a) *Programming and project formulation.* The present programming procedures of the UN development system do not adequately reflect the real needs of the developing countries, nor is there any form of integrated approach to the problems of each country. All too often, projects are the results of Agencies' "salesmanship" rather than a response to priority needs, and this is encouraged by the "project-by-project" approach adopted for the Special Fund component. The consequence is "scatterization" of effort, less than effective impact, and a tendency to the self-perpetuation of projects.

(b) *Execution.* Difficulties here stem largely from the heavy operational burdens which have devolved so suddenly on the Specialized Agencies and which surpass the present capacity of several of the larger ones. This leads not only to delays in delivery but also to a decline in quality, especially as regards project personnel who are often not suited or prepared for assignments which exact so much more than technical expertise.

(c) *Evaluation.* Quantitatively, so much evaluation is now being attempted that it almost amounts to international hypochondria. It is a definite brake on the capacity of the system. Qualitatively, the position is the more disturbing, for very few people have the necessary experience and understanding to undertake this exacting function successfully.

(d) *Follow-up.* What should be the most important phase of the programme is often its weakest link, and insufficient attention is paid to it as an integral phase in the whole process of development.[9]

To the LDC leadership, foreign assistance transfers appear as straightforward business transactions involving no sense of obligation beyond the terms of the agreement. Donors who think in terms of LDC gratitude or similar attitudes are deluding themselves. As the LDCs see it, loans are negotiated at conventional rates. Other transfers are sometimes made in the interests of particular foreign policies which recipients are expected to help implement. This too is in the nature of a transaction. Borrowers from the international development banks view these credits as no less than their due; assistance from the UN, the UN Development Programme, and their affiliates is viewed in the same light. Indeed the LDCs are increasingly inclined to dictate the terms and purposes of assistance.

Less developed countries have become familiar with donor agency practices. At least some of them regard with cynicism the requirement tying loan proceeds to purchases within the donor country. They see well enough that this enables suppliers to enjoy monopoly prices at their expense. The Pearson report estimated that this practice has raised costs to recipients more than 20 percent.[10]

A further reduction in the amount of effective assistance is the return flow from LDCs of interest and amortization of previous advances from both public and private sources. This flow has to be funded out of LDC general foreign exchange resources. But these foreign exchange balances are related to LDC exports, the bulk of which are in the form of agricultural commodities. Such exports frequently encounter adverse world market prices as well as protectionist tariffs of the developed countries.

> The important impact of loan terms on the debt service ratio is, in our view, a very strong reason to urge that future development assistance be extended on highly concessional terms. Also, economic growth in many developing countries calls for large and sustained investment in areas where increased productivity is not immediately reflected either in increased revenue (e.g., education, roads, agriculture, public health, research, et cetera) or a sufficient improvement in balance of payments. This means debt service on borrowing for investments in these areas must be financed by the debtor country out of its own foreign exchange earnings or by the lender. When the borrower's ability to finance these investments is limited, concessional aid becomes not only desirable but necessary. This will be true even when the investments lead to rapid increases in production and revenue if there are structural problems in the domestic or international economy which prevent these increases from being translated into foreign exchange earnings adequate to service commercial debt.[11]

The conclusions of the Pearson Commission report lean in the direction of increasing the proportion of soft loans and grants to hard loans.

In appraising the impact of foreign assistance, an often overlooked aspect is the heavy administrative burden it imposes on LDC government personnel. Skill of a high order is required by those LDC officials who direct foreign assistance flows and manage the resulting obligations. They have to judge not only the specific merit of the purpose for which the advance is made but terms for each separate advance in relation to the entire range of outstanding obligations. In some cases it may become necessary to juggle repayment terms by renegotiating original agreements to extend amortization periods and reduce hard interest rates to soft. This may entail a series of other shifts. There is also a certain amount of pressure on these financial managers by the continual competitive selling efforts of donor representatives, in combination with efforts of their own officials to promote particular projects. These schemes all require counterpart funding to be allocated from slender local resources. Competition for project approval frequently involves bickering among representatives of the several UN agencies and LDC ministries. The LDC financial managers have to handle all these problems in conjunction with an always precarious balance of trade. Some of the development schemes and policies proposed by donors have not worked well.

T. W. Schultz has been critical of USAID programs.[12] Originally these had the effect of discouraging agricultural development by keeping food prices low in order to encourage industry. He thought that American advisors had not placed enough emphasis on investment in agricultural research and technology and that control of amounts spent and manner of spending was inadequate. This criticism could also be applied to numerous small, scattered, more or less ad hoc undertakings of both multinational and bilateral official agencies. Too often these undertakings result from scholarly predilections and forceful personalities. In Tanzania in 1970, 24 different countries were engaged in rural assistance programs in addition to the programs of the multinational agencies (author observation). This amounted to over 100 separate rural development projects, each with its own criteria.

Question of Reform

None of the institutions for international assistance has forthrightly endorsed or promoted measures for the reform of the inequities that impede rural development. All have repeatedly implemented conventional forms of rural assistance and farming in circumstances where benefits would accrue to only a minority and the majority could suffer additional deprivations. They seem to have proceeded on the assumption that assistance would benefit everyone equally and have not recognized that rural underdevelopment was partly due to profound inequities in the rural system. Thus they did not see that development required removal of these inequities simultaneously with improved agricultural technology and infrastructure. To the luckless majority, implementation of rural development schemes must have appeared as designed by elites for elites.

Although the United States was involved in three successful land reforms (Japan, South Korea, and Taiwan), it has refrained from using its leverage in favor of land reform in Latin America and other regions. In June 1970 the Agency for International Development devoted its entire *Spring Review* to land reform. Thirty USAID missions were polled to determine their activities in support of land reform: 19 missions reported *no* support, 6 reported *little* support, and only 6 reported *substantial* support activity (although this included taking credit for reforms in Japan, Korea, and Taiwan under other auspices).[13]

In contradiction to students of land tenure as related to agricultural productivity, AID missions to Latin America saw no difficulty with existing land tenure in relation to agricultural development.

> Most significantly *no* mission, with the possible exception of Brazil, sees land tenure patterns as a basic and controlling impediment to development which, unless changed, calls into question the country's basic development policies.[14]

One gains the distinct impression that for most AID missions land reform has overtones of social disturbance, if not of communism. But failing to favor land reform in Latin America is almost tantamount to acquiescence to a system that impedes agricultural development. By its neutral stance, both politically and administratively, the United States, in its AID missions and perhaps in its embassies, accepts prevailing land tenure status quo in underdeveloped countries and so stands aside as land reform becomes a spreading and acute political issue.

The United States took a similar attitude toward land reform in South Vietnam, despite its experience in Japan, Korea, and Taiwan. This position is hard to reconcile with U.S. involvement against the

Viet Cong, who made expropriation of landlords and redistribution of land the cornerstone of their appeal to South Vietnamese farmers.

Initial land reform legislation under the Diem regime in 1956 was imperfect; it provided an ownership ceiling of 100 hectares when average farm operating units in the southern region of the country, with two-thirds of the country's population, were under 3 hectares and were only 1 hectare in the more densely populated central lowlands. This measure, even if it had been efficiently implemented, would have fallen far short of effective land reform.

Lands acquired by this legislation together with lands from former French owners provided a total inventory of about one-third of tenant lands in South Vietnam. The distribution phase of this original reform was low. By 1966 less than half of the expropriated lands had been distributed, and both the United States and the government of Vietnam apparently considered land reform a dead issue. Rather it was an issue by default, conceded as a principal political weapon of the Viet Cong.

Early in 1966 Orville Freeman, then U.S. Secretary of Agriculture, visited South Vietnam. In ensuing discussions the issue of land reform was raised. After a short but intensive review it was concluded that the land tenure situation in South Vietnam corresponded closely to conditions formerly prevailing in Japan and other rice-growing regions of the Far East. A proposal was drafted for immediate implementation of a major and drastic land reform program financed largely by the United States (prepared by author).

Up to this point, the USAID agricultural program followed lines that had become traditional—fertilizer and pesticide distribution along with new rice varieties and advisory services. Both the United States and the government of South Vietnam apparently failed to recognize that inequities of land tenure, high rent, and exorbitant credit —in fact all the disabilities of tenant farming—were deeply resented by a majority of rural people. Because they did not prosecute land reform, both the United States and their government appeared to many small farmers as supporters of the system.

In late spring and summer of 1966, as the issue of land reform and its importance were sharply defined for U.S. authorities, it seemed to evoke positive enthusiasm. But opposition favoring the status quo strengthened, and the issue entered a period of drift. There seemed little will to proceed on what some considered a revolutionary course. No one in responsible positions in the Vietnamese government, the U.S. mission, the military, the State Department, or the

White House undertook decisive action. Rather lengthy discussions about the merits and demerits of the scheme ensued. There was considerable anxiety lest the matter reach either the press or Congress. Informal inquiries from Senator McGovern and staff members of the Foreign Operations Subcommittee of the House Committee on Government Operations were turned aside. Finally a decision was reached to employ the Stanford Research Institute to undertake a study of Vietnam land tenure and to make recommendations about the need for land reform. The SRI study in 1967 and 1968 endorsed the 1966 proposals. Nearly four years after the issue was first presented for action, President Thieu signed the Land-to-the-Tiller Bill (March 26, 1970), and a powerful U.S. bipartisan congressional group introduced legislation to provide $200 million supporting assistance to Vietnam land reform.[15]

The new law is brief and clear. Properly and speedily implemented it should, in the terms of Douglas MacArthur in his March 15, 1946, directive to the Japanese on a similar occasion, "uproot and destroy the various evils which had for so long blighted the lives of the peasantry."[16]

We do not know to what extent the government and President Thieu have implemented or will implement the Land-to-the-Tiller Bill at long last. We can be sad that the initiative came from President Thieu and was only reluctantly accepted by U.S. officials. It is even sadder to contemplate the failure of U.S. officials who let a dozen or more years go by without raising the issue of land reform. Conclusions derived from the SRI study imply that omission of forthright dealing with the land tenure issue caused much of the U.S. effort and investment in South Vietnam rural development to be wasted insofar as it had any effect on changing the loyalties of rural population.

Perhaps the South Vietnam case is extreme. Nevertheless, it does illustrate a deficiency affecting all rural development assistance. This deficiency consists in using conventional western methods and avoiding institutional change.

Assistance Institutions and Rural Manpower

The assistance agencies, binational and international, have not tackled exploding LDC rural unemployment. Yet during the entire period of overseas assistance, now approaching a quarter of a century, rural unemployment has continually increased in most if not all the LDCs. It is doubtful if any of these agencies or the LDCs themselves know the full dimensions of the unemployment. Yet we see evidence of this misuse of rural manpower on all sides, and we know that it is a characteristic of rural society in many LDCs. The incompatibility of rural development and increasing waste of manpower has not been considered sufficiently.

There is little consolation in pointing to increases in the agricultural components of the Gross National Product of the LDCs if at the same time rural unemployment increases by leaps and bounds. The real implication of this contrast is that while some people are better off, a considerable number are becoming worse off. Unemployment represents a waste of precious human resources; hence rural development schemes failing to take unemployment into account may not contribute very much to economic growth.

The endless ranks of LDC rural unemployed stand aside from the procession of active life. Like prisoners they are deprived of participation in human affairs. Their existence has been discounted almost to zero; they barely exist at all. As more and more human beings are committed to this dreadful death-in-life existence, the problem of rural manpower should become a central issue in planning LDC rural development. The assistance agencies should develop analytical procedures for testing manpower aspects of LDC rural development schemes and insist that their LDC clientele provide the necessary safeguards against increasing unemployment and undertake measures for its amelioration.

Assistance institutions must face the fact that rural unemployment in the LDCs is already too large to respond to any single solution. Partial measures may afford some relief on particular occasions and in particular places, but delaying or impeding technological advance in agriculture is not a satisfactory solution to countries in desperate need of increased food output. Nor in the short run is an increase in urbanward migration a likely answer. The current pressure of new residents arriving in large LDC metropolitan centers dangerously stretches their administrative and economic capacity. The respective dimensions of a very large redundant rural labor force and any realistic migration flow, even if that were substantially increased (and even if the primary cities could absorb the increase) deny the reality of the migration alternative.

In this situation government policy is highly important. Since some rural unemployment probably results from the structure of the rural economy, government policy could be directed toward structural modification of the rural sector. Structural imbalance is exhibited primarily in disparity in land occupancy and income between middle and larger farmers and the much larger mass of traditional small-scale peasants including totally and partially unemployed as well as mini-operators.

In contrast to these suggestions, government policy has too often been directed toward an aggravation of existing disparities. This misdirection has taken the form of agricultural subsidies primarily benefiting larger producers. For example, irrigation water is often substantially underpriced, and cheap credit (provided out of the national budget or the central bank) to commercial farmers facilitates purchase of import-tax–free fertilizer and machinery. Subsistence farmers obviously receive little benefit from these subsidies. Moreover, subsidies to commercial producers are not compensated but rather are exacerbated by uniformly low land taxes and the absence of income taxes on the rural sector.

Thus profit margins for larger and medium-size farms result from artificially low input costs. No effort is made to mobilize a part of these profits for solution of rural problems or particularly for alleviating the lot of the unemployed or small holders. Rural land taxes are not progressive, and revenue is disproportionate to cost of subsidies. Stanley Please indicates that underpricing of irrigation water is equivalent to 40 percent of land taxes in some parts of India.[17] At the same time, savings from untaxed agricultural profits move out of agriculture or into conspicuous consumption partly because of abnormally low depositor rates in rural areas resulting from low, subsidized official loan rates. Thus steps taken by government to directly assist peasant producers or to alleviate rural unemployment represent deficit treasury financing or a transfer of resources from other sectors; the cost does not accrue to rural wealth.

To a considerable extent agricultural production escapes indirect control by national policy, and few LDC governments are strong enough to implement direct or fiat measures. This means that resources devoted to agricultural production may not be applied in a fashion consistent with the national interest; returns to farmers tend to avoid any form of mobilization to mitigate unemployment. Since savings tend to flow out of the rural sector, there is small prospect for voluntary establishment within it of institutions for the mobilization of sector resources.

Rectification of this situation would not cure rural unemployment but might narrow those gaps in the economic structure tending to promote additional unemployment and hindering amelioration. Such measures ought to be undertaken; they would help governments to obtain resources needed to control, for example, overhasty mechanization for operations where labor would be equally efficient. The assistance agencies should lend their support to these policies and urge their adoption.

Only if government can mobilize resources in agriculture—its largest and most productive sector—should it intervene in market and price situations in behalf of agricultural producers or for implementation of agricultural policy. The prescription for intervention is threefold: revision of agricultural subsidies to favor *all* producers, not just the 5–10 percent who dominate commercial production; design of a progressive land and income tax on agricultural producers; and revision of agricultural lending rates and encouragement of institutions that could retain rural savings within that sector.

Only when hard-pressed and recently emerged LDC governments mobilize substantial rural resources can they afford to finance rural public works and infrastructure to modify rural unemployment without unduly draining resources from other sectors. Expenditures for these purposes within the rural sector also provide employment in the construction stage and stimulate rural production of consumer goods, but care must be taken to maintain an appropriate wage structure. Public works wages to rural workers should be equitable: if they are too high the result could be acceleration of agricultural mechanization by commercial farmers to replace labor; a subnormal wage structure increases the existing subsidy situation at the expense of labor.

John P. Lewis suggested that redundant Indian rural labor might be redeployed by enlarging employment opportunities in traditional rural market centers if these could be enlarged to encompass additional service, industrial, and commercial activities.[18] Edgar Johnson had a more general proposal: rural landscapes could be deliberately planned to provide a hierarchy of central places as part of overall rural development. At present the rural sector suffers from a dearth of alternative employment opportunities and services which such employment envisioned by Lewis and Johnson might stimulate. This does not necessarily involve any great increases of capital above that already planned but rather greater awareness of the significance of location and preparation of needed planning guidelines. Currently LDCs have relatively few central places separated by large areas of rural space occupied by fields and small primitive villages with marginal employment opportunties. The proliferation of markets and market towns would provide the essential dynamic for development and dissolution of the unemployed mass.[19] Thus location, size, and function of new, larger centers should be a principal concern in designing efficient national development and employment policy.

On the other hand, Norton Ginsburg is of the opinion that establishment of such urban centers on a national scale would be enormously costly and perhaps unnecessary. He argues for development of rural-urban regions. As these metropolitan centers expand in conjunction with a developing rural hinterland, the entire region would become progressively urbanized. Ginsburg believes this could not be undertaken nationwide but rather in selected regions. The remainder would have to endure "benign neglect" until its turn was reached.[20] These views agree that one aspect of the solution of rural employment is a transformation to *rural urbanization*.

Throughout this discussion the role of government has been emphasized. But government must function in a political context. The opposition to government action necessary for mobilizing resources would be very great from politically powerful commercial farmers, and few LDC governments have undertaken to challenge them. In the case of development of market towns, government action would be essential to control and supervise the conduct of the markets. The subsequent economic development of such centers would follow a demonstration of benefits of regulated markets.

Assistance and International Trade

Assistance to LDC rural development involves trade and balance of payments. Foreign exchange problems can become exceedingly burdensome to the LDCs and can interfere with rural development. The LDCs can be helped or hindered by assistance agency policy. Thus an important aspect of the formulation of assistance agency policy should be a general understanding among donors of LDC balance of payment problems and agreement on common criteria for implementing assistance. This is a complex matter. It may involve important foreign policy considerations of individual donor countries, constraining their ability to enter into common agreement. Moreover, international trade volume originates in transactions of individual traders who can circumvent consortia criteria.

For those LDCs with petroleum resources, balance of trade problems are less severe. They have latitude for negotiation and can maneuver to assist their rural sectors if they wish to use their power for that purpose. However, this latitude is denied that group of LDCs primarily dependent on agricultural exports for foreign exchange earnings. This latter group needs to import capital goods, for the most part administratively priced by producers; but their agricultural exports are priced in world markets beyond the control of individual countries or may encounter severe constraints in the form of protective trade barriers.

When world prices for agricultural products shift with devastating suddenness, central planning and budgeting must be adjusted accordingly. When world sisal and coffee prices dropped drastically as they did a few years ago, the entire Ethiopian economy was affected, as was that of neighboring Kenya and Tanzania. Sugar-producing countries are periodically exposed to shifts in U.S. and British sugar quotas. This can be an extremely serious matter, as in the case of tiny British Honduras where nearly a quarter of the total labor force is directly or indirectly concerned with the sugar industry. And this export, completely dependent on U.S. and British quotas and negotiated prices, represents over half the value of exports in a country whose existence is dependent on foreign trade.

It is in this context that production increases of cereals from the Green Revolution occur. India and Pakistan, along with Brazil, Mexico, Kenya, Thailand, Indonesia, Malaysia, and the Philippines, are likely to become competitors in world trade for the new cereal varieties. These countries may at least temporarily have solved their internal food problems; it is also possible that a world cereal surplus associated with drastic price reductions may be created.

Another aspect of world trade among LDCs is that overseas assistance agencies may unintentionally promote intraregional competition for foreign markets. Thus assistance is given to both Ethiopia and Tanzania coffee production and perhaps to Brazil and other Latin American countries as well. India's important cashew nut export may be affected by that of Tanzania financed or assisted from multilateral or bilateral sources. Wherever production of one product in the export trade of one country is assisted, it is possible that the same product may be pushed with similar assistance in another or several other countries.

Trade policies of developed nations include protective tariffs and internal price-support programs. Both devices confront LDCs in their efforts to increase development through export of primary products. One of the clearest cases of this is presented by rice. As former rice-deficit countries achieve self-sufficiency with the high-yielding varieties and develop a surplus, the world price of rice drops and their surplus has a lower trading value. They also find that the world market for rice has become smaller, partly because of protection. And protection, as in the case of Japan, may be related to an inordinately high internal support price. At one time this support price was nearly triple the world market price.[21] Another area presenting less developed regions with problems is the European Common Market. European countries have deliberately followed the policy of food self-sufficiency, with the result that European domestic grain prices have been very high and surplus stocks have accumulated. The net effect is to shut that market to nonindustrial regions.

It seems contradictory for the developed countries to provide a trickle of development assistance flows to LDCs only to block the resulting return flow as the development potential is realized. But the political procedure is plain: in the developed regions farmers are well organized politically, and the wealthier regions can afford the additional cost of subsidy and, at least in the short run, encouragement of inefficient production.

A few answers to this dilemma have been suggested. The first is obvious: nonindustrial agrarian development should seek to diversify rather than to depend solely on one, two, or even three exports. This suggestion is difficult to follow because the shift to other products takes time and may include expensive preparation, different inputs, additional research, and possibly specialized training. Moreover, markets for diversified food production do not just appear; they have to be identified and promoted. In addition scant resources really do not permit the launching of very many trade missions in the underdeveloped nations.

Another suggestion is that the developed countries arrange among themselves to set aside import quotas for developing regions. The Pearson Commission report recommended:

> that developed countries draw up plans in respect of protected commodities designed to assure that over time an increasing share of domestic consumption is supplied by imports from developing countries.[22]

Such an undertaking will require heightened international cooperation. A proliferation of international agreements and agencies in addition to those already existing—including the United Nations Conference on Trade and Development (UNCTAD) and the General Agreement on Tariffs and Trade (GATT)—will become necessary, as will the organization of consortia, perhaps under leadership of the World Bank. [23] However, underlying all such arrangements will be the domestic politics and administrative vision of the constituent nations.

VII

INTERNATIONAL STRUCTURE FOR RURAL DEVELOPMENT

INTERNATIONAL TRADE DIRECTLY affects the economic condition of underdeveloped nations. These nations seek foreign markets for their raw materials, mostly farm products and minerals; earnings from sales of these products provide the means to acquire capital goods necessary for industrial expansion. In turn industrial expansion is expected to provide employment for a redundant rural labor force. Thus LDC planners come to think of foreign trade as a principal development factor particularly important to the rural sector. As they conceive it, an LDC should increase rural sector output of export items in order to provide increased imports of capital goods.

This generally accepted development formula depends on a continually expanding demand among industrial regions for LDC raw material exports, and this assumption may be too optimistic. More likely the prospects for increased trade with developed countries are limited both by their falling rates of population increase and by lowered demand for some farm products.[1]

At the same time that birthrates fall in the industrial countries, per capita earnings may rise; as they do, the demand for bulk staple foods and natural fibers typically produced in the LDCs will shift to fruits, vegetables, poultry, dairy products, and synthetic substitutes. These may be products the LDCs have difficulty in producing in substantial quantity—at least without a considerable time lag. As export markets narrow and competition intensifies, one country's exports may also be threatened by those of another. Thus increasing exports of African coffee might hurt Brazilian coffee producers more than it would profit African producers, and increasing East African tea exports by amounts equal to 10 percent of the world supply might cause equivalent losses in the Indo-Ceylon tea trade.[2]

There may be some exceptions to the generally doubtful prospects of LDC trade with developed countries. Even more doubtful, however, is whether these exceptions will have widespread effects. Among the oil-rich Arab nations petroleum sales to developed countries could provide a substantial base for importing industrial capital goods helpful to both rural and industrial development, but there is little evidence that this is happening or is likely to happen. East African countries may be able to ship frozen mutton carcasses across the Red Sea and the Mediterranean to the Near East, Greece, and Yugoslavia. Some Central American countries enjoy a U.S. and Caribbean market for truck crops. Similar instances of comparative advantage may open opportunities for export of limited amounts of specialty crops from Southeast Asia and the Philippines to Japan. Unfortunately these opportunities may be confined to small areas and special circumstances. The ensuing foreign exchange earnings may not be channeled into productive investment; they may be spent instead for conspicuous consumption or remain abroad in overseas investment. The effect on rural development may be quite limited.

These limited foreign trade prospects are not sufficient for LDC development. A quantum jump in volume of exports, substantial shift in the composition of trade, and great improvement in the terms of that trade are required. This is the challenge confronting the LDCs. They must seek new and much larger trade outlets for new commodities produced with innovative, labor-intensive methods and under conditions of more equitable distribution and more encouragement to savings.

These requirements in LDC foreign trade differ sharply from those of the conventional LDC commerce of today. As things now stand, LDC farm exports are produced under conditions not greatly different from the colonial period. Today's LDC trading partners are often the former colonial powers; in order to compete in today's markets, producers must conform to a production technology and scale economy tending to reproduce colonial conditions of employment, wages, and working conditions. Thus for LDC farmers producing for today's export market the change from colonial conditions is formal, not substantive. In Asia and Africa the former colonial theme has ended but the original economic farming system still lingers, and for millions the change is not distinguishable.[3]

It is primarily in a world order of nation-states that the massive rural misery of the LDCs escapes general notice or concern. Rich nations, secure within their own borders, seem not to recognize their responsibility for handling foreign trade in a manner that benefits more than it harms the people of poorer countries. Developed nations should be continually reminded that a system of foreign trade not deliberately aimed at helping the LDCs will serve to perpetuate backwardness and widen the scope of rural misery.

As a group the LDCs cannot now determine the terms of their foreign trade. Instead these terms tend to be set for them by their rich and powerful trading partners. Among these powerful nations welfare considerations extend only to their own citizens; poverty and misery of their own seem more poignant and more dreadful than similar conditions among people in other countries. In the sphere of international commerce the only fear for rich nations is of retaliatory trade measures by their equals. This policy—or lack of policy—puts all rich and powerful nations on one side of the trading counter and all LDCs on the other. Unfortunately the LDCs pursue the same or similar tactics with respect to each other. They cannot afford to do this; their hope is for comprehensive cooperation among LDCs, furtherance of a common LDC interest in securing better terms of trade, and expanding the horizons of their export trade. Not only their geographic location but the irrationality of national frontiers laid down in colonial times recommends the formulation of integrated patterns of LDC regional trade as an alternative to the present stifling conventional configuration.

Malthusian predictions may ultimately have to be faced by the LDCs. But the present reality that accounts for rural distress is poverty, largely resulting from sheer lack of purchasing power, along with ignorance. The overriding consideration is not scarcity but (1) the lack of institutions to offset inequities arising from the socioeconomic structure of the LDCs and (2) the persistence of political rigidities inherent in aggressive nationalism.[4] Montague Yudelman voices a similar view about Latin America; Rene Dumont says of Africa that men, not resources, account for underdevelopment.[5]

Trade Concessions

Exports of LDC agricultural products to developed countries will tend increasingly to be confined to noncompeting items. The most important of these for many LDCs are the beverage commodities

—coffee, tea, cocoa, and kola. Demand is not likely to be a problem for these commodities, although competition among LDCs may result in long-term price declines. Two additional problems remain—sharp short-term price changes due to weather and restrictions by importing countries. The Pearson report (see Chapter 6) suggests that aid-giving countries consider the possibility of lowering such duties.[6] Some effort has been made in this direction through international agreements seeking to modify some of the ill effects of short-run changes in supply conditions—e.g., the International Tea and Coffee Agreements.

Several significant LDC world trade commodities like sugar, rice, vegetable oils, cotton, and tobacco are to some extent competitive with farmers of developed regions. It seems probable that LDC export trade in these commodities will be subject to more or less continual harassment through one protective device or another as farm blocs in developed regions exert political pressure. To what extent concessions would be made to favor LDC exporters above those already in effect as a result of efforts by the UN Conference on Trade and Development (UNCTAD) and the General Agreements on Tariffs and Trade (GATT) is conjectural.

Although the LDCs are not presently in a position to make their own decisions about foreign trade policy, these decisions represent for them partial determinants of their rate of rural development which in turn depends partly on imported technical input. Even trade concessions to the LDCs and their monopoly on tropical agricultural products would tend at best toward economic growth at about existing levels. This still leaves regional economic integration among LDCs as the principal prospective growth alternative.

The lack of any serious intention by the industrial nations to undertake adjustments in their policies to significantly improve the LDC trade position in spite of clearly articulated LDC appeals was made quite clear in 1964 and again in 1967. In 1964 in the Charter of Altagrácias, initiated at the Geneva UNCTAD conference, a number of Third World nations laid out their trade problems and fundamental economic demands in a petition for consideration of the developed nations. Eventually 77 nations of the Third World joined in this petition spelling out the need for modification of prevailing trade and tariff conventions and for preferential tariff treatment for their primary exports together with better terms of international finance. These statements, based on a portrayal of the great economic differences between developed and less developed countries and the need for changing these conditions, were almost completely ignored. Again presented in 1967 at the second UNCTAD conference in New Delhi, India, these pleas received some slight attention, but little real benefit resulted. Instead the developed nations continued to insist that the remedy was for the LDCs to improve their internal economic affairs and to develop by means of capital importation. Both these suggestions ignore the realities of LDC economics, and in taking this attitude the industrial nations closed the door on the possibility of significant reorientation "in the focus of international relations."[7]

PROSPECTS FOR REORIENTATION OF AGRICULTURAL EXPORT PRODUCTS

The continental regions of Asia, Africa, and Latin America may enjoy vast latent comparative advantages with respect to each other, and in the exploitation of these great opportunity for rural transformation and improvement may exist. What now appears as an enormous mass of poverty-stricken people also represents potentially large continental markets, but the determination to develop these markets and the necessary supporting infrastructure is missing. The comparative advantages of yet undetermined commercial agricultural specialization of subregions within these continents need exploration and research to provide alternatives to the prospective weakening of demand for LDC exports by the developed countries.

In conceptual terms what is involved is a recognition, on a continental scale, of the potentials among the LDCs for a rationalized system of agricultural productivity at increasingly higher technical levels through regional economic integration and stronger institutions for equalizing the distribution of consumer benefits. Such a planning framework gives significance to principles of environmental protection and the need for taking them into account as larger quantities of fertilizers and pesticides are introduced. It is doubtful in the present atomistic arrangements of uncoordinated national units that threats of potential deterioration of the ecosystem will receive much consideration. Only when the rate of resource exploitation on a regional or continental scale is deliberately planned can appropriate levels of waste control be appreciated. Closely related to planned levels of energy utilization are population levels. Perhaps one reason for the slow progress of global population control efforts is that the problem, like that of the environment, has not been put in the appropriate regional context.

One may indeed have misgivings about the viability of a system of continental and intercontinental regional trading units within the present system of separate nation-states. Increasingly virulent nationalism among the newly independent countries of Africa and Asia tends to work against the establishment of regional free-trade areas or the more advanced common market form of regional economic development. Moreover, with rising nationalism there is a growing tendency toward protectionist tariff and import substitution policies. In Latin America there are also problems associated with well-established industrial and commercial vested interests. Further aggravating the Latin-American situation is disparity between richer, partly urbanized and poorer, more rural countries. It would be very difficult in these circumstances to design regional trading policies that would not injure less-developed, agricultural countries more than they would benefit better balanced national economies. Additional obstacles to Latin American regional trade development are lack of transport, communications, and power facilities, although these obstacles are also present in parts of Africa and Asia. To some extent all the LDCs share a common lack of product diversification resulting from the present orientation of foreign trade.[8]

The rich resources of Africa are divided among numerous small states and a profusion of separate markets. This balkanization of African countries tends to hinder development because of duplicated functions and an uneconomic scale of enterprise.[9] Moreover, the colonial heritage is now apparent in irrational national boundaries that enable foreign interests to play one nation against another. These impediments culminate in the irrational location and size of intermediate processing and manufacturing establishments, with resultant lowered added-value benefits and higher costs for supplier goods such as fertilizers. Moreover, efforts to change or alter trade flows and to reorient production might challenge current arrangements with foreign firms and investors located within a particular country. This condition is more typical of the African situation, but these trade rigidities exist in the other two continents as well.

One difficulty confronting efforts to develop Asian regional trade is absence of a tradition of social and economic intercourse between nations.[10] Difficult language barriers contribute to the limited personal contacts of people among cities of the different Asian countries. Agricultural products with little complementarity make up the bulk of the export trade of Asian countries. Commonwealth preferences tend to tie some individual Asian members to participation in that trade orbit; similarly several Southeast Asian countries have French and, more recently, Japanese ties.

Perhaps political differences between Asian countries are the most significant obstacles to regional trade; among them is a wide spectrum of political forms ranging from communism to military dictatorship to representative democracy. Also present are widespread mistrust and even hostility between several Asian nations and sometimes within them. The Asian countries have developed a wide divergence of relations with the major powers—China, the Soviet Union, Japan, and the West. Thus Asian countries have to formulate their foreign policy and attendant foreign trade negotiations in continual adjustment to the ups and downs of the power struggles among the major powers and their satellites.

A dominant factor in Asian relations is the preponderant size of India and its apparent disinterest in integrated regional trade development despite intense Indian concern with bilateral trade.[11] With the great land mass of China and the Indian subcontinent thrust through the center of Asia, and with neither country having regional trade identification, it is inevitable that regional economic integration in Asia has been confined to subregional national groupings on the western and eastern edges of the continent.

Difficult as prospective regional trade development on a continental scale may be for the LDCs, existing alternatives may be still less attractive. Already internal domestic trade suffers from limitations of poverty and relatively small markets. External trade with developed regions along traditional lines affords little opportunity to escape from neocolonial patterns, and even these limited export outlets seem likely to narrow with increasing self-sufficiency of major food and fiber importers and inelasticity of demand for food in these external markets.[12]

Still another set of factors requiring adjustment and realignment of LDC interests may emerge with major shifts in international alignment resulting from the end of the Vietnam war; a cold war detente; resumption of more normal U.S.-Chinese relations; a considerable expansion of the scope of the European Common Market; and the possibility of freer trade among Iron Curtain countries, the West, and Japan. Out of such realignment it is possible that several new spheres may emerge, each with potential attendant repercussion on LDC agricultural export trade. Without the existence of substantial regional and continental trade, the LDCs will have to participate in the new configurations, and probably not on their own terms.

Efforts to Promote Regional Economic Integration

Organizational activity to promote regional and subregional trade seems to occur almost constantly in Latin America, Asia, and Africa.

The three UN regional commissions—the Economic Commission for Latin America (ECLA), the Economic Commission for Asia and the Far East (ECAFE), and the Economic Commission for Africa (ECA) —have continuous operations centering on regional trade. Activities include periodic conferences of commission members, special committee meetings, preparation of studies, collection of statistical material, and publication of materials. The work of the commissions is supported by staffs who serve as investigators, researchers, and technical advisors.

These regional commissions helped launch the three regional development banks. They have also provided a central institutional framework for discussion and negotiation leading to formation of subregional trade associations as well as development of intraregional political and economic policies and organizations. Finally regional commissions serve to decentralize UN deliberations, to interpret UN policy decisions in regional terms, and to feed back information to the parent body.

LATIN AMERICA. In Latin America the cause of regional trade and economic integration has been promoted by ECLA and, since 1961, by the U.S.-sponsored Alliance for Progress and its affiliate the Organization of American States (OAS). In addition these major bodies have "spun off" a number of other groups. One of these is the Latin American Institute for Economic and Social Planning, affiliated with ECLA and supported jointly by the UN Development Programme and the Inter-American Development Bank.[13] The OAS is financed by the U.S. Agency for International Development (USAID), but its operations also involve cooperation with ECLA, the Inter-American Development Bank, the World Bank, and the UN Development Programme.

Both the multinational groups and the U.S.-financed groups have focused their efforts on promotion of regional economic integration in Latin America; ECLA provided initial technical support for the Latin American Free Trade Association (LAFTA), the Central American Common Market (CACM), the Caribbean Free Trade Association (CARIFTA), and the East Caribbean Common Market.

A review of ECLA operations and those of its affiliates indicates that they have served well as institutions for consultation among Latin American countries and for providing a substantial flow of information. Beyond this, ECLA has prepared recommendations for action at both national and international levels. Perhaps more important is that ECLA's work has made apparent to many Latin American leaders, thinkers, and officials the steps necessary for regional economic integration. Moreover, groundwork laid by ECLA provided much of the foundation for the Alliance for Progress and OAS programs.

In its proceedings and discussions the ECLA group has consistently emphasized the social and welfare aspects of Latin American development. Particular attention has been directed toward disparities in rural income and rural poverty. The Social Affairs Division of the commission has voiced doubts about the ability of the Latin American economies, under existing national policies, to ever provide broad social participation.[14] Thus ECLA has conceived regional economic integration not as an isolated policy of trade but rather in the broad context of overall economic development and social justice.

Some may feel that the Alliance for Progress has mounted a more vigorous effort toward Latin American economic integration than the ECLA group. This opinion would tend to reflect basic differences between a primarily multinational body limited to ministerial functions and the Alliance for Progress functioning through economic development as an instrument of national policy. Although initially the Alliance for Progress was conceived as a multilateral agency, it has not worked out that way, partly because the United States saw the Alliance not only as an instrument for Latin American economic development but also as a means for containing the spread of Castroism. Thus early on it became plain that the Alliance would not adopt anti-U.S. or leftist postures even though these might have reflected public opinion of some constituent countries. Perhaps of equal importance in defining the eventual role the Alliance was the extreme nationalism of the constituent nations—particularly the two largest, Brazil and Argentina—who refused to countenance multilateral judgments on their financial proposals for development.

These several constraints were compounded in their effect by ambiguities in the basic Alliance charter and by U.S. unwillingness to relinquish approval authority for its financial advances to member countries.[15] Thus the Alliance has not worked very well as an instrument for promoting regional trade. The volume of regional trade (with the exception of some Central American trade) has not increased, and the member countries have made almost no effort toward restructuring tariffs. With the tentative exception of Central American countries, no Latin American country has developed a plan for regional integration or any program for advancing it.[16]

If the Alliance has not worked well, it may also be said that ECLA has done little better in terms of specific achievement. It may be some consolation that an intense discussion of regional economic integration has been under way and that a lot of pertinent information has been produced and exchanged. Perhaps we can find some comfort too in observing, in spite of disappointment and nonachievement, that the combined ECLA-Alliance effort is the longest sustained effort on a large scale to promote the idea of regional integration as one of the essentials for LDC development.

Until recent hostilities the CACM had reportedly made some progress in regional agricultural integration. The reasons for the progress, in contrast to LAFTA's stagnation, are unclear. One factor may have been CACM's concern for agricultural commodities in contrast to LAFTA's preoccupation with industry. Another may have been the small geographic area encompassed by Central American countries compared with the enormous geography of the LAFTA nations as well as the great size discrepancies among them and the dominance of Brazil and Argentina.[17]

ASIA. The Economic Commission for Asia and the Far East seems to have a central concern about the role of farming and farm products in regional economic integration. At the 27th session of the commission attention was directed to the possible effect on international trade of increased cereal production and the need for consultation among producer countries. At the same time emphasis was placed on the need for restructuring land tenure systems and improving cooperatives, credit, and price policies. The commission also supported proposals for convening a number of experts to help arrange periodic intraregional consultations for liberalization and development of the rice trade.[18]

The commission has received from its membership fairly definite guidelines for planning its work. Apparently these commissioners, representing a number of Asian countries, have strong views about the direction of ECAFE policy and operations. The 4th session of the Council of Ministers for Asian Economic Cooperation meeting at Kabul, Afghanistan, December 16–19, 1970, expressed a need "to examine guidelines and negotiate an agreement for the early establishment of an Asian clearing union and an intergovernmental committee to examine principles for a trade expansion program in the ECAFE region." Guidelines for the establishment of an Asian Reserve Bank were also to be further examined by an intergovernmental committee.

Continued concern with farm commodities stresses assistance to member countries in the stabilization and expansion of regional trade in these commodities. The commission urged that national development plans be in harmony with anticipated market conditions.[19] It seems to view its principal agricultural objective as the mutual rationalization among the nations in Asia of the programming and implementation of agricultural development.

Both commission members and ECAFE's technical staff have sought to make an intelligent and enlightened contribution to the cause of Asian regional integration. Unfortunately these efforts have been made under a cloud of major uncertainties. No one can foresee the full significance of the recent Indo-Pakistan conflict or what is in store for newly emerging Bangladesh. India appears to lend nominal support to the concept of Asian unity, but she is too large, too powerful (and possibly too proud) to see much value in being an equal partner in a continental economic system. Another uncertainty is Taiwan's future relations with mainland China—an important factor because of Taiwan's substantial export trade. Realignments of trade following a possible economic entente between China and Japan could greatly affect the Philippines and the whole of Southeast Asia including Indonesia and Malaysia. Still to be reckoned with are trade potentials and the market situation proceeding from a rapprochement between North and South Korea as well as the near-future prospect of a greatly reduced U.S. official presence in the region.

These several possible shifts in trade and political alignment weigh heavily on the future prospects of several Asian regional organizations attempted or achieved in the last quarter-century. Both the Southeast Asia Treaty Organization (SEATO)—established in 1954 and including the United States, UK, Thailand, French Indo-China, the Philippines, and Pakistan—and the Central Treaty Organization of the Middle East (CENTO)—established in 1959 and including UK, Pakistan, Turkey, and Iran among others—were cold war, political, and military alliances; neither has achieved significance as an agent of economic development.[20] The British Commonwealth Colombo Plan has channeled technical and financial assistance to southern and southeastern Asian countries. The principal donors were Britain, Australia, and New Zealand; the recipients were mostly former colonies in the British Commonwealth.

Alongside these quasi-military and political alignments have been a procession of regional trade schemes involving Asian and Southeast Asian countries. Some of these have gone out of existence (MAPHLINDO—Malaysia, the Philippines, and Indonesia) or have been succeeded by other groupings and altered objectives. The Southeast Asia Agricultural Development Conference established a regional agricultural development fund administered by the Asian Development Bank. The Association of Southeast Asia (ASA) had a checkered and uncertain existence until it was succeeded by the more comprehensive and successful Association of Southeast Asian Nations (ASEAN) in 1967. An even more carefully worked out scheme of trade collaboration resulted in creation of the Asian and Pacific Council (ASPAC) in 1966 with members including among others South Korea, Malaysia, Thailand, and the Philippines.

All these efforts have been handicapped—first by the war in Southeast Asia, second by the lack of national integration and uncertain political leadership of some of the constituent countries, and finally because of the overriding trade policies and ambitions of Japan, Australia, and the West. It is doubtful that these developed countries would relish economic confrontation with an independent, well-organized, and efficient Asian trading bloc.

The procession of these trade groupings and their evanescent existence causes one to wonder whether they were ever intended to be the permanent instruments of economic integration or were not rather ad hoc products of short-term political maneuvering. They all seem to share equally short term objectives set by the ideological and political struggle among the West, the Soviet Union, and China and to be involved in the growing Japanese economic hegemony in the region.

Out of this history of shifting and uncertain efforts to integrate regional trade a very large regional trade area could emerge in Asia to include the Korean peninsula, China, Japan, and all the remaining mainland and island countries as far south as Malaysia and Singapore. In such a grouping Japan's role might be that of middleman and processor, with China exercising background control to assure that the terms of regional trade would not be divisive nor at the expense of rural masses and that more backward areas were protected against exploitation.

AFRICA. The Economic Commission for Africa faces formidable problems in its efforts to expand African trade on an intracontinental scale. To begin with, the map of Africa reveals a bewildering pattern of relatively small states. One is unable to account for this apparent balkanization of the African landscape by the newly emergent states except in terms of historical accident and a strange form of chauvinism. Apparently these new nations failed to comprehend in establishing their jealously guarded frontiers that they were in effect accomplishing a scheme of political and economic gerrymandering that would leave them permanently weak and in jeopardy of intermittent embroilment with their neighbors. At any rate the political subdivision of Africa among the new nations compounds the difficulties of economic development, particularly of establishing interregional trade. This atomization of nationalities is further complicated by tribal conflicts and a rapid succession of coups d'etat and radical shifts in government policy.

Some of these new countries may never become fully viable in economic terms. Nevertheless, they exist and will continue some form of existence in the future. The price of this separate existence is likely to be increasing poverty and increasing belligerence by their national leaders. These leaders will be just as demanding and vocal as the elites of more viable national entities, and the insolubility of their problems will not reduce the burdens of the ECA.

Then there is the major regional separation of the continent into a white south and a black north. As things stand now, differences between these two major regions are completely insoluble short of major armed conflict. Regional divisions also separate the northern tier of African states fronting on the Mediterranean from Morocco to Egypt from the almost equally distant regions of East, West, and Central Africa—each with its own distinct and different economic and trade orientation.

These differences are exacerbated by geographical barriers and lack of ameliorating physical infrastructure, particularly communications and markets. Some of these may be overcome in time—for example, construction of rail connections between Zambia and Tanzania and the highway link between Addis Ababa and the coast in Ethiopia. Others are less certain and in any event will take at least another generation before they can begin to make significant changes in current trade patterns. Meanwhile the ECA can do little to expedite infrastructural change.

It has to be remembered too that the makeup of the ECA and its secretariat is African. Thus the commission members reflect in their own attitudes the biases and aspirations of their countries of origin. The fact that these are all bright people anxious to do something for Africa increases the burden of frustration that commission members and staff must carry.

All these limitations, constraints, and frustrations need to be borne in mind in reviewing the commission's record over the dozen years of its existence. The task has not been easy. However, the commission has materially contributed to establishment of the African Development Bank and has helped to create the African Institute for Economic Development and Planning and to train technicians at the regional and subregional levels. It has been involved in numerous studies and negotiations on the development of hydroelectric energy and on creating a West African Rice Development Association. In its deliberations the commission has been concerned with African agricultural development and the environmental aspects of that development.[21] Still these meritorious undertakings have not contributed much to implementation of regional trade. Perhaps it was a sense of lack of accomplishment in this last respect that caused members of the commission recently to express the wistful view that the commission's work should be more operational. These members felt that the commission should directly assist African states to arrive at common positions leading to restructuring their foreign trade relations and formulating demands to carry out these objectives.[22]

The African Development Bank in its short life has achieved a record of vigorous efforts toward integrated regional trade. It has carried out a number of specific studies of subregional economic potentials and has sought ways and means for more effective coordination with ECA.[23]

In view of the difficulties and actual barriers to the establishment of major intercontinental trade in Africa, it will probably be strategic to stress trade integration at subregional levels. This orientation would be more feasible since several subregional political and economic organizations already exist—the West African Regional Group; the Central African Customs and Economic Union; and the Entente Council comprising Dahomey, Ivory Coast, Nigeria, Togo, and Upper Volta. At one time the East African Community composed of Kenya, Uganda, and Tanzania seemed a very hopeful omen of international economic cooperation, but recent hostilities between Uganda and Tanzania have probably diminished or retarded further accomplishment in this region.

Several African countries have economic ties with European countries. These ties originated in the colonial period (such as the relation between Belgian interests and the Congo and those between France and its former colonies in the Communaute Francais) and are well established and make it difficult for African countries to contemplate any changes in the direction of stronger regional trade. It is possible that these black countries, in their distrust for and dislike of white nations, would be willing to make some economic sacrifices in seeking to establish a larger intra-African regional economic integration, but this is a doubtful prospect.[24]

Evaluation of Efforts toward Regional Integration

Concern with regional economic integration efforts in Asia, Africa, and Latin America arises in the context of the massive poverty and misery of the majority of the population of these three great land masses. This population is predominantly rural and depends on agricultural production as the principal source of income and employment. We believe that poverty and hunger of the population arises not only from current overpopulation and lack of capacity to produce food and fiber but primarily from lack of employment and income.

The industrial-commercial sector in many LDCs does not expand fast enough to absorb the redundant rural labor force or to raise the level of per capita earnings and is limited by narrow foreign trade based on agricultural exports. However, LDC trade with the developed regions of Europe, North America, and Japan does not, even under more liberal terms, afford a prospect of trade volume proportional to foreign trade needs. New regional, interregional, and intercontinental markets in Africa, Asia, and Latin America need to be created. Development of this trade could stimulate the stagnant LDC economies. The inherent capacity of agriculture could be exploited to a much greater extent with a consequent increase in the total volume of food and fiber and in employment.

This hypothesis apparently accounts to a considerable extent for the efforts at regional integration of the UN regional economic commissions, the Organization for Economic Cooperation and Development, the three regional banks, the World Bank, regional and subregional trade association plans and programs, the Organization of African Unity, the Organization of American States, and the Alliance for Progress.

The regional economic integration concept has influenced U.S. foreign policy for Latin America in supporting plans for a Latin American free-trade area. Efforts in Southeast Asia have a similar origin, as does the Colombo Plan. Similar undertakings have been initiated in Africa both by the ECA and the Asian Development Bank. A very sizable corps of statesmen, politicians, diplomats, national leaders, planners, and professional and technical people have been deployed around the world in an interlocking organizational network to implement the regional economic integration objective. Many, many meetings and conferences have been held, involving at one time or another all the heads of state and the principal political and administrative leaders of both the developed and less developed countries, including the Soviet Union and its satellites. Whole libraries of reports, plans, statistics, drafts of declarations, and minutes of meetings bearing on regional economic integration have been accumulated. Thousands, perhaps millions, of miles of official air travel have been logged for attendance at meetings and conferences, and countless man-years of hard work have been involved in the service of this concept.

Unfortunately these efforts toward LDC regional and interregional economic integration have occurred in conjunction with preoccupation of traditional bilateral trade relations between developed and underdeveloped countries. Thus convocations of UNCTAD and the several sessions on GATT have become sounding boards for complaints of the LDCs over their export trade disabilities vis-à-vis developed country import restrictions. The most recent of these (April 1972) was the UNCTAD Conference at Santiago, Chile, at which several Latin American countries criticized U.S. economic policies. Behind these expressions are business interests whch constitute an important component of the social, political, and economic configuration of each individual country. These interests would probably be unwilling to modify existing trade relations with the United States, Japan, or the European Common Market for the sake of the concept of regional economic integration. Thus an immediate obstacle to a rationalization of regional trade or of the evolution of a common market is the existence of substantial vested interest in the status quo of international trade. The problem is an old one—the conflict between sacrifice of a short-run vested advantage for longer-run social gains. This is the dilemma confronting those concerned with furthering regional economic integration.

The real issue is alleviation of LDC agricultural stagnation, rural poverty, and unemployment. The vested interests that control existing LDC export trade are not primarily rural or agricultural, nor do they speak on behalf of the millions in the LDC rural hinterlands. The social objectives of regional economic integration probably would not influence their behavior. Thus if the issue of relief of poverty, unemployment, and social disadvantage underlies the concept of regional economic integration, there must be some specific arrangement to insure that implementation of the integration concept will have the desired effect—that anticipated benefits would in fact relieve the hunger and malnutrition of the rural masses.

The LDC socioeconomic systems manifest rapidly increasing population and mounting rural unemployment; indeed these characteristics are to some extent produced by the LDC systems. In that sense these systems possess a regressive, not a progressive, dynamic. Moreover, the gap between LDC rich and poor is large, and the rich in consequence have great economic and political power. In this setting the working of Myrdal's "principle of interlocking circular inter-dependence within a process of cumulative causality"[25] reinforces the negative processes of LDC systems.

Thus regional economic integration cannot stand alone as a solution to LDC ills; it must be part of a total policy. Without complementary support regional economic integration would increase disparities of income; existing weakness would create further weakness among nations, groups, and individuals. Poverty and unemployment for the many could increase simultaneously with increasing power and wealth of the few. What is more, the machinery for international economic assistance and cooperation would hardly be in a position to redress these imbalances once set in motion. Part of their appeal, and at the same time part of their weakness, is their ministerial and advisory role. All their action-oriented institutions are appendages of a central body operating through parliamentary procedures among a membership of theoretically equal sovereign states.

Thus regional economic integration as a process must incorporate countervailing safeguards to offset the negative dynamics of existing LDC rural systems. As a beginning, land reform has a vital role in regional economic integration; without it existing land tenure arrangements will work to force small farmers and tenants off the land. The authority of the central government must be brought strongly into play to erect a system of subsidies and prices that protects agricultural producers against adverse effects of regional imports. Government will have to take positive steps to insure that credit is available on reasonable terms to all producers regardless of size of enterprise. The marketing of agricultural products and the sale of agricultural supplies cannot be turned over to private enterprise; rather farmer cooperatives should be promoted, supported, and strengthened. This approach will require governmental mobilization of resources.

Unfortunately discussions, debates, and proceedings of the UN regional commissions create the impression that reliance has been placed on gradual accrual of benefits to the rural sector through some sort of automatic "spreading" effect. Thus regional economic integration tends to be conceived as a roundabout process that eventually conveys benefits to the rural sector. Such working of an unseen hand is a very unlikely outcome; more likely is a strengthening of negative forces presently afflicting the rural sector.

VIII

An Alternate Proposal for Regional Integration

CERTAIN NATURAL RESOURCE areas of the world should be developed only in terms of what Elisabeth Mann Borgese calls "social property." These vast resource regions are so located that their optimum development transcends traditional concepts of national or private ownership. The major potential benefit from these developments can be realized only through international efforts. For one thing, capital costs exceed what concerned nations can command individually or collectively. For another, technological requirements of development call for organization and management on a scale exceeding national resources of finance and professional training. Moreover, these regions possess an inherent environmental integrity requiring that they be developed as total regions.

Therefore, the products these resources are capable of generating command an approach in legal, fiscal, and organizational terms accommodated to the environmental imperatives. More bluntly, these regional resources must be developed as integrated units or lose their most significant and unique potentials. Development schemes based on chopping off bits and pieces of the integrated whole will be self-defeating because of costs, because of technical obstacles, or because of self-evident harm to other claimants. Consequently the only sensible view is that these resources constitute a common heritage for the entire region and to some extent for the world.

Mrs. Borgese says that answers to the legal and administrative problems posed by resource development on this scale will not be found in present forms of international cooperation.

> What the world community has been doing, in fact, was to try to build an old constitutional structure, inherited from the international organizations of the first half of the twentieth century, on the new basis of the Common Heritage of Man. . . . When the structure does not fit its base there is trouble.[1]

Her view is pertinent to our earlier discussion of the limited value of traditional parliamentary forms in pursuing solutions to regional economic integration through establishment of common markets and free trade associations. These forms more often than not have seemed to inhibit definition of purpose and to prevent reasonable action. Whatever may be their eventual value for rationalizing trade and tariffs, they are not suitable as models for structuring administration of international development efforts of large international resource regions. Thus one is forced to the conclusion that because no organizational model for such an undertaking exists it will be necessary to invent one or to adapt some antecedent organizational form to fit the case. The latter is a more likely course.

Long ago Stringfellow Barr suggested that the Tennessee Valley Authority as an organizational form provided a model for what he called a *World Development Authority*. As he conceived it, this was to be a public corporation. Barr had a wholesome disrespect for the past behavior of some American private corporations, but he also credited them as the chief modern device for getting big jobs done. His somewhat dated language is still pertinent to the challenge presented by the potentials of major geographic resources:

> Congress recognized this when it set up TVA as a *public* corporation, responsible to Congress. This pamphlet suggests that the U.N. set up a public corporation to do a job for the people of the world and that they give it so much money that men and women in every country will know that they mean business and can deliver. On the day that money was set aside, and long before the WORLD DEVELOPMENT AUTHORITY could plan its wise investment, hope would sweep the world where now fear holds it paralyzed. That day would be one of the great historic dates of the present century.[2]

A practical modification of Barr's concept might be conceived as a series of regional development authorities directed or licensed by a parent World Development Authority. The principal members of regional authorities would be those nations most immediately affected, e.g., riparian nations in the case of an international river. These authorities could incorporate organizational and procedural safeguards to national pride and against outside domination. Special emphasis would be placed on attaining specific practical objectives; programming and scheduling would be designed to produce some early, even if small-scale, demonstrations of visible implementation. On the other hand, the rationale of integrated development of an international region by international cooperation because of the environmental imperatives of a natural system would be a central concept underlying all planning criteria of the authority, whose powers would include provision for large financial support from multilateral and bilateral sources through public bond issues backed by international guarantees.

One essential characteristic of such an undertaking is that development plans in accord with the character of the resource require a cooperative regime. Therefore, use of the regional development authority instrumentality should be restricted to those natural regions where recoupment of principal benefits by any participant requires total cooperation and involvement of all participants.

A situation somewhat parallel to this is found in the development of federal irrigation projects in the western United States. Here irrigation water is not the commodity provided but rather its use. To some extent the physical unit, the acre-foot of water, somewhat answers to Mrs. Borgese's concept of "social property." The fee paid for the right to use a specified unit of service does not convey title to the water itself; that ownership is vested in the sovereign.

This principle is inherent in the arrangements for construction by the federal government of the transmountain diversion system known as the Colorado–Big Thompson project in Colorado. This system takes water out of the Colorado River on the western slope of the Rockies and conveys it through the Continental Divide for service to irrigated agriculture in northern and eastern Colorado. Before the system commenced to function it was necessary for all interests benefiting from this irrigation to create a regionwide corporate entity to distribute the water among thousands of users. To this end a great deal of time and energy went into the establishment of the Northern Colorado Water Conservancy District embracing a number of Colorado counties and municipalities. Thus the Northern Colorado Water Conservancy District undertakes actual distribution of water service and collects irrigation service charges from individual users and finally reimburses the federal government for its bulk water service deliveries.

Without the cooperation and integration of many often conflicting interests in the irrigation service area, the project, which has contributed many millions of dollars to the economy of the South Platte Valley, would not have been possible. Further, the undertaking was possible because socialization of the physical ownership of water was an accepted legal principle. In another sense creation of this district depended on voluntary abdication of political powers of a number of independent political entities and the concurrent imposition on them of new responsibilities in behalf of the district.

These considerations possibly apply to several regions in Asia, Africa, and Latin America where opportunities exist for integrated international development efforts. These natural resource regions physically encompass several nations on not very good terms with each other; in some instances there are even marked ideological disagreements not only among the nations immediately concerned but also possibly with respect to potential donors of financial and technical support. However, the tremendous scale of the challenge presented by development potentials of those regions might outweigh mutual animosity and could enlist a degree of world support. From the experience of working together toward a common goal, these many conflicting interests might arrive at a modus vivendi with far-reaching implications for common benefit.

Lower Mekong Basin

Planning for development of the Lower Mekong Basin has involved sustained international cooperation for more than fifteen years. The large scale of this effort is the result of the dimensions and location of the region and the tremendous Mekong River itself. From the outset environmental factors have commanded human response, because the basin itself presents an interplay of natural forces and planning necessarily conforms to this interplay.

The raw power of the resource is compelling, for the Mekong is a mighty river—third longest in Asia and eighth in the world. At its mouth on the South China Sea in Vietnam its minimum discharge is twice that of our own magnificent Columbia. The lower river extends 1,500 miles from the junction of the Chinese, Burmese, and Laotian borders to its mouth; it traverses in this distance Thailand, Laos, Cambodia, and Vietnam with a drainage area of 236,000 square miles. That is 60 percent of the land area of the riparian countries with 25 million inhabitants—just under 50 percent of their combined populations. Agriculture dominates the economy of the basin and provides the largest proportion of employment.[3]

Initial interest in development of the Lower Mekong originated with the UN Economic Commission for Asia and the Far East. A 1952 ECAFE study noted the source and irrigation potentials of the lower basin. This was followed by U.S. Bureau of Reclamation studies pursuant to an agreement with the riparian countries and a 1957 ECAFE study on hydroelectric, irrigation, and flood control potentials of the basin.

> The 1957 ECAFE report was an important milestone because it provided a conceptual framework for the planning that has since taken place. It emphasizes that if optimum use was to be made of the Basin's water and related resources, a broad river basin approach would be required and, as a corollary, close cooperation in planning and development between the nations sharing the Basin. Several of the major projects mentioned in the report would be located at points where the Mekong forms a boundary between two countries sharing the Basin. Moreover, some of the projects, even though located in one country, could benefit several others by providing hydroelectric power or irrigation water, or by regulating flows which might permit increased power production downstream, reduce flood losses and improve navigation. The report noted that international cooperation will be required not only in planning and development but in basic data collection as well. In calling for uniform standards in the collection of hydrologic and other data and in the leveling and mapping, the report emphasized that "the accuracy of such measurements should be beyond doubt, the figures should be acceptable to all countries at all times."[4]

A succeeding step and an important outcome of this report was the establishment in 1957, by formal adoption of ECAFE and the four riparian country representatives, of the Statute of the Committee for Coordination of Investigations of the Lower Mekong—a permanent body known generally as the Mekong Committee. This committee with its extensive secretariat has guided the entire work of development planning for the lower basin to the present time. Among its early activities the Mekong Committee requested two missions to prepare fundamental reports. These were undertaken and provided the basis of much subsequent activity. The Wheeler Mission report in 1958 made specific recommendations covering hydrologic, meteorologic, photographic, topographic, and hydrographic requirements as well as site identification and studies relating to fisheries, agriculture, forestry, mineral resources, navigation, transportation, power markets, flood damage, soil surveys, geology, and preliminary planning of promising projects. France, the United States, Canada, and Japan undertook the financial support for the work these recommendations encompassed.

In 1961 the Ford Foundation sponsored a mission by Gilbert F. White to assess the requirements for investigations of socioeconomic aspects of this Lower Mekong development. The White Mission's recommendations included appointment of several scientists to the committee staff, training programs, market studies, national accounts, examination of economic feasibility methods, administrative organization, a basic land inventory, training of extension personnel, establishment of a demonstration project, and several other similar activities. Not all of these studies could be undertaken, but apparently support has been found for a substantial part of the $15 million estimated cost of implementing the White report.

Thus from small beginnings the Mekong Committee has achieved a remarkable record of international cooperation in a region noted for mistrust. Work has gone forward in the face of guerrilla activity and open warfare. Also worth noting are the considerable amount of legal work done for the committee by the UN Office of Legal Affairs and the continued close association and support of the committee by the UN and its affiliates.[5]

The funding of the Mekong Committee's activities also reflects a substantial amount of what might be called "international conscience." As of December 31, 1970, total Mekong project resources were $202.7 million: grants totaled $152.2 million and loans $50.5 million. Funds totaling $99.7 million had been contributed by 26 nonriparian nations, $89.1 million came from the four riparian nations, 12 UN agency contributions totaled $13.6 million.[6] These contributions represented not only monetary flows but the money equivalent of machinery, tools, supplies, and personal services.

While there have been clashes and conflicts—particularly among the riparian nations but also to some degree among technicians of other nationalities—this extensive mixture of nationalities, agencies, and organizations has managed to run at least as smoothly as some orthodox and conventional arrangements. As it stands, the Mekong project is "about as composite a job of multinational mutuality as the contemporary world has yet seen," and is an illustration of functional international cooperation.[7]

> For one of the first and smallest of the projects, Nam Pong in northeast Thailand, Japan provided the original reconnaissance report, France the pedological investigations, the United States the power study, the United Nations the feasibility survey,

West Germany the loan ($17 million), the Thais the local cash (the equivalent of $13 million) and the continuing push, while a Danish and a Japanese firm did the actual construction. For Tonle Sap in Cambodia, India has contributed the feasibility survey and the preliminary engineering designs, France has completed a study on fisheries and sedimentation, the Philippines has done the topographical investigation, and New Zealand is supplying some equipment. For Prek Thnot, also in Cambodia, a consortium of nine nations (Australia, Canada, India, Israel, Japan, the Netherlands, Pakistan, the Philippines, and the United Kingdom) has raised almost the full required amount of foreign exchange ($29.3 out of $33 million)—but each member, incidentally, is demanding rather more say in management than the Cambodians are willing to concede.

The most noteworthy achievement to date under the Mekong Project has been the creation of a functioning if still far from ideal organization. In procedural as in substantive matters, the sponsors of the Mekong Project have had to feel their way without much in the way of precedent to guide them. Indeed, the present arrangements seem almost as much the result of chance as of evolution in accordance with anyone's vision of present requirements, let alone those of the future. But what started out twenty years ago as a minor, minute bureau of E.C.A.F.E., tentatively proposing busywork for itself, has now developed into a semi-autonomous, four-nation committee, with a permanent Secretariat staffed by some thirty international experts, a fund of $155 million, and a rapidly growing program spread through the four riparian countries.[8]

So far accomplishment on the Mekong project has been largely limited to planning and investigation; construction has been limited to a few small tributary dams built by the riparian countries. Thus the Mekong undertaking has yet to face the stern tests of construction and operation of the enormously costly main-stem works. Perhaps the first great test will come when work starts on the giant multipurpose Pa Mong project above Vietiane in Laos, which may commence in the mid-70s at an estimated cost of $600 million. Pa Mong is designed to irrigate 2 million hectares, to improve navigation for 200 miles upstream, to generate 20 billion kilowatts of firm power annually, and to provide important downstream navigational and flood control benefits over a 100-mile reach. Willard Hanna cites a $600 million cost estimate which applied only to the major structures.[9] The irrigation system will cost another $1 billion; associated administration, education, transportation, and industrialization necessary to capture the full benefit of Pa Mong will increase these base costs five times. The estimated $6–7 billion structural costs of the Mekong project will ultimately total $30–35 billion at 1968 prices.

No one knows whether a market can be developed for the tremendous hydroelectric energy potential of the Mekong project or even of Pa Mong itself. However, as in the case of the Columbia Basin project in the state of Washington and of the TVA, the existence of an available large amount of cheap electrical energy acts as a stimulus to create new demands. Agricultural potentials are not so nebulous. In the project region more than half of the arable land is not cropped; only about 3 percent of the cropped area is irrigated, and this mostly on a single-crop basis. Under irrigation rice yields could double and multiple-cropping would be possible. It is believed that present per capita annual incomes of $50 could triple.[10]

The Mekong Committee will somehow have to fund construction costs of at least $7 billion (1968 estimate) in the next ten years and perhaps five times that much within the next quarter-century. Moreover, planning for the basin requires an integrated approach; real worth of Pa Mong depends on construction of other major works both upstream and downstream. The heights and lengths of dams and their storage capacities are all related throughout the system to the Pa Mong key; but if Pa Mong is built and the other relevant structures are not, the whole scheme fails. This could easily happen as a result of jealousy among the riparian countries because, for example, a major structure was not built in their territory despite their much greater benefits. It is "a clear-cut case of cooperating or not developing at all."[11]

There is a question too about the capacity of the Mekong Committee to absorb the enormous additional administrative, organizational, and technical strains as the development phases succeed one another. Such considerations have led to review of the committee's role and discussion of possible alternates, such as the creation of a regional authority with broader decision-making powers. In order to achieve this the riparian countries would need to make some further compromise with their cherished sovereign autonomy.

The Mekong Committee's legal advisor has studied the issue of sovereignty that is bound to arise among the riparian nations as the work of development proceeds. This study concluded that the conventional concepts of absolute territorial sovereignty cannot be applied. What emerges is the need to make water sovereign. Thus it will be necessary to operate the project and the river by some kind of international mainstream authority with delegated responsibility for construction, operation, and maintenance of main-stem works. These responsibilities would probably have to extend to equitable distribution of power and water. Moreover, such a corporate entity would probably need quasi-sovereign authority over areas immediately surrounding major installations. Thus the kind of authority contemplated is not multinational but supranational. There is little if any precedent for this kind of corporate entity, so it will be necessary to invent it.[12]

There are other uncertainties. One of these is the role that China, now a member of the UN, may propose to play in ECAFE of which it also becomes a member. The Soviet Union has indicated some sympathy with the Mekong project but has not yet actively participated in it. Burma is still an unknown quantity although it has a concern as a riparian country, and the cloud of war still hangs over Vietnam.

In spite of misgivings, those who are most familiar with the Mekong project operations and have been touched with the "Mekong spirit" feel that:

> the mere existence of a continuing body which includes men who can approach problems in a spirit of cooperation, with primary emphasis on technical rather than political ends, is a giant step forward, and one much more likely to lead to satisfactory solutions than if problems are left to haphazard decision at the diplomatic level as they arise.[13]

AMAZON BASIN

It may be just as well that the working of an effective international planning and development organization should take place on the Mekong. If this effort could succeed there, it might be adapted to more complex conditions in Latin America, primarily in the Amazon Basin. This vast continental waterway serves as both a physical and political obstacle to unification of South America and possibly contributes to the political and economic disarray of that region.

Not enough is yet known about the physical makeup and economic potentials of the Amazon Basin to enable more than a superficial assessment of the realities of basinwide development. It is evident, however, that the location and physical characteristics of the Amazon River and adjacent territory separate the continent north, south, east, and west. This fact has led some observers to speculate on long-range possibilities following opening up the Amazon through a major international development scheme. Perhaps a preliminary requirement would be a detailed inventory of the resource potentials for agriculture, electrical energy, transportation, flood control, commerce, and industry.

Physically the Amazon and its tributaries cover an area of wilderness and semiwilderness comparable in extent to the area in the United States between the Rockies and the Allegheny. The Amazon region includes the greater portion of Brazil; a part of Venezuela; a large portion of Colombia; and important portions of Ecuador, Peru, and Bolivia.[14]

Politically, development of the Amazon might encounter even more difficulties than those among the Mekong riparian nations. The principal political considerations would be the location in Brazil of key parts of the basin and the acute national sovereignty sensibilities of Brazil and to some extent of the other basin countries as well. No one can question Brazil's perfectly proper sensitivity toward suggestions for international development of the Amazon which would affect over half its sovereign territory. At the same time Brazil probably could not mobilize resources sufficient for full-scale investigation and planning efforts of the Amazon; such an effort would have to be international.

The physical dimensions of an Amazon investigation would far exceed those involved on the Mekong. The Amazon Basin occupies 2 million square miles of largely unexplored and uninhabited land; its population is about 5 million inhabitants, most of it in a few riverbank towns and communities such as Belem (600,000) and Manaus (250,000).[15] The river extends for 3,000 miles and has 1,000 tributaries, some of them comparable to major North American rivers including the Mississippi. At its mouth the Amazon approximates 180 miles in width, and its discharge is twelve times as great as the Mississippi.

Scant information credits the basin with vast timber resources, large areas adaptable to a variety of agricultural commodities, and petroleum now being extracted in portions of Ecuador and Colombia, though not on an impressive scale. Other mineral potentials are tin, manganese, bauxite, copper, gold, and diamonds, although information is uncertain and even speculative. On the other hand, these interior lands are infested with a number of tropical diseases; malaria is particularly prevalent. In some areas rain is incessant and the climate is hot, humid, and enervating.

Brazil's current development plans for the Amazon tend to be projects based on exploitation of natural resources, agriculture, food processing, timber, and forest products. These efforts are promoted by a Brazilian government development corporation which has approved more than 200 projects of moderate size with an investment of over $200 million. So far, actual experience with agriculture is only moderately encouraging, largely due to climatic conditions but possibly also because of the absence of substantial factual information to permit selection of top-quality locations.

One gains the impression that the current development approach is ad hoc and piecemeal and that the concept of the region as an integrated environmental unit has not yet emerged in Brazilian policy formulation. International contributions to development have taken the form of enlargement of American investments—e.g., timber research by Georgia-Pacific Corporation of Portland, Oregon, and mineral exploration by Bethlehem Steel Corporation of Pennsylvania. Suggestions for comprehensive resource development planning have aroused the strident nationalism of Brazilian politicians.

In 1965 and 1966 a Walter Lippmann article and a speech by Senator Robert F. Kennedy pointed out the Amazon Basin resource potentials. These expressions of interest resulted in a Johnson administration Amazon Study Commission and a campaign statement by Richard Nixon favorable to opening up the Latin American interior by means of a highway down the center of the continent.[16]

In a similar vein a vast almost visionary proposal has been made to create a series of dams in Colombia which would open up a waterway from the Pacific to the Caribbean, providing electrical energy and better access to interior lands. This scheme, estimated to cost (1969) $3 billion, in effect proposes creation of a series of six great lakes linking the Orinoco and an Amazon tributary, the Rio Negro. Other proposals are to create a north-south waterway, to connect the Guapore and Paraguay river systems for another waterway across Bolivia, and finally to erect a major dam on the Amazon.[17]

Clearly needed at this time are not proposals for development which are little more than sketches but rather some form of international organization that could undertake preliminary investigations in an orderly sequence. Far too little is known about the real potential of the Amazon to support even the most preliminary outlines of schemes. By the same token, far too little is known to justify the present piecemeal Brazilian ventures. These may even run counter to the imperatives of the environmental system. For example, logging in the riparian jungles would probably have to be a clear-cutting operation opening up the tropical soil to direct rays of the sun. Enough is now known about tropical soil characteristics to suggest that such soils must be very carefully handled lest they completely lose any agricultural value. Consequently their ruthless exposure as a result of clear-cutting could become a sacrifice of their productive potentials. At the same time encouragement of riparian industrial settlement may create vested interests opposed to any riverine structures involving inundation.

As an alternative to this approach, the Mekong experience might be used as a model. The ECLA might undertake to persuade the Amazon riparian countries to establish a counterpart to the Mekong Committee. Undoubtedly this would require a great deal of delicate negotiation and much legal innovation by UN legal technicians. However, such an organizational framework could then be used to sponsor reconnaissance engineering and physical resource surveys similar to the work on the Mekong of UN's Wheeler Mission in 1957 and socio-economic investigations along the lines of Ford Foundation's White Mission in 1961. These two missions proposed investigation activities for the Mekong to cost about $26 million; an Amazon investigation would probably begin with $100 million and quite possibly a good deal more (the 3,000-mile Amazon main stem is twice as long as the Lower Mekong). The Amazon Basin contains 2 million square miles, over eight times the size of the Lower Mekong Basin. The greater portion of possible financing would have to be provided from nonriparian country sources as in the case of the Mekong.

Development of the Amazon no matter how undertaken represents exploitation of one of the world's last great resource frontiers. Properly handled, Amazonian development might contribute much toward providing food and fiber for the world. This increment would not necessarily be entirely from Amazonian production but in part from the overall stimulus to Latin American agriculture resulting from a more closely knit continental economy.

Congo Basin

In terms of volume the River Congo is second only to the Amazon; its basin's extent—from the borders of Zambia, Ruanda, Tanzania, and Burundi on the east and south to the Atlantic on the west—is 1,425,000 square miles compared to the Amazon's 2 million square miles.[18] The longest portion of this basin is located in the sparsely populated Democratic Republic of the Congo (Zaire) and a lesser portion in the Republic of the Congo. As in the case of the Amazon the natural resources endowment is enormous. The hydroelectric potential equals that of the United States and is greater than that of the entire Soviet Union.

Soils of the Congo Basin, classified as latosols, constitute the largest contiguous soil body in Central Africa.[19] According to Charles Kellogg, these only moderately productive soils have benefited from a physiographic and climatic interaction. Constant electrical storms continually fix and contribute atmospheric nitrogen, while dust from deserts on the north and south and volcanoes on the east have maintained high levels of calcium carbonate in the forest cover. Kellogg visualizes the Congo Basin as "eventually the garden spot of the world."[20]

Unlike those of the Amazon, the numerous tribes of the Congo Basin have practiced a semiprimitive slash-and-burn agriculture rather well adapted to environmental conditions throughout most of the region. However, the tremendous agricultural potentials of this underdeveloped area have not generally been appreciated. The other productive factor in this region, also not fully recognized, is the extraordinary availability of solar energy.

> A much larger part of sunshine received is available for photosynthesis in the tropics than in temperate zones because temperatures of the tropics are above the minimum for plant growth.[21]

The limiting factors to agricultural development of the Congo Basin are not land and water but economic, social, political, and institutional problems—particularly rampant tribalism and political instability. Considerable background agronomic knowledge already exists. Kellogg alludes to considerable soil management research in the Congo between 1935 and 1958:

> The very important research and experiences of the Institut National pour l'Etude Agronomique du Congo has recently been summarized and illustrated in considerable detail by Jurion and Henry (1967). Settlers on well-selected newly developed arable soils in the Tropics need not go through all the steps between primitive and fully developed modern systems. The beginning level of soil management can be at whatever level the settlers have *both* the skills to handle and the industrial and agricultural services to support.[22]

Perhaps there is no great urgency in developing the Congo Basin. However, the very great potential importance of the resource both to the riparian nations and to the world food supply does argue for prompt initiation of work to determine the order and scope of supporting measures and institutions. Possibly this approach will have to be geared to the emergence of politically stable regimes in these new postcolonial countries.

It is important for these countries and for Africa as a whole that development planning and implementation be programmed to accord with the environmental system. The first step might be to determine through research the implications of that environment for agricultural and soil management systems. Some attention is also required to foresee what institutional and infrastructural supports are required.

While Zaire occupies a dominant position as principal occupant of the region, it probably does not command sufficient resources to undertake significant development efforts. Also the Congo Basin has great significance for all nations of the entire central African region extending from the Indian Ocean to the Atlantic. Any real African unity will depend to a considerable degree on some nodal ingathering of national interests surrounding and occupying the basin. Such considerations might persuade regional interests to engage the ECA and the Organization of African Unity in discussions leading to a Congo Basin Committee along the lines of the Mekong Committee. Efforts might also be made by such a group to secure international financing for a series of physical, economic, and environmental studies of the basin which could be scheduled as parts of a comprehensive undertaking over a period of several years.

IX

Role of Energy in LDCs

Wealthy industrial nations view with trepidation the prospects of a shortage of hydrocarbon energy, but poor less developed countries of the world already receive an energy ration well below levels consistent with even moderate rates of progress. Since most of these nations are predominantly rural, their development depends on their ability to transform their traditional, static, sometimes involuted agriculture into more dynamic, innovative systems. At the same time they must somehow develop a much more substantial industrial sector. Adequate supplies of energy are critical to development in either sector.

Farm commodities presently provide the economic backbone of a number of LDCs, so energy requirements of rural sectors represent a priority development factor. One reason LDC farmers do not receive a better energy ration is that they do not have the money to buy it. Without access to more energy supplies, development rates will barely keep up with rates of population growth.

Current discussions of the "energy crisis" are based largely on comparison of the energy needs of rich countries and the present and prospective supplies of hydrocarbon fuel from the producing countries. It would be interesting to compute this balance sheet on the assumption that the LDCs were viable customers in the energy market. What is worrisome about the estimates now being prepared is the assumption that energy consumption levels of the intensely rural LDCs will not substantially increase; that assumption implies a future world in which the gap between wealth and poverty steadily widens.

Energy Needs for Rural Development

One striking characteristic of LDCs is their relative energy poverty: energy consumption equivalents per capita occur in a descending scale as does income per capita, with LDCs consuming less than 5 percent per capita of the average amount of energy consumed by developed regions.[1] This comparison, with the United States and Europe at the top of both income and energy consumption scales, would undoubtedly reflect an even greater disparity if it were between rural sectors of respective national groups, since urban-industrial consumption accounts for most of the LDC energy consumption.

Energy poverty can be overcome by investment in energy production; and this potential has attracted the attention of planners concerned with raising LDC welfare levels. But the problem is not simply that of providing large blocks of energy to the dominantly rural LDCs. Megawatt transmission systems hooked up to conventional or nuclear generation are not likely to solve LDC energy problems. Undoubtedly megawatt systems are needed to provide industrial energy and to satisfy urban needs, but these forms of energy consumption are a small fraction of the theoretical requirements of the rural sector.

Rural energy requirements are more difficult to satisfy and the distribution of rural energy is more costly than that for urban-industrial sectors. This perhaps explains the discrepancy in some LDC energy plan allocations, where the preponderance of energy is earmarked for urban-industrial use and smaller fractions go to the rural sector. Also, more than conventional engineering and conventional economics are involved in designing appropriate rural energy systems. Such systems must conform to rural configurations.

Thus at the outset a consideration of the energy needs of agricultural and rural development poses policy dilemmas. Experience has already demonstrated that the unplanned introduction of modern technological processes to rural areas (as in the case of high-yielding varieties of grain) can aggravate maldistribution of incomes, displace smaller cultivators, increase unemployment and rural poverty, and intensify agrarian disorganization. An inevitable result of this process, now appearing on a worldwide scale, is to swell the volume of migration from rural areas and increase urban problems. On the other hand, modern agricultural technology does promise a greatly increased food supply, mitigating for a time at least the threat of a world food shortage.

Policies are needed to cushion the shock of agrarian innovation so that disadvantaged rural people are not forced into urban slums. With few exceptions customary government policies should be changed, but unfortunately such policies often remain unformulated. Very few proposals have been made for halting the negative social thrust of agricultural innovation or for incorporating social costs into the scaling of enterprise. The form of energy distribution for rural development will probably tend to correspond to that of modern large-scale agricultural technology, at least in free enterprise LDC economies.

The general impression (unfortunately not based on hard information) is that China has elected not to follow the large-scale enterprise model of Western technical agriculture.[2] In that case the energy requirements of Chinese rural development might correspond to its unique rural communal system. If this system should spread to other developing regions, a competitive model of small-scale technology with unique energy requirements might evolve.

At the other extreme would be the giant farm enterprises of the United States and of the Soviet Union. Here the agricultural power tools would be large and agricultural mechanization would be almost universal. Perhaps a principal use of energy would be to drive large, deep well pumps delivering hundreds of cubic feet per second of water to irrigate thousands of acres cultivated with big motorized equipment. Large-scale refrigeration plants, dehydrating equipment, and blowers would require additional energy. Such enterprises would provide their own step-down transformer equipment and possibly their own circuitry.

In such large-scale systems of industrialized agriculture the resident labor force, consisting primarily of technical personnel, would be centrally housed. Thus the rural landscape would contain widely dispersed population centers; smaller communities would disappear. The power delivery system would be designed to meet moderately large service needs. Patterns of energy utilization would correspond to large-scale centralized energy generation and high-tension transmission—i.e., electrified industrial agriculture.

Under these circumstances no great ingenuity is required to design and construct the energy delivery system or energy-using devices. Power generation would be conventional—a question of selection among hydrogeneration, thermal generation, a hydrothermal complex, or thermonuclear generation. Problems of adapting such systems to climate or geographic variations are all soluble.

A basic assumption of imposing this type of system on a less developed society is that the configuration of that society can be changed to fit the technological needs of conventional energy generation and distribution systems with respect to scale, population, distribution, and method of energy use. To put it succinctly, *existing rural society can be made to serve the needs of conventional energy systems by radical social transformation and displacement.*

One consideration is the relation of the scale of the energy system to costs. Generally speaking, low-cost energy means large-unit generation and high-tension transmission. It is this aspect that frustrates thinking about the linkup of cheap energy with rural development conceived as an improvement in the quality of life of rural people. The difficulty arises at the point of energy application; if we do not wish to greatly shock or destroy the existing socioeconomic configuration, the scale of energy application must be small. The problem is not to electrify the aggregate Indian rural landscape or energize Asian or African agriculture in vast plantations but rather to distribute energy in a usable form to small rural population centers—a local agricultural base that may not exceed one or two thousand acres divided into very small farms. Some countries have made progress in this respect. A substantial number of small motors are used to power pumps and agricultural machinery in Chinese rural communities.

The need is for units of energy suitable to small-scale use, at the same time avoiding the distribution costs of stepping down a high-tension transmission system to feed a myriad of local distribution systems with a maximum 10KV capacity. One solution, avoiding the need for hooking villages to a megawatt grid, is to provide a flexible energy package or module specifically designed for the needs of rural villages and small-scale agriculture. Such a package would provide energy to small electric pumps for irrigation, small-scale farm cultivating and harvesting machinery, residential lighting, refrigeration, air-conditioning, cinemas, radios and TV sets, small-scale provision of and handling of agricultural commodities such as oilseed presses. Hence the requirement would be to design an energy technology based on actual rural community needs rather than to force existing rural structures to fit the technical requirements of conventional energy systems. Energy distribution should serve the needs of the rural configuration, not vice versa.

In the early 1960s at a UN conference a representative of one of the LDCs admitted he was overwhelmed by technical discussions of large-scale multipurpose dams. His interest was in a small hydroelectric generator to "bob up and down" in jungle streams providing sufficient current for minimum village needs for lighting and perhaps for a cinema projector. Being able to read something after their day's work might help people to produce more efficiently. In time a larger generator could be acquired for a village industry out of market surplus.[3]

Such devices seem practicable. What is needed first, however, is a definitive, detailed analysis of local rural needs for energy and the strategic roles that a small power cell could play in improving the quality of rural life and small-unit farming. Surely the present advanced stage of technology could design an appropriate energy element. Unfortunately the technology-rich countries have tended to think exclusively in terms of bigness. The term "economy of scale" usually refers to large-scale efficiency; very little intensive research has been devoted to efficiency at the small end of the scale. In Japan small powered agricultural equipment has been successfully used for a number of years. This equipment uses fossil fuels, but it should be possible to design small-scale, inexpensive, battery-powered equipment with relatively infrequent recharge requirements.

While the incremental benefits would not be initially large in a single village, the aggregate of these increments over an entire rural sector would represent a significant advance. Of equal importance, however, is the need to rationalize and control the impact of energy technology on the rural landscape. Eventually the LDC rural sector must be fully modernized with all that this implies for technological advance. The appeal here is not to deny the benefits of modernization but rather to avoid the adverse shock and dislocation of sudden exposure to the full impact of advanced technology on traditional rural configurations. If western commercially dominated energy technology cannot or will not concern itself with this kind of problem, perhaps it is time for international cooperative institutions to take over.

On-Farm Energy Utilization

The problem of meeting or even ameliorating the agricultural energy needs of Africa, Asia, and Latin America is complex. Economic progress of these regions requires a rate of agricultural production attainable only through improved technology involving sharply increased energy consumption. Widespread rural unemployment is already a stark reality in some LDCs and is likely to increase. Increased mechanization simultaneously carries the threat of lowered labor requirements and the promise of better farming and increased yields. Heavy soils can be plowed deeper, weeds can be controlled better, and crops can be harvested more quickly with machinery, along with sharply reduced losses in threshing, storage, and transport.

Labor-intensive farming tends to be traditional and static. Modernization of farming methods with mechanization and energy inputs introduces a dynamic quality to the rural sector and opens the door to innovation. Without the economic and social dynamism created by energy-consuming agricultural technology, the densely populated areas of the LDCs may become increasingly stagnant. More and more traditional hand labor will be utilized on a fixed agricultural land area. This process has been described as "agricultural involution."[4] Clifford Geertz has described the process as it occurred in the rice fields of Java. There, as population expanded, with no outlet for employment except in the paddy fields, more and more labor was absorbed without lowering marginal productivity or seriously decreasing per capita income.

The difficulty is that this process eventually becomes institutionalized, and the resulting socioeconomic structure becomes permanently rigid and irreversible. Change is foreclosed. To paraphrase Geertz's eloquent description, the process of involution foredooms the future.[5] Thus the Java experience could be repeated among the densely populated rural areas of Asia, Africa, and Latin America in the absence of increased levels of on-farm energy consumption and accompanying technological breakthrough.

The alternative is to devise a system that corresponds to LDC capacity to compromise technology and employment. The Chinese have reportedly developed a form of rural social organization that permits increase in on-farm energy utilization represented by a 1,600 percent increase in electricity consumption from 1957 to 1963 alongside a rise in farm machinery horsepower from 0.56 million in 1957 to 7.0 million in 1964.[6] This accomplishment was accompanied by the development of decentralized light industry in rural areas with corresponding opening of employment opportunities.

China, like other Asian countries, will ultimately have to provide a rational plan for absorbing some part of its rural population in an urban-industrial sector. At the same time an intriguing possibility for increased rural employment opportunities may be afforded by development of a rural services sector along the lines currently reported from both Tanzania and China. But policies of agricultural production should not deny the use of advanced technology in an effort to solve the population problem. An important element in adjusting to the advent of agricultural innovation in tropical and subtropical farming is reform of the socioeconomic structure to prevent monopolization of the benefits of technology by a minority of large landowners at the expense of increased unemployment and poverty for the majority. For the time being, China (doubtless at some considerable cost) seems to have developed an approach to this problem through its rural communal system.

Even with substantial improvements in LDC ability to mobilize resources, the minimum energy requirements for the agro-rural sector will have to cope with the prospective world energy shortage. The LDCs will face stiff competition for fossil fuel from the developed industrial regions. This condition can be mitigated in the agricultural sectors of the Organization of Petroleum Exporting Countries (OPEC) in the Middle East and North Africa. It is possible (but not likely) that world fossil-fuel exploration may provide a breakthrough in hydrocarbon energy supplies. It is also possible that hydro-energy developed on Latin American rivers and in Southeast Asia on the Lower Mekong may be substituted for fuel energy. Even so, many LDCs may have to choose between costly hydroelectric development, rising fuel energy costs, and fission or fusion energy. While nuclear energy may prove less costly to manufacture, it will still be costly to distribute among rural populations.

In assessing the need for energy the LDCs will have to make a hard choice between energy for industry and energy for farming. Farm energy inputs are closely related to the modernization of agriculture and the emergence of a dynamic rural system, but industrial progress is also required, not only to provide an increased flow of production but also to provide expanding employment opportunities for the urbanward migration of displaced rural people. It is doubtful that even a dynamic rural sector can absorb all prospective labor force increments or that, even under the best of conditions, considerable technological displacement will not occur. The problem for planners is to devise a pragmatic and viable balance between rural and industrial sectors, avoiding rural stagnation on the one hand and reducing urbanward migration on the other.

The FAO Indicative World Plan emphasizes the energy consumption needs of LDC agriculture. In contrast to the availability of 0.93 HP per hectare on European farms and 1.03 HP per hectare on U.S. farms, Africa had 0.05 HP, Asia 0.19 HP, and Latin America 0.27 HP per hectare. Energy capacity of the LDCs will have to be increased to an average of 0.50 HP per hectare in order to achieve annual increases of 3.4–3.9 percent on the gross value of agricultural production. These rates of increase are critical if farm production is to keep abreast of population growth and contribute to overall development.[7]

The theoretical magnitude of fuel needed to activate minimum powered farm machinery for the 563 million hectares of LDC arable land by 1985 will be about 3 billion barrels of diesel fuel, or 12 percent of the estimated 1985 world oil production.[8] By 1985 world fuel consumption will have expanded so that severe competition for fuel energy will probably be reflected in steeply rising fuel prices. Thus one of the factors to be weighed in the development of foreign assistance programs may well be to supplement LDC fuel supplies. Even with such assistance LDC energy needs of this magnitude almost certainly cannot be met from traditional sources. Most of the LDCs are in the lower latitudes and thus receive enormous quantities of solar energy. Present efforts at efficient utilization take the form of multiple-cropping. Techniques for capture of additional solar energy for direct utilization are still in an experimental stage.

Overcoming this energy deficiency would make possible the progressive mechanization of LDC agriculture—largely in the form of tractors, improved tillage, cultivating and harvesting equipment, and trucks. This power equipment was estimated to have a value in 1962 of $875 million, increasing to $2.675 billion in 1985 (at 1962 prices)— an increase of 227 percent.[9] Increments of power and corresponding investments in this order of magnitude are needed to overcome the serious deficiency in the LDC ability to farm at critical periods. Inasmuch as the IWP increases in farm production are anticipated to follow more intensive use of land and the more precise specifications for agricultural practices associated with production efficiency, the degree of mechanization indicated is critical. This degree of mechanization will facilitate not only increased cropping intensity, seedbed preparation, and planting but also better cultivation and harvesting practices. Power inputs thus become one of the preconditions of modernization of LDC agriculture, which include increased use of improved seeds, chemical fertilizer, irrigation, and pest control methods.

The kind of energy application contemplated in these projections is tractive power, and for the foreseeable future such equipment will be designed primarily for fossil fuels. Those LDCs not possessing a supply of this form of energy will probably have to import it. Thus these countries will have to increase their foreign exchange now used primarily for industrial inputs to purchase inputs to expedite agricultural modernization. This policy change in turn may require an upgrading of national ability to mobilize agricultural incomes for investment in agriculture, not only for mechanization but also for increasing expenditure for motor fuel.

Energy and Water in Agriculture

Wherever farmers toil throughout the world, they have a constant preoccupation with water. Whether consciously formulated or not, the schedule of their lives is largely influenced by the interaction of soil and water on plant life. For millions the energy requirements are supplied by their own labor. For the more fortunate, irrigation, flood control, and drainage schemes provide more precise controls. But universally the ability to deal with water constraints is a major factor in survival. Too little water means a poor crop or none at all; too much water floods croplands, drowns livestock and people, washes away homes and farm structures. Torrential downpours wash away topsoils and convert fields into hopelessly eroded landscapes.

The pattern of rain-fed agriculture is defined by rainy seasons. Cropping systems relate to the succession of wet and dry periods. The movement of livestock herds from one watering point to the next forms the nomadic pattern of several African tribes. Indeed much of human history, and perhaps its prehistory, is partly related to changes in the distribution of water.

In the natural hydrologic system, water vapor is drawn from the earth's surface and later released as rainfall. This phenomenon involves enormous amounts of energy. Under natural conditions the system is uncontrolled; efforts to bring it under control for agricultural purposes require irrigation, flood control, and drainage.

Gravity irrigation schemes involving massive dams or simpler river diversions largely use the natural gradient of the landscape to lead water into canals and thence into minor distribution channels to the cultivated area. Such systems have formed the backbone of the great river irrigation systems from the ancient systems of the Near East and Egypt to such giant systems as those of the Indus and its tributaries.

As these schemes have become more sophisticated, the association with energy has become more direct. The energy in the water falling from high dams is used to generate electricity, which in turn operates pumps to bring water from underground aquifers to the surface and to drain water from irrigated fields to prevent waterlogging and accumulation in the soil of injurious salts.

A great deal of the irrigated farming of the world has been in river valleys—the Jordan, the Euphrates, the Caudery, the Colorado, the Nile, the Indus, the Menam Chao Phya, and so forth. However, irrigation schemes based on water pumped from underground aquifers are also very old. In the Indus Basin gravity irrigation water is combined with water pumped from underground sources so that the gravity supply of the Indus River is supplemented by water from underground aquifers. In the plains of northern India a vast underground sheet of water originates in the snow melt of the Himalayas. This groundwater now provides a pumped irrigation supply for many thousand acres of land. The energy to operate the pumps is partly hydroelectric power generated in the Bakhra Dam on a tributary of the Indus and partly from diesel fuel.

Thus irrigation water from underground sources depends on energy to lift water to the surface—to overcome gravity. These pumps vary from crude waterwheels lifting water from a shallow well to powerful electric pumps with a lift of a thousand feet or more. The interplay between energy costs and farm income directly determines the number of feet of lift. For some crops the limit is a few hundred feet and for others much greater lifts. Thus the economics of pumped irrigation are linked with the entire framework of farming systems. The relative value of pumped irrigation water affects the extension of modern agricultural technology and innovation. As better seeds, chemical fertilizer, and pesticides become available, the effect is to increase both the demand for water and the associated demand for powered pumping.

Large quantities of groundwater exist throughout the world. Although the precise location and depth of aquifers have not been universally established, the total amount of groundwater stored within 2,500 feet of land surface probably is greater than 30 times the amount stored in all freshwater lakes today.[10] Recent exploration for oil in the Sahara has uncovered a vast underground aquifer, the Albienne Nappe.

> As recently as 1950 the suggestion that there was a great freshwater sea "under the Sahara" was derided as a geological legend. Today, the Albienne Nappe is a truth made manifest in the swimming pools in the heart of the desert, and in the man-made oases that are providing food for the growing oil-townships. When the drillers went down 11,000 feet into the oil formations they passed through the aquifer, a vast reservoir of fresh water. When water is recognized as being at least as valuable as oil, "legends" will become economic fact and the vast underground reserves which are now known to exist will make the wastelands productive.[11]

One might speculate that locally produced fossil fuel could provide energy for an irrigated Saharan agriculture if a similar speculation might envision a corresponding transport and marketing system. The mere existence of an extensive underground aquifer removes only one constraint in the way of a developed agriculture. There remains a very large energy constraint and beyond that the economic and technical features of a modern agronomic system. However, with available water *and* energy, speculation moves toward reality. This means that there must be some correspondence between the cost of electricity (capital plus operation and maintenance) and the value of the final output—the agricultural commodity. Finally we are faced with the need for cheap energy. It is possible to conceive schemes whereby fossil fuels and water production are parts of the same complex. For example, when the fossil fuel lies below the water-bearing aquifer, the capital cost of drilling for water could be shifted to the oil drilling cost, or there might be a dual pumping system with oil pumping bearing the cost of water pumping. In strict accounting this amounts to subsidizing water production at the expense of fuel production, but the enormous profit margins of fossil fuels are probably sufficient to bear such costs.

There seems to be some correspondence between the existence of large underground water bodies and desert conditions. The North African artesian basin mentioned above covers an area of one million square kilometers and underlies parts of Morocco, Tunisia, Algeria, and Central Africa.[12] Other subterranean sources underlie Libya (from drainage in the Sudan, Ethiopia, and Central Africa), parts of the Arabian Peninsula, India, Pakistan, and possibly portions of the Gobi Desert.[13] In these cases energy would be required to lift water from the underground source to the land surface except where artesian pressure was sufficient. However, before a successful irrigated agriculture can be established, many factors in addition to moisture must be available—chemical fertilizer, appropriate tillage methods, and improved seeds as well as full knowledge of their interaction from appropriate research.

It is difficult and perhaps unproductive to make generalizations about energy in relation to agricultural water management. The problems tend to be location-specific and regionally disparate. Globally the population/land resource ratio looks more favorable than it does in Asia generally or in specific African or Latin American locations.

The potential arable land of the world is three times the area cultivated in a single year. Over 4 billion acres—more than half the world's arable potential—are located in the tropics. Perhaps a third of this land may require irrigation. On the other hand, very little potentially arable land is available in Asia. Thus the choices for extending cultivation in Asia depend on increasing the intensity of cultivation by improved practices. Water management, including new and supplemental irrigation and drainage, will be important in specific locations. The energy component will tend to be a function of water management.[14]

In contrast to the pressing land needs of Asia, the extensive arable potentials in Africa and South America have a greater time horizon. Large potentially arable areas in these continents lie within humid and subhumid zones. Constraints to more intensive cultivation of these lands seem to be not physical but socioeconomic. In some cultivated areas in these regions the use of supplemental irrigation to overcome the stern limitations imposed by seasonal rainfall may require pumping from adjacent streams or from wells. Any extensive development along these lines will probably depend on regional economic and social development.

RICE PRODUCTION. Nowhere is the complex interplay of population, food supply, farming, water, and energy as vivid or as pressing as in the rice-growing regions of Asia. Ninety-five percent of the world's rice is produced and eaten there and thus supports a third of the world's population.

Rice production dominates farming from the Yangtse Basin in China to the South China Sea, east to the Philippines, to all of Southeast Asia and much of South Asia. The characteristic features of the rural landscape of this vast, densely populated region are an intricate pattern of waterways, terraced paddy fields, ditches, drains, ponds, and reservoirs. Rice is everywhere, and everywhere rice grows there must be water. Since rice has been cultivated for thousands of years in this region, further increases in production must come from more intensive cultivation or by extending the rice acreage. In either case a change in the water regimen will be necessary. If additional acreage can be put into rice, new sources of water will be required. This is a less likely alternative than bringing a more advanced technology to the existing paddy fields.

A specific proposal is to utilize rice varieties with a short growing season, so that two crops per season can be produced on the same acreage in place of the native varieties having an exceptionally long growing season. Such a proposal requires that the first crop be harvested and the second crop planted in a very short interval; timing and precision become important, and several operations must succeed each other in a tight schedule. Water used for the first crop must be drained off; the standing rice must be cut and then threshed; the land must be flooded again for a second crop.

This series of operations involves a rapid mobilization and deployment of manpower—an undertaking greatly facilitated by power machinery. Particularly helpful would be a proliferation of small, powered lift pumps for prompt flooding of paddy fields. It might be possible to use the same power unit for mechanical threshing. This would overcome the present time lag in some areas where lower-lying paddy terraces have to wait for water until higher levels are flooded and where harvesting operations by hand are time-consuming.

In China it was estimated that the 1958 rural energy supply was about 1.6 million HP. In the succeeding six years this supply was increased nearly four times, principally for electric and diesel-powered pumps for irrigation and drainage.[15] There has been a continual emphasis on rural electrification in the Chinese agrarian program. It has been estimated that in 1965 the rural power supply had increased 25 times since 1957; this would have amounted to about 5.4 million kilowatt-hours. While the success of this program has probably been uneven, it is nevertheless significant that the effort to increase power-driven irrigation and drainage pumps has been persistent.[16] Apparently the Chinese have recognized that energy applied to irrigation not only releases labor for other tasks but also does a better job, thus permitting better results from advanced technology, including the use of chemical fertilizer. Probably such considerations have caused the Chinese to accord to irrigation priority of use of rural electricity, not only because of the greater efficiency of electrically powered irrigation pumps but also because it is easier to manufacture these in appropriate small units and they do not require expensive fuel oil.

The significance of these observations on Chinese use of energy for rice production is a probable increase in the energy demands of the entire Asian rice economy. Efforts to raise rice yields to levels higher than population increases will be reflected in the widening adoption of advanced technology dependent on efficient water management and in turn on powered water controls.

The research efforts of the International Rice Research Institute in the Philippines have resulted in producing strains of rice with much higher yields than the native varieties in many areas of Asia. However, these miracle strains presuppose precise technical methods and inputs; a central basic requirement is precise water management. Once introduced over a wide area, these high-yielding varieties enforce technological imperatives that may not be denied; there is no possibility of return to older, less productive strains and to traditional farm practices. The initial investment of each farmer makes it essential that the water in his paddy field be quantitatively precise in accordance with a rigid delivery schedule. The prospect for progressive improvement in the rice yields of Asia may be directly related to the availability of energy to power pumps that could provide such a water supply.

ARID REGIONS. The prospect of reduced energy costs along with improved water desalting technology has resulted in a number of proposals for agriculture. These proposals take two forms: (1) reclamation of desert wastelands by irrigation with new fresh water produced by desalting sea water; (2) reduction of excessive salt content of present irrigation supplies through desalting.

Enhancing these prospects is the possible use of low-cost nuclear energy—either presently available fission energy or anticipated very low cost fusion energy. In either case substantial amounts of energy are required, and the fixed charges (capital costs plus depreciation) will be an important factor. It is impossible to generalize about the case for or against desalting. The particular regional circumstances, the available alternatives, and the relative urgency of the need for water tend to make for unique solutions.

Israel probably has no alternative to desalted water for replenishing existing water supplies and for extending its irrigated area.[17] Israel will also substantially increase its electrical output rate, and this rate will be greater than the rate of increase of its water supply. Wasowski has outlined the arguments for conventional production of energy compared with nuclear energy: for the large-scale plant requirements for Israel a dual-purpose thermonuclear plant (electricity and water) would be most economical. However, part of this analysis is based on the economies of scale of the dual-purpose plant. Peterson indicates that Israeli costs for desalted water were about $0.25 per 1,000 gallons, but water was sold for $0.06–0.10 per 1,000 gallons; this differential represented a subsidy to water users out of electricity revenue. This calculation is based on a plant generating 500 megawatts, and part of the subsidy is represented by cutting electrical output to 300 megawatts, thus permitting production of 100 million gallons of water per day (the trade-off between water and electricity is about 100 megawatts for 50 million gallons per day).[18]

The acre-foot cost at $0.10 per 1,000 gallons is over $32.00. In U.S. terms this cost would be possible only for relatively high value crops such as citrus fruits or vegetables. At the actual cost of $0.25 per 1,000 gallons, the acre-foot cost is over $70.00. In U.S. terms this would be prohibitive if farmers paid the entire amount and if this water represented the full supply.

A somewhat different situation is presented where the more costly supply represents an increment to a deficient base supply; the deficiency may be in either quality or quantity. The value of a marginal increment may be sufficiently large, as it is in the case of some crops, to justify the addition of high-cost supplemental water.

The constraint imposed by high-cost desalted water may be relaxed (as in the case of Israel) when water is produced jointly with electricity, because the demand for electricity apparently is relatively inelastic. In such a situation electric consumers carry part of the water costs. This arrangement is common practice for the multiple-purpose water projects in western United States.

A somewhat similar situation arises when the initial or base supply of irrigation water contains an excessive concentration of harmful minerals. Through desalting methods toxic waste water (from collector drains) is recycled to reduce toxicity levels. The recycled water is then reintroduced to the system and mixes with the higher toxicity base supply with a resulting reduction in toxicity levels to tolerable ranges. While the cost of this desalted supply is high, the rise in cost of the resulting mixed water is within economic limits, or so the theory appears to run.

A case study along these lines, based on the use of nuclear energy, was made in the lower Colorado River Basin in the United States. The site selected was an arid irrigated farming area of 10,570 acres, where irrigation supplies were subject to increasingly higher levels of toxic concentration.[19] The study included a number of alternative schemes—varying concentrations of chemical salts, cropping patterns, and desalting methods. Investment costs per acre were very high, ranging from $5,000 to $8,200. Benefit/cost ratios were from negative to a high of 1.72. Only in two alternatives was the benefit/cost ratio positive. The investigation also revealed that a very long growing season was essential to favorable returns. This study used a very nominal interest rate of $3\frac{1}{4}$ percent and a fixed charge factor of 5.62 percent to capital costs. For many countries these rates may be much too low; in such cases costs would be substantially higher. However, the length of growing season would probably be fairly typical of a number of arid areas in tropical regions. The model was a single-purpose desalting plant. No effort was made to develop a combined electricity-water production system. Consequently all benefits are based on increased agricultural production. It is also worth mentioning that this study is based on U.S. conditions of high levels of agricultural technology and infrastructure.

A more ambitious international study was undertaken in 1967-68 of the potentials of a hypothetical joint nuclear electric generating and desalting plant in northern Mexico just south of the international boundary with the United States. The hypothetical model had a freshwater capacity of 1 billion gallons per day and 1,700-1,867 megawatts to supply electricity and water to the northern states of Mexico and Arizona and California.[20] In general outline the installation would take salt water from the Gulf of Lower California and discharge brines back into the gulf. Electricity would be tied to U.S. and Mexican grids, and fresh water would be dispatched to central distributing points in both countries.

This large system would apparently produce water at costs of U.S. $0.16-0.40 per 1,000 gallons (U.S. $49-130 per acre-foot) based on 1966-67 price level and electricity at U.S. $0.0018-0.0031 per kilowatt-hour. The principal problem to be overcome by this installation is a lowering of the water table on both sides of the border as a result of overpumping in areas already well-developed and prosperous. The prospective higher water prices for this supplemental supply may be tolerable not only in terms of increasing production but also in preserving large-scale investments. The proposed initial installation would offset a substantial portion of this overdraft in the 1980 time period. An additional plant of equal capacity would probably be needed to meet water deficits in 1995, due to expansion of irrigated acreage and increased municipal and industrial water demand, probably stimulated by the expansion of the agricultural plant.

The total initial cost of the plant might be $800-1,000 million, with annual costs running $80-180 million. The electricity product might provide an opportunity for shifting part of the water cost to electricity consumers.

Additional preliminary investigations involving water desalting by nuclear energy in industrial and agro-industrial complexes were reported by the Oak Ridge National Laboratory, drawing on prior nuclear desalting studies and industry experiences.[21] The study contains several critical considerations:

1. Nuclear-powered energy generation is "footloose"—not fastened to locations based on the availability of raw natural energy sources such as fuel or hydroelectric sites.

2. By combining desalting operations with energy-consuming industries in a complex of substantial scale, economies may result, thus reducing the cost of energy and in turn substituting it for raw materi-

als. Energy would be used partly as electricity for conventional purposes and partly as heat for desalting.

3. With economical desalted water several of the world's coastal desert areas might be reclaimed for irrigated agriculture.

4. A component of the industrial complex might be large-scale production of nitrogenous fertilizers.

These considerations, while provocative, are not entirely consistent. Some of the advantage of the flexibility of nuclear energy is offset by the need to locate complexes on the shore of coastal deserts. The study identifies as possible locales western Australia, the Kutch Desert of India, Baja California, the Sechura Desert of Peru, and the Sinai-Negev region of the Near East.

However, such locales may not prove economical for industrial production, so the scheme might have to depend entirely on the economic returns of a water-only operation. At this point the study seems to turn on the anticipated returns from advanced irrigated agricultural technology—particularly the interrelation between climate, chemical fertilizer, soil moisture, and improved high-yielding plant material.

This investigation can be considered only as suggestive of the direction to be taken by subsequent study and investigation. It does not make clear that the costs of desalted water in the near future are very high. Moreover, it does not offer insight into the actual farm operation or the resulting settlement pattern. Apparently a very high degree of mechanization and accompanying considerations of the benefits to be derived from large-scale farming are assumed. In fact the term "food factory" is used to emphasize the degree of industrialization involved.[22] The capital costs for such an installation would probably be beyond the means of some developing countries, and so would the managerial, technological, and infrastructure requirements (Israel and OPEC countries excepted).

The investigation is aimed primarily at showing how nuclear energy can be aimed at increasing the world food supply. It is not intended as a proposal for national economic development policy in the designated areas. The selection of desert areas as model locations is probably viewed as desirable partly because they are largely unoccupied and thus the installation of the desalted water-based food factories would entail a minimum of social and economic dislocation and partly because "the food factory concept would appear to be the reverse of agrarian reform programs in many countries."[23]

Peterson has said that income distribution aspects of this scheme are bothersome. "If 40,000 workers on an agro-complex produce enough food for 30 million people, how do the 29,960,000 others get the money to buy it?"[24]

These are not the only disturbing aspects of this desert locale model. All the energy generated in the complex or in the water-only alternative would seem to be consumed on-site. No opportunity, perhaps because of the isolated locale, is indicated for electrical transmission or the revenues it might produce. In the water-only model all returns depend on the results of a high-technology agricultural food factory; in the complex model the returns would come from both farm produce and industrial products, and these apparently would have to be exported. Thus, in addition to the investment costs of this seaside agro-industrial complex, the costs of port facilities would have to be added.

This investigation assumes the energy source to be a nuclear *fission* reactor. One might conjecture that a system built around *fusion* energy would have much lower costs. Even so, the capital investment would be substantial; without some better estimate of how the desert agricultural scheme might work, conclusions are entirely hypothetical. The investigation calculates that costs of water at $0.20/ 1,000 gallons (1967 prices) are "in the ball park." This means that water would cost around $70 per acre-foot—very high by U.S. standards for irrigated agriculture, even for high-value fruit and truck crops. Israel would probably have trouble selling its water above $0.10/1,000 gallons.[25] At that price energy costs would have to be zero, because costs of amortization of the capital would be $0.10/1,000 gallons ($32 per acre-foot). Thus the water costs derived from the Oak Ridge study are very high relative to Israeli conditions; Israeli irrigation water rates may come close to water costs of the costless fusion power model.

The conclusion one reaches from this study even with very low cost fusion energy is that desalted irrigation water cannot be considered as a viable prospect in the near future for rapidly increasing agricultural production except in special circumstances and for a limited range of high-value commodities. The prospect for irrigated agriculture by desalted seawater and fission or fusion energy seems brighter if the locale is already developed, as in the southwestern United States–northern Mexico model or in India and Pakistan where the economic impact of higher-cost water would be modified by its use for mixing or blending purposes. Moreover, the existing social and economic organization might provide a favorable market for energy and the opportunity for cost-sharing between water and electricity. The prospect for desalted irrigation water production to reclaim unpopulated coastal desert areas is somewhat conjectural in the Oak Ridge studies because their cost predictions seem optimistic. Among the proponents of nuclear energy, professional objectivity sometimes borders closely on advocacy.

Prospects

The energy requirements of the Third World agro-rural sector depend on and are created by relative rates of community and economic development. This is also true of the urban-industrial sector, which generally among Third World countries has received the major allocations of available energy supplies, perhaps because it is relatively more modern and productivity rates respond fairly quickly to increments of energy. But in the long run, national interests are not well served by achieving high-productivity urban-industrial communities alongside large numbers of relatively backward rural communities.

On the other hand, most of the Third World has had little or no voice in the distribution of world energy flows. The developed regions have so completely appropriated energy sources and monopolized distribution and use that Third World prospects for energy policy formulation have been reduced to very few alternatives.

A global view of current energy sources and energy distribution is not encouraging either for the Third World or its rural sector. Fossil fuels are the dominant source of world energy. At present neither the logistics of fossil fuel production nor its economics favors Third World rural people. Latin America is a case in point. The large Venezuelan production is sold principally to North America. At the same time the rapidly expanding industries of Brazil and Argentina depend on African and Mideast supplies. A similar pattern of off-shore distribution applies to Trinidadian and Colombian sources. Mexican production is used largely for its industrial sector. Very little Latin American fossil fuel finds its way to the large, poor rural sector of that region. Similarly African and Mideast production goes to Europe, North America, and Japan. The Soviet Union's potentials seem likely to go to overseas markets and Europe.

In the present world order of sovereign nation-states and multinational corporate power, the richer and more highly industrialized regions and subregions have consistently outbid poorer rural regions for the world supply of fossil fuels. It is an anomaly that Persian Gulf oil goes to distant Europe and North America (meanwhile flaring its natural gas deposits) rather than to South Asia, just across the Arabian Sea. Even if this source of energy were to be diverted to these nearby energy-poor regions, the industrial-urban sector of these deficit regions would probably have priority over the poorer agro-rural sector.

Of course fossil fuel deposits may yet be discovered in energy-deficit regions. These regions are vast in geographical extent and geological diversity. Exploration now going forward in these nations may prove fruitful. Yet such potentials, if realized, would under the present world system likely become instruments of national power policy rather than be used for broader, more global, more humanitarian ends. Fossil fuel deposits are always location-specific, meaning that they are always properties of sovereign states.

A great danger lurks in the nationalistic, industrial dedication to fossil fuels. First, technology and organization based on fossil fuels become highly specialized with limited convertibility and built-in rigidity. Second, the industrial commitment being inherently expansive requires ever increasing amounts of fossil fuel from a finite source. The tip of this iceberg of hazard to the fuel-consuming, heavily industrialized regions is now becoming apparent. This threat, though distant, is even now causing a frantic search for new discoveries and crash programs for advanced transport techniques. The United States is considering revision of its national environmental policies as well as its conservation policies by opening up lands for strip-mining of coal and by reducing air pollution standards so that lower-quality fuel may be used. The less industrialized, albeit poorer, countries do not share either the hazard or the need for making drastic policy changes detrimental to the environment. In this respect the Third World is in a much better position. They are not harnessed to the rigidities of a fossil fuel–based industrial culture. Their options, currently limited, are in the longer run not foreclosed by prior technological commitments. They are not fenced into a narrow range of conventional technological alternatives. Their horizons of creative imagination are wide open; they are not presented with the burden of massive investments of capital or of its carrying costs.

In the final analysis energy problems are an intellectual challenge, and the domain of human intellect is universal and cosmic in scope. The components of thought are the heritage of all humanity. This heritage and its fruits—technology, invention, and innovation—properly belong, and should be universally vested as a worldwide social property, in a world institution dedicated to the promotion of energy research and development designed to meet the specific needs of energy-deficit regions. Such an institution should place considerable emphasis on the invention and design of energy units compatible with agro-rural configurations and devote intensive effort to finding appropriate devices for rice culture, water control, desalination, and amenities to improve the quality of life in rural communities. These advances might lead to the orderly organization of rural space and regional development.

Our hypothetical institution would have the great advantage of freedom from the inhibitions of conventional technology and the preoccupation of the fossil fuel syndrome. It could then capitalize on and expand the frontier of knowledge in nuclear fission and fusion. It could explore the potentials of solar, geothermal, oceanic, and chemical synthetic sources of energy. It could design and construct models of appropriate devices for supplying rural energy needs and construct appropriate working models for subsequent manufacture by licensees—revenues and royalties from such licenses going toward support of the central institution.

Nor would this supposition arise only in utopian altruism. An important practical aspect is that world needs for food are growing by leaps and bounds, and the world capacity to meet this demand is showing signs of strain. We have known for some time that the world needs for energy and protein food have not been met. The incremental contribution of presently energy-deficit agro-rural regions could improve possibilities for a peaceful world order.

NOTES

Chapter 1

1. Adapted from *World Food Problem*, 2:47.
2. Ibid., p. 76.
3. Ibid., p. 5.
4. Lord Ritchie-Calder, "Famine at the Feast," Center Conference, pp. 7–8.
5. *World Food Problem*, p. 9.
6. Howard T. Odum, "Energetics of World Food Production," *World Food Problem*, 3:55–56.
7. Ibid., p. 63.
8. Herman E. Koenig, William E. Cooper, and James M. Falvey, "Industrialized Ecosystem Design and Management," p. 8.
9. Ibid., pp. 8–9.
10. National Science Foundation, National Science Board, *Environmental Science*, p. 1.
11. Charles E. Kellogg and Arnold C. Orvedal, "Potentially Arable Soils of the World and Critical Measures for Their Use," *Advan. Agron.*, 21:109–70.
12. Ibid., p. 113.
13. Ibid., p. 112.
14. S. Herbert Frankel, *The Economic Impact on Underdeveloped Societies*, p. 146.
15. H. Thompson Straw, review of Allan Wood, *The Groundnut Affair, Geograph. Rev.*, 41(4):676–77.
16. Kellogg and Orvedal, p. 113.
17. *World Food Problem*, 2:407–8.
18. Ibid., p. 408.
19. Ibid., pp. 439–40.
20. Dean F. Peterson, "Water as a Factor in Development of World Agriculture," Center Conference, p. 5.
21. United Nations, FAO, *Provisional Indicative World Plan for Agricultural Development*, 1:39.
22. *World Food Problem*, pp. 446–47.
23. Peterson, pp. 19–20.
24. Ibid., p. 2.
25. United Nations, pp. 47–48.
26. Perry R. Stout, "Agricultural Requirements for Nitrogen Fertilizers in the USA," Center Conference, p. 1.
27. Ibid., p. 22.
28. Calculated from Stout, Table 4.
29. Derived from Stout, Table 4.

Chapter 2

1. Lester R. Brown, "Human Food Production as a Process in the Biosphere," *Sci. Am.*, 223(3):161, 163.
2. Clifton R. Wharton, Jr., "The Green Revolution: Cornucopia or Pandora's Box?" *Foreign Affairs*, 47(3):464–76.
3. *World Food Problem*, 1:87.
4. United Nations, FAO, *Provisional Indicative World Plan for Agricultural Development*, 1:175–77.
5. Ibid., 2:468–73, Tables Af, A5.
6. Ibid., Tables A4, A5, and A6.
7. William J. Staub and Melvin G. Blase, "Genetic Technology and Agricultural Development," *Science*, 173(3992):119.
8. J. George Harrar, "The Green Revolution in Perspective," pp. xx, xxi.
9. Ibid., pp. xxii–xxiii.
10. Jonathan Garst, *No Need for Hunger*, pp. 3–4.
11. Jonathan Garst, "Chemicals for Conservation," Center Conference, p. 3.
12. Perry R. Stout, "Agricultural Requirements for Nitrogen Fertilizers in the USA," Center Conference, pp. 14–15.
13. U.S. Dept. Health, Education and Welfare, *Report of the Secretary's Commission on Pesticides and Their Relationship to Environmental Health*, pp. 55–56.
14. Ibid., pp. 84–87.
15. *Los Angeles Times*, Mar. 10, 1972, p. 5.
16. Emil M. Mrak, "Pesticides, Herbicides, and the Contamination of the Ecosystem," Center Conference, p. 2.
17. *World Food Problem*, 1:95.
18. G. F. Sprague, "World Research Needs for Increasing Corn Production," *Agr. Eng.*, 51(2):71.

Chapter 3

1. United Nations, FAO, *Provisional Indicative World Plan for Agricultural Development*, 1:17.
2. United Nations Statistical Yearbook and Yearbook of National Accounts Statistics, 1969; World Bank, cited by Jimmye S. Hillman, "Increasing Agricultural Productivity vs. Environmental Protection in Developing Countries," Center Conference, Table 1.
3. Theodore W. Schultz, "Food, Population and the Ecosystem," Center Conference, p. 10.
4. Howard T. Odum, "Energetics of World Food Production," *World Food Problem*, 3:56 ff.
5. Yujiro Hayami and Vernon W. Ruttan, *Agricultural Development*, p. 169.
6. Peter Dorner, "Needed Redirections in Economic Analysis for Agricultural Development Policy," *Am. J. Agr. Econ.*, 53(1):9.
7. Martin E. Abel, "World Needs for Food and Fiber," Center Conference, p. 13.
8. Schultz, pp. 5–6.
9. Dorner, pp. 11–12.
10. Abel, p. 22.
11. Hillman, p. 11.
12. Hayami and Ruttan, p. 169.
13. Schultz, pp. 16–17.
14. Ibid., p. 18.
15. D. Gale Johnson, "International Trade and Other Economic Relations Affecting the World Food Supply," Center Conference, p. 14.
16. Clifton R. Wharton, Jr., "The Green Revolution: Cornucopia or Pandora's Box?" *Foreign Affairs*, 47(3):467–68.
17. Wolf Ladejinsky, "Ironies of India's Green Revolution," *Foreign Affairs*, 48(4):763.
18. Ibid., pp. 764–65.
19. Hayami and Ruttan, p. 191.

20. Ibid., p. 217.
21. Ibid., p. 169.
22. Abel, p. 24.
23. M. L. Dantwala, "From Stagnation to Growth," *Indian Econ. J.*, 19(2):186–87.
24. Abel, p. 18.
25. Schultz, p. 19.
26. Hillman, pp. 17–18.
27. Earl O. Heady, "Alternatives in Environmental Control through Agriculture," Center Conference, p. 2.
28. Ibid., pp. 10–15.
29. Hillman, p. 11.

Chapter 4

1. Alexis de Tocqueville, *Democracy in America*, Henry Reeve text as revised by Francis Bowen, now further corrected and edited with Introduction, Editorial Notes, and Bibliographies by Phillips Bradley, Alfred A. Knopf, 2 Vols., New York, 1945, 1:62–68.
2. Gunnar Myrdal, *Asian Drama*, pp. 293, 300, 888, 891–98. Also see Edgar Owens and Robert Shaw, *Development Reconsidered*, D. C. Heath, Boston, 1972, Chs. 1 and 2.
3. Stefan H. Robock, *Brazil's Developing Northeast*. The acronym SUDENE stands for Superintendency for Development of the Northeast.
4. Hiram S. Phillips, *Guide for Development*, pp. 10–11.
5. Lester R. Brown, "Human Food Production as a Process in the Biosphere," *Sci. Am.*, 223(3):170.
6. David Hopper, recorded comments at Center Conference.
7. Laurence I. Hewes, Jr., *Japan—Land and Men*, pp. 78–83, 142–46. Also his *Japanese Land Reform Program*, General Headquarters, Supreme Commander for Allied Powers, Natural Resources Section, Rept. 127, Tokyo, Japan, 1950, pp. 34–48.
8. *Main Conclusions of the Joint OECD Development Center/IBRD Seminar on Rural Development Problems* (Paris, May 15, 16, 1972).
9. USAID/India Office of Rural Development Adviser, *Long Range Rural Development Policy Analysis*, New Delhi, India, 1964 (preliminary draft, unpublished), mimeo., p. 24.
10. *Joint OECD/IBRD Seminar*.
11. M. L. Dantwala, *Brief Outline on the Concept of Rural Development*, OECD Development Center/IBRD Seminar.
12. Imperial Ethiopian Government, *Third Five-Year Plan: 1968–1973*, Berhanem Selam H.S.I. Printing Press, Addis Ababa, 1968, pp. 187, 188.
13. Government of Tanzania, *Tanzania Second Five-Year Plan for Economic and Social Development, 1 July 1969–30 June 1974*, Government Printer, Dar Es Salaam, 1970, Vol. 1, Ch. 2.
14. John P. Lewis, *Quiet Crisis in India*, p. 168.
15. E. A. J. Johnson, *The Organization of Space in Developing Countries*, p. 227.
16. Frances M. Foland, "Agrarian Reform in Latin America," *Foreign Affairs* (Oct. 1969), p. 97.
17. Dale W. Adams, "Leadership, Education and Agricultural Development Programs in Colombia," *Inter-Am. Econ. Affairs*, 22(1):87.
18. Ibid.
19. Cf. Phillips, p. 18.
20. TANU stands for Tanzania African National Union, the official political party of Tanzania.
21. Permanent Settlement Act of 1793.
22. Iftikhar Ahmed and John F. Timmons, "Current Land Reforms in East Pakistan," *Land Econ.*, 47(1):55.
23. Paul H. Appleby, *Public Administration in India*, p. 45. Appleby, since deceased, was at the time Dean of the School of Public Administration, Syracuse University, New York. His letter of transmittal on this report was dated Jan.

15, 1953. Appleby was a warm friend and ardent supporter of India, which he regarded as one of the great working democracies of the world.
24. Francine R. Frankel, *India's Green Revolution*, p. 206.

CHAPTER 5

1. The respective allocations to highways, electrical development, etc. and between rural and metropolitan areas in the Government of India's Second Five-Year Plan bear out this point. The current Five-Year Plan of Tanzania has a very large allocation for main highways and a much smaller allocation for rural roads. In both cases there are perhaps overriding reasons for this policy other than purely economic and developmental considerations.
2. See Kusum Nair, *Blossoms in the Dust*, Praeger, New York, 1962, pp. 28-29, 31-34, 47-49, 69, 70.
3. John R. Commons et al., *History of Labor in the United States*, Macmillan Co., New York, 1918, 1:6.
4. *Market Towns and Spatial Development in India*, New Delhi, National Council of Applied Economic Research, 1965.
5. John P. Lewis, *Quiet Crisis in India*, pp. 50-69, 169-201.

CHAPTER 6

1. 1966 commitments by these countries were estimated at $1.3 billion. See Jagdish N. Bhagwati, *Amount and Sharing of Aid*, p. 6.
2. World Bank, *Annual Report Fiscal Year 1970*, Washington, D.C., 1970, p. 46.
3. Ibid., p. 7.
4. Ibid, pp. 47-48.
5. USAID, *Fiscal Year 1970 Operations Report*, Washington, D.C., 1970, p. 5.
6. Lester B. Pearson, *Partners in Development*, p. 145.
7. Clive S. Gray, *Resource Flows to Less Developed Countries*, p. 91.
8. Susan Aurelia Gitelson, "Multilateral Aid for National Development and Self-Reliance."
9. United Nations Development Programme, *Study of the Capacity of the United Nations Development System*, 1:10-11.
10. Pearson, p. 172.
11. Ibid., p. 162.
12. T. W. Schultz, "The Malinvestment Trail," *Economic Growth and Agriculture*, pp. 36-41.
13. USAID, *Spring Review of Land Reform*, Background Paper 1: AID Support for Land Reform, Washington, D.C., 1970.
14. Jerome T. French, *Views of the Latin American AID Missions on Land Reform*, USAID, Washington, D.C., 1970, p. 3.
15. A good deal of the foregoing is based on personal recollections of events in 1966. These have been brought up to date in articles by William Bredo and Roy R. Prosterman in *Asian Survey*, Aug. 1970.
16. Laurence I. Hewes, Jr., *Japan—Land and Men*, pp. 53-54.
17. Stanley Please of the World Bank provided several of the ideas expressed in this section, both in personal conversation and from his "Capital Flows and Income Transfers within and between Nations to Sustain the Agricultural Revolution."
18. John P. Lewis, *Quiet Crisis in India*, Ch. 3.
19. E. A. J. Johnson, *The Organization of Space in Developing Countries*, pp. 178-207.
20. Norton Ginsburg, "Regional and Urban Planning for National Development and Environmental Conservation."
21. Pearson, Ch. 4.
22. Pearson, p. 85.
23. Ibid.

NOTES

Chapter 7

1. The U.S. Bureau of the Census reported a 0.98% population growth rate for 1971 (*Los Angeles Times*, Part I, p. 2, Apr. 24, 1972): "The birth rate of 17.2 per thousand in 1971 was the lowest ever reached [in the U.S. presumably]." The *Times* also cited a NATO study showing that birth rates in the Soviet Union dropped from 26.7 per thousand in 1965 to 18.4 and in satellite countries from 24.4 to 16.0.
2. Reginald H. Green and Ann Seidman, *Unity or Poverty?*
3. Ibid., p. 47. This comment applies specifically to Asia and Africa, but the conditions are as true or even more so in Latin America.
4. Cf. Gunnar Myrdal, *Asian Drama*, 2:1260.
5. Montague Yudelman, *Agricultural Development and Economic Integration in Latin America*, p. 33; Rene Dumont, *False Start in Africa*, p. 32.
6. Lester B. Pearson, *Partners in Development*, p. 162.
7. Gustavo Romero Kolbeck, "The Plight and the Plea: A Third World View," *One Spark from Holocaust*, Elaine H. Burnell (ed.), CSDI, 1972, pp. 150–52.
8. Cf. Roy Blough and Jack N. Behrman, "Regional Integration and the Trade of Latin America," p. 49 ff.
9. Green and Seidman, Part One, Ch. 3.
10. This discussion is largely based on Lalita Prasad Singh, *The Politics of Economic Cooperation in Asia*, Ch. 14.
11. Shin Joe Kang, in collaboration with Klaus Boeck, *Economic Integration in Asia*, p. 47.
12. Green and Seidman, Part One, Ch. 3.
13. United Nations, Economic Commission for Latin America, *Annual Report*, 1971, 1:78, 79, 87.
14. Ibid., 2:72–73.
15. This position was later relaxed.
16. Harvey S. Perloff, *Alliance for Progress*, p. 154.
17. This paragraph draws heavily on Montague Yudelman's discussion of the Central American Common Market; cf. his *Agricultural Development in Latin America*, p. 219 ff.
18. United Nations, Economic Commission for Asia and the Far East, *Annual Report*, 1971, p. 48.
19. Ibid., p. 139.
20. This discussion of Asian efforts at economic integration is based on Shin Joe Kang and Klaus Boeck.
21. United Nations, Economic Commission for Africa, *Annual Report*, 1971, 1:57, 59, 102.
22. Ibid.
23. Ibid., pp. 103–4.
24. The growth and power of European and U.S. transnational corporations such as Unilever in international trade present newly emerging African countries with a serious threat. These concerns can control the African export trade in agricultural commodities but can also influence the structure of agricultural production and the terms of trade, and they may well be on the way to doing just that.
25. Gunnar Myrdal, *Economic Theory and Underdeveloped Regions*, Chs. 2 and 3.

Chapter 8

1. Elisabeth Mann Borgese, "Yugoslav Constitutional Law as a Model for World Law and the Law of the Seas," paper presented at CSDI, Oct. 13, 1972.
2. Stringfellow Barr, *Let's Join the Human Race*, p. 26.
3. Much of the factual material for the foregoing and subsequent discussions is based on Department of the Army, Engineer Agency for Resources Inventories, *Development of the Lower Mekong Basin*.
4. Ibid., p. 24.

5. Virginia Morsey Wheeler, "Co-operation for Development in the Lower Mekong Basin," *Am. J. Intern. Law*, 64(3):596, 597.
6. P. K. Menon, "Financing the Lower Mekong River Basin Development," *Pacific Affairs*, 44(4):569–79.
7. Willard A. Hanna, *The Mekong Project*, Part II: "The Evolution of the Design," 16(11):1.
8. Ibid., pp. 1–3.
9. Hanna, Part V: "The Prize at Pa Mong," pp. 3, 7; Wheeler, p. 601.
10. Hanna, Part V, p. 9.
11. Hanna, Part I, "The River and the Region," p. 9.
12. Hanna, Part III, "The Agency and the Rationale," p. 3.
13. Wheeler, p. 602.
14. Harvey Perloff, *Alliance for Progress*, p. 176.
15. This and subsequent physical data relating to the Amazon are from *Wall Street Journal*, Dec. 3, 1968, article by Bowen Northrup with a Manaus, Brazil, dateline.
16. Editorial Research Reports, *Amazon Basin Development*, Washington, D.C., 1969, 2:692.
17. This scheme was authored by Robert B. Panero of the Hudson Institute. Cf. Editorial Research Reports, *Amazon Basin Development*, pp. 695–96.
18. These and subsequent geographical details are from *Encyclopaedia Brittanica*, 1972, 6:313–23; Marvin P. Miracle, *Agriculture in the Congo Basin*, p. 3.
19. Charles E. Kellogg and Arnold C. Orvedal, "Potentially Arable Soils of the World and Critical Measures for Their Use," *Advan. Agron.*, 21:142, Fig. 8 ff.
20. Center Conference discussion; see also Kellogg and Orvedal, p. 149.
21. *World Food Problem*, 2:474.
22. Kellogg and Orvedal, p. 163.

Chapter 9

1. Cf. "Science and Technology for Development," report of Conference on Application of Science and Technology for the Benefit of the Less Developed Areas, *World of Opportunity*, United Nations, New York, 1963, 1:38.
2. Cf. Audrey Donnithorne, *China's Economic System*, Praeger, New York–Washington, 1967.
3. "Science and Technology for Development," p. 47. Also cf. Ritchie-Calder, *Two-Way Passage*, Heinemann, London, 1964, p. 149.
4. Clifford Geertz, *Agricultural Involution: The Processes of Ecological Change in Indonesia*, University of California Press, Berkeley and Los Angeles, 1963.
5. Ibid., p. 123.
6. I have used the data reported by Michel Oksenberg, *China's Developmental Experience*, Proc. Academy of Political Science (March 1973), 31(1):64.
7. United Nations, FAO, *Provisional Indicative World Plan for Agricultural Development*, 1:197; Summary and Main Conclusions, p. 3.
8. This estimate is based on LDC power equipment of .5 HP per hectare (assuming farms averaging 15–25 h.) and 40 hours of machinery use per hectare at 5 gallons of fuel per hectare. See FAO, *IWP*, 1:225–31. World oil production estimates are based on M. King Hubbert, "The Energy Resources of the Earth," *Sci. Am.* (Sept. 1971), 224(3):61–70.
9. *IWP*, Summary and Main Conclusions, Appendix Table 5.
10. Raymond L. Nace, "Water of the World," *Natural History,* 74(1):10–19, as cited by Dean F. Peterson, "Water as a Factor in Development of World Agriculture," Center Conference, p. 2.
11. "Science and Technology for Development," p. 241.
12. Ibid., pp. 225–26.
13. Ibid.
14. This discussion follows closely *World Food Problem*, Vol. 2, Ch. 7.
15. Dwight H. Perkins, *Agricultural Development in China, 1368–1968*. Aldine Publishing Company, Chicago, 1969, p. 58.

NOTES 171

16. Cf. Donnithorne, pp. 124–25, 133–35.
17. Stanislas Wasowski, *U.S. Aid for an Israeli Desalination Plant,* Institute for Defense Analysis, July 1966, p. 9.
18. Dean F. Peterson, letter of March 20, 1973, in response to inquiry.
19. John T. Maletic et al., "Desalting Saline Irrigation Water Supplies for Agriculture: A Case Study on Nuclear Desalination—Lower Colorado River Basin, U.S.A.," paper for symposium sponsored by International Atomic Energy Agency, Madrid, Spain, Nov. 18–22, 1968.
20. Joint United States–Mexico–International Atomic Energy Agency Study Team, *Nuclear Power and Water Desalting Plants for Southwest United States and Northwest Mexico: A Preliminary Assessment,* 1968.
21. Oak Ridge National Laboratory, *Nuclear Energy Centers—Industrial and Agro-Industrial Complexes, Summary Report,* July 1968, ORNL 4291.
22. Ibid., p. 27.
23. Ibid.
24. Letter to the author, Mar. 20, 1973.
25. Ibid.

BIBLIOGRAPHY

NOTE: Papers presented at the Conference on Expanding World Needs for Food and Fiber and Protection of the Ecosystem, Center for the Study of Democratic Institutions, Santa Barbara, Calif., Aug. 9–13, 1971, are cited in the references as Center Conference.

Abel, Martin E., "World Needs for Food and Fiber: Some Economic Aspects of Science Requirements, Resource Development, and the Environment," Center Conference.

Adams, Dale W., "Leadership, Education and Agricultural Development Programs in Colombia," *Inter-Am. Econ. Affairs* (Summer 1968), 22(1):87–96.

African Development Bank, *Report by the Board of Directors of the African Development Bank Covering the Period from 1st January to 31st December 1969,* Abidjan, 1970.

Ahmed, Iftikhar, and John F. Timmons, "Current Land Reforms in East Pakistan," *Land Econ.* (Feb. 1971), 47(1):55–64.

Appleby, Paul H., *Public Administration in India: Report of a Survey,* Government of India, Cabinet Secretariat, Organization and Methods Division, New Delhi, 1957.

Asher, Robert E., et al., *Development of the Emerging Countries: An Agenda for Research,* Brookings Institution, Washington, D.C., 1962.

Asian Development Bank, *Annual Report for 1970,* Manila, 1971.

Bansil, P. C., *Agricultural Statistics in India,* Dhanpat Rai & Sons, Jullundur-Delhi, 1970.

Barnes, J. M., *Toxic Hazards of Certain Pesticides to Man,* World Health Organization, Monograph Ser. No. 16, Geneva, 1953.

Barr, Stringfellow, *Let's Join the Human Race,* University of Chicago Press, Chicago, 1950.

Bhagwati, Jagdish N., *Amount and Sharing of Aid,* Monograph No. 2, Overseas Development Council, Washington, D.C., 1970.

———, *The Economics of Underdeveloped Countries,* McGraw-Hill, New York, 1966.

Bhagwati, Jagdish N., Ronald W. Jones, Robert A. Mundell, and Jaroslav

Varek (eds.), *Trade, Balance of Payments and Growth,* North-Holland Publishing Company, Amsterdam, 1971.
Blough, Roy, and Jack N. Behrman, "Regional Integration and the Trade of Latin America: Problems of Regional Integration in Latin America," CED Suppl. Paper No. 22, Committee for Economic Development, New York, Jan. 1968.
"A Blueprint for Survival," *The Ecologist* (Jan. 1972), 2(1).
Borgese, Elisabeth Mann, "The Ocean Regime," background paper for Center Conference.
Boulding, Kenneth, *Economics as a Science,* McGraw-Hill, New York, 1970.
———, "Fun and Games with the Gross National Product—The Role of Misleading Indicators in Social Policy," in Helfrich, Harold W., Jr. (ed.), *The Environmental Crisis,* Yale University Press, New Haven, 1970, pp. 157–70.
Bredo, William, "Agrarian Reform in Vietnam: Vietcong and Government of Vietnam Strategies in Conflict," *Asian Survey* (Aug. 1970), 10(8):738–50.
Brown, Lester R., *Seeds of Change: The Green Revolution and Development in the 1970's,* Overseas Development Council, Praeger, New York, 1970.
———, "Human Food Production as a Process in the Biosphere," Center Conference and *Sci. Am.* (Sept. 1970), 223(3):160–70.
———, "The Agricultural Revolution in Asia," *Foreign Affairs* (July 1968), 46(4):688–98.
———, "The Social Impact of the Green Revolution," *International Conciliation,* No. 581 (Jan. 1971).
Burnell, Elaine H. (ed.), *One Spark from Holocaust: The Crisis in Latin America,* Interbook Incorporated, New York, 1972.
Ciriacy-Wantrup, S. V., "The Economics of Environmental Policy," *Land Econ.* (Feb. 1971), 47(1):36–45.
Dantwala, M. L., "From Stagnation to Growth," *Indian Econ. J.* (Oct.–Dec. 1970), 18(2):165–92.
Department of the Army, Engineer Agency for Resources Inventories, *Development of the Lower Mekong Basin: A Report to the Chief of Engineers,* Mar. 1970.
Department of Technical Co-operation, "Technical Co-operation under the Colombo Plan: Report for 1962–63 of the Council for Technical Co-operation in South and South-East Asia, Colombo, October 1963," Her Majesty's Stationery Office, London, 1963.
Dorner, Peter, "Needed Redirections in Economic Analysis for Agricultural Development Policy," *Am. J. Agr. Econ.* (Feb. 1971), 53(1):8–16.
Dorner, Peter, and Juan Carlos Collarte, "Land Reform in Chile: Proposal for an Institutional Innovation," *Inter-Am. Econ. Affairs* (Summer 1965), 19(1):3–22.
Dumont, Rene, *False Start in Africa,* Praeger, New York, 1966. (Translated from French by Phyllis Nauts Ott.)
Ehrlich, Dr. Paul R., *The Population Bomb,* Sierra Club/Ballantine, New York, 1968.

Fadiman, Clifton, and Jean White (eds.), *Ecocide—And Thoughts Toward Survival*, CSDI, Interbook, Inc., New York, 1970.
Foland, Frances M., "Agrarian Reform in Latin America," *Foreign Affairs* (Oct. 1969), pp. 97–112.
Frankel, Francine R., *India's Green Revolution: Economic Gains and Political Costs*, Princeton University Press, Princeton, 1971.
Frankel, S. Herbert, *The Economic Impact on Underdeveloped Societies*, Harvard University Press, Cambridge, 1955.
Garst, Jonathan, "Chemicals for Conservation," Center Conference.
———, *No Need for Hunger*, Random House, New York, 1963.
Ginsburg, Norton, "Regional and Urban Planning for National Development and Environmental Conservation," paper prepared for Seminar on Development Planning and the Environment, cosponsored by National Academy of Sciences and Central American Institute for Industry and Technology, Antigua, Guatemala, July 25–30, 1971.
Gitelson, Susan Aurelia, "Multilateral Aid for National Development and Self-Reliance: A Case Study of the UNDP in Uganda and Tanzania," Ph.D. thesis, Columbia Univ., New York, 1970.
Glade, William P., *The Latin American Economies: A Study of Their Institutional Evolution*, Van Nostrand, New York, 1969.
Gray, Clive S., *Resource Flows to Less Developed Countries: Financial Terms and Their Constraints*, Praeger, New York, 1969.
Green, Reginald H., and Ann Seidman, *Unity or Poverty? The Economics of Pan-Africanism*, Penguin African Library, Baltimore, 1968.
Green, Reginald H., and K. G. V. Krishna, *Economic Cooperation in Africa: Retrospect and Prospect*, Oxford University Press, Nairobi, 1967.
Haas, Ernst B., and Philippe C. Schmitter, *The Politics of Economics in Latin American Regionalism: The Latin American Free Trade Association After Four Years of Operation*, University of Denver, 1965.
Hanna, Willard A., *The Mekong Project*, American Universities Field Staff Reports, Southeast Asia Series, Vol. 16, Nos. 10–14, New York, 1968.
   Part I: The River and the Region
   Part II: The Evolution of the Design
   Part III: The Agency and the Rationale
   Part IV: The Test at Nam Ngum
   Part V: The Prize at Pa Mong
Harrar, J. George, "The Green Revolution in Perspective," *President's Review and Annual Report*, Rockefeller Foundation, New York, 1970.
Hayami, Yujiro, and Vernon W. Ruttan, *Agricultural Development: An International Perspective*, Johns Hopkins Press, Baltimore, 1971.
Hazlewood, Arthur (ed.), *African Integration and Disintegration: Case Studies in Economic and Political Union*, Oxford University Press, London, 1967.
Heady, Earl O., "Alternatives in Environmental Control through Agriculture, Comparative Trade-offs in Developed Countries," Center Conference.
Hewes, Laurence I., Jr., *Japan—Land and Men: An Account of the Japanese Land Reform Program 1945–51*, Iowa State College Press, Ames, 1955.

Hewes, Laurence I., Jr., "Administrative and Political Aspects of the Impact of Science and Technology in Agrarian Societies," Center Conference.
Hillman, Jimmye S., "Increasing Agricultural Productivity vs. Environmental Protection in Developing Countries: Analyses of Alternatives," Center Conference.
Hirschman, Albert O., *Development Projects Observed*, Brookings Institution, Washington, D.C., 1967.
Holdren, John P., and Paul R. Ehrlich (eds.), *Global Ecology: Readings Toward a Rational Strategy for Man*, Harcourt Brace Jovanovich, Inc., New York, 1971.
Inter-American Development Bank, *Agricultural Development in Latin America: The Next Decade*, Washington, D.C., April 1967.
———, *Eleventh Annual Report, 1970*, Washington, D.C., 1971.
International Bank for Reconstruction and Development, International Development Association, *Annual Report 1971*, Washington, D.C., 1971.
Johnson, D. Gale, "International Trade and Other Economic Relations Affecting the World Food Supply," Center Conference.
Johnson, E. A. J., *The Organization of Space in Developing Countries*, Harvard University Press, Cambridge, 1970.
Kang, Shin Joe, in collaboration with Klaus Boeck, *Economic Integration in Asia*, Hamburg Institute for International Economics, Hamburg, 1969.
Katz, M., *Measurement of Air Pollutants: Guide to the Selection of Methods*, World Health Organization, Geneva, 1969.
Kellogg, Charles E., and Arnold C. Orvedal, "Potentially Arable Soils of the World and Critical Measures for Their Use," Center Conference and *Advan. Agron.* (1969), 21:109–70.
Khusro, A. M. (ed.), *Readings in Agricultural Development*, Allied Publishers, Bombay, 1968.
King, John A., Jr., *Economic Development Projects and Their Appraisal: Cases and Principles from the Experience of the World Bank*, Economic Development Institute, International Bank for Reconstruction and Development, Johns Hopkins Press, Baltimore, 1967.
Koenig, Herman E., William E. Cooper, and James M. Falvey, "Industrialized Ecosystem Design and Management" (Mimeo.), Michigan State University, 1971.
Ladejinsky, Wolf, "Ironies of India's Green Revolution," *Foreign Affairs* (July 1970), 48(4):758–68.
Lewis, John P., *Quiet Crisis in India*, Brookings Institution, Washington, D.C., 1962.
Lipset, Seymour Martin, and Aldo Solari, *Elites in Latin America*, Oxford University Press, New York, 1967.
Maass, Arthur, *Muddy Waters: The Army Engineers and the Nation's Rivers*, Harvard University Press, Cambridge, 1951.
Man and the Ecosphere: Readings from Scientific American, W. H. Freeman & Co., San Francisco, 1971.
Man's Impact on the Global Environment, reprint issued by the Library of Congress, Congressional Research Service, Mar. 25, 1971, by permission of MIT Press, Cambridge, copyright 1970.
Maritano, Nino, *A Latin American Economic Community: History, Policies, and Problems*, University of Notre Dame Press, Notre Dame, 1970.

Mathis, F. John, *Economic Integration in Latin America: The Progress and Problems of LAFTA,* Bureau of Business Research, University of Texas, Austin, 1969.

McCaull, Julian, "Conference on the Ecological Aspects of International Development," UNESCO, *Nature and Resources* (June 1969), 5(2):5–12.

McKinley, Charles, *Uncle Sam in the Pacific Northwest,* University of California Press, Berkeley, 1942.

Menon, P. K., "Financing the Lower Mekong River Basin Development," *Pacific Affairs* (Winter 1971–72), 44(4):566–79.

Menz, John A., "Some Aspects of Land-Use Planning in Peasant Cultures," *Land Econ.* (Feb. 1971), 47(1):46–54.

Miracle, Marvin P., *Agriculture in the Congo Basin: Tradition and Change in African Rural Economies,* University of Wisconsin Press, Madison, 1967.

Mrak, Emil M., "Pesticides, Herbicides, and the Contamination of the Ecosystem (Including Contamination from Other than Agricultural Sources)," Center Conference.

Mudd, Stuart (ed.), *The Population Crisis and the Use of World Resources,* Indiana University Press, Bloomington, 1964.

Myrdal, Gunnar, *Asian Drama,* 3 vols., Pantheon, New York, 1968.

———, *Economic Theory and Underdeveloped Regions,* Gerald Duckworth & Co., Ltd., London, 1957.

National Science Foundation, National Science Board, *Environmental Science: Challenge for the Seventies,* GPO, Washington, D.C., 1971.

Odum, Howard T., "Energetics of World Food Production," *The World Food Problem: Report of the President's Science Advisory Committee,* 3:55–94, GPO, Washington, D.C., 1967.

Organization for Economic Co-operation and Development, *Activities of OECD in 1970, Report by the Secretary General,* Paris, 1971.

———, *Aid to Agriculture in Developing Countries,* Paris, 1968.

Organization of American States, *Report of the Secretary General, July 1969–December 1970,* Washington, D.C., 1971.

Organization of American States, General Secretariat, *Physical Resource Investigations for Economic Development: A Casebook of OAS Field Experience in Latin America,* Washington, D.C., 1969.

———, *Survey of the Natural Resources of the Dominican Republic,* Washington, D.C., 1969.

Pacific Northwest River Basins Commission, Urban and Rural Related Lands Committee, *Ecology and the Economy: A Concept for Balancing Long-Range Goals: The Pacific Northwest Example* (discussion draft), Vancouver, Washington, 1972.

Pearson, Lester B. (chairman), *Partners in Development: Report of the Commission on International Development,* Praeger, New York, 1969.

Peeler, John A., "Foreign Aid, Influence, and Tax Administration in Peru," *Inter-Am. Econ. Affairs* (Spring 1969), 22(4):19–30.

Perloff, Harvey S., *Alliance for Progress: A Social Invention in the Making,* Resources for the Future, Johns Hopkins Press, Baltimore, 1969.

Peterson, Dean F., "Water as a Factor in Development of World Agriculture," Center Conference.

Phillips, Hiram S., *Guide for Development: Institution-Building and Reform,* Praeger, New York, 1969.
Planning and Development Collaborative International, *Report on Technical Assistance Requirements for Integrated Rural Development in Tanzania: A Report to the Administrator of the United Nations Development Programme in New York,* Washington, D.C., Dec. 1970.
Please, Stanley, "Capital Flows and Income Transfers within and between Nations to Sustain the Agricultural Revolution," *Agricultural Development,* Proceedings of a Conference Sponsored by the Rockefeller Foundation Apr. 23–25, 1969, at Villa Serbelloni, Bellagio, Italy, Rockefeller Foundation, New York, 1969.
Prosterman, Roy L., "Land Reform in Vietnam," *Focus* (Jan. 1972), 22(5):1–7.
———, "Land-to-the-Tiller in South Vietnam: The Tables Turn," *Asian Survey* (Aug. 1970), 10(8):751–64.
Ritchie-Calder, The Right Honorable Lord, "Famine at the Feast," Center Conference.
Robock, Stefan H., *Brazil's Developing Northeast: A Study of Regional Planning and Foreign Aid,* Brookings Institution, Washington, D.C., 1963.
Rockefeller Foundation, *Agricultural Development,* Proceedings of a Conference Sponsored by the Rockefeller Foundation Apr. 23–25, 1969, at Villa Serbelloni, Bellagio, Italy, New York, 1969.
Sauchelli, Vincent (ed.), *Fertilizer Nitrogen, Its Chemistry and Technology,* Reinhold Publishing Corp., New York, 1964.
Schultz, T. W., *Economic Growth and Agriculture,* McGraw-Hill, New York, 1968, pp. 36–41.
———, "Food, Population and the Ecosystem," Center Conference.
———, "The Food Supply—Population Growth Quandary," background paper for Center Conference.
———, "Reflections on the Economics of Fertilizers," Center Conference.
Singh, Lalita Prasad, *The Politics of Economic Cooperation in Asia: A Study of Asian International Organizations,* University of Missouri Press, Columbia, 1966.
Sprague, G. F., "World Research Needs for Increasing Corn Production," *Agr. Eng.* (Feb. 1970), 51(2):71, 90, 91, 108.
Sprout, Harold and Margaret, *The Ecological Perspective on Human Affairs: With Special Reference to International Politics,* Princeton University Press, Princeton, 1965.
Staub, William J., and Melvin G. Blase, "Genetic Technology and Agricultural Development," *Science* (July 1971), 173(3992):119–23.
Stout, Perry R., "Agricultural Requirements for Nitrogen Fertilizers in the U.S.A.," background paper for Center Conference.
———, "Fertilizers, Food Production and Environmental Compromise," Center Conference.
Straw, H. Thompson, review of Allan Wood, *The Groundnut Affair* (Bodley Head, London, 1950), *Geograph. Rev.* (Oct. 1951), 41(4):676–77.
Task Force on International Development, *U.S. Foreign Assistance in the 1970's: A New Approach,* Report to the President from the Task Force on International Development, Mar. 4, 1970, GPO, Washington, D.C., 1970.

United Nations Conference on Trade and Development, "Report of the Trade and Development Board: 24 September, 1969–13 October, 1970," General Assembly, Official Records, 25th Session, Suppl. No. 15 (A/8015/Rev.1), New York, 1971.

United Nations Development Programme, *A Study of the Capacity of the United Nations Development System,* Vols. I and II combined, Geneva, 1969.

———, "Financial Report and Accounts for the Year Ended 31 December, 1969, and Report of the Board of Auditors," General Assembly, Official Records, 25th Session, Suppl. No. 7A (A/8007/Add.1), New York, 1970.

———, "Report of the Governing Council," 11th Session (14 Jan.–2 Feb., 1971), Economic and Social Council, Official Records, 51st Session, Suppl. No. 6, New York, 1971.

———, "Report of the Governing Council," 12th Session (7–23 June, 1971), Economic and Social Council, Official Records, 51st Session, Suppl. No. 6A, New York, 1971.

United Nations, Economic Commission for Africa, *Annual Report* (15 Feb., 1970–13 Feb., 1971), Vols. I and II, Economic and Social Council, Official Records, 51st Session, Suppl. No. 5, New York, 1971.

United Nations, Economic Commission for Asia and the Far East, *Annual Report* (1 May, 1968–28 Apr., 1969), Economic and Social Council, Official Records, 47th Session, Suppl. No. 2, New York, 1969.

———, *Annual Report* (28 Apr., 1970–30 Apr., 1971), Economic and Social Council, Official Records, 51st Session, Suppl. No. 2, New York, 1971.

———, *Regional Economic Co-operation in Asia and the Far East: The Second Ministerial Conference on Asian Economic Co-operation and the Asian Development Bank,* Regional Economic Co-operation Ser. No. 4, New York, 1966.

United Nations, Economic Commission for Latin America, *Annual Report* (8 May, 1970–8 May, 1971), Vols. I and II, Economic and Social Council, Official Records, 51st Session, Suppls. No. 4 and 4A, New York, 1971.

———, *Development Problems in Latin America,* Institute of Latin American Studies, University of Texas Press, Austin, 1970.

United Nations, FAO, *Production Yearbook, 1969,* Vol. 23, Rome, 1970.

———, *Provisional Indicative World Plan for Agricultural Development: A Synthesis and Analysis of Factors Relevant to World, Regional and National Agricultural Development,* Vols. I and II, Rome, 1970.

———, *Report of the Fifteenth Session of the Conference,* 8–27 Nov., 1969, Rome, 1969.

———, *The Selective Expansion of Agricultural Production in Latin America,* New York, 1957.

———, *The State of Food and Agriculture 1970,* Rome, 1970.

———, *World Agriculture: The Last Quarter-Century,* Rome, 1970.

United Nations, General Assembly, "An International Development Strategy for the Second United Nations Development Decade (Resolution 2626 [XXV])," *U.N. Monthly Chronicle* (Nov. 1970), 7(10):105–20.

U.S., AID, *The Foreign Assistance Program: Annual Report to the Congress, Fiscal Year 1970,* GPO, Washington, D.C., 1971.

U.S. Department of Agriculture, ERS, *Economic Progress of Agriculture in*

Developing Nations 1950–68, Foreign Agricultural Economic Rept. No. 59, Washington, D.C., 1970.

U.S. Department of Health, Education and Welfare, *Report of the Secretary's Commission on Pesticides and Their Relationship to Environmental Health,* Parts I and II, GPO, Washington, D.C., Dec. 1969.

Volkner, H. E., *Social Factors in Reservoir-Settlements, Relocation and Costing Factors: An Adaptation of Scaleogram Analysis Using Aerial Photography and Ground Survey Data, Applied to the Mekong Basin Pa Mong Dam Project,* Prepared for AID, Department of State and Mekong Committee, 1972.

Wharton, Clifton R., Jr., "The Green Revolution: Cornucopia or Pandora's Box?" *Foreign Affairs* (Apr. 1969), 47(3):464–76.

Wheeler, Virginia Morsey, "Co-operation for Development in the Lower Mekong Basin," *Am. J. Intern. Law* (July 1970), 64(3):594–609.

World Food Problem: A Report of the President's Science Advisory Committee, GPO, Washington, D.C., 1967, Vols. I, II, and III.

Worsnop, Richard L., "Amazon Basin Development," *Editorial Research Reports* (Sept. 17, 1969), 2(11):689–708.

Yudelman, Montague, with Frederic Howard, *Agricultural Development and Economic Integration in Latin America,* George Allen and Unwin, Ltd., London, 1970.

INDEX

Afghanistan, Helmund Valley development, 11
Africa
  balkanization, 124–25
  ECA, 124–27, 143
  intracontinental trade, 124–25
  land reform, 76–77
  Organization of African Unity, 127, 143
  regional economic integration, xxvii–xxviii, 124–27
  rule by elites, 58–59
  subregional trade integration, 126
  trade reorientation, 118
African Development Bank, 125, 126
AID. *See* USAID
Albienne Nappe, 153
Alliance for Progress, 120, 121, 122, 127
Amazon Basin, development of, 138–41
  Kennedy, Senator Robert F., 140
  Lippmann, Walter, 140
American Farm Bureau Federation, 97
Army Corps of Engineers, 19
ASEAN (Association of Southeast Asia Nations), 124
Asia
  land reform, 122
  regional economic integration, xxvii–xxviii, 122–24, 127
  regional trade obstacles, 118–19
  regional trade schemes, 123–24
  rules by elites, 58–59
Asian Development Bank, 123, 127
ASPAC (Asian and Pacific Council), 124
Assistance, overseas, xxiii–xxv
  accomplishments, 95–100
  as business transactions, LDCs, 101–2
  donor agency practices, 102
  donors' perspectives, 96–97
  donor targets, 97
  LDC administrative burden, 103
  and LDC fuel supplies, 151
  and LDC rural unemployment, 106–7
  and LDC trade, xxv–xxvii, 110–12
  review of programs, xxiv
  "soft" loans, xxiv, 103
Aswan Dam, 64, 94

Bakhra Dam, 153
Banks, regional, xxv, xxvi, 127
  African Development Bank, 125, 126
  Asian Development Bank, 123, 127
  Inter-American Development Bank, 120
Brazil, SUDENE program, 63, 63 n
British Commonwealth Colombo Plan, 123, 127

CACM (Central American Common Market), 120, 122
CARIFTA (Caribbean Free Trade Association), 120
CENTO (Central Treaty Organization of the Middle East), 123
Charter of Altagrácias, 116–17
China, People's Republic of
  aid to LDCs, 96
  and energy, 146, 149–50, 156
  Mao Tse-tung, 77
  rural communal system, 77, 146, 149–50
  rural services sector, 149
  urban-industrial sector, 149
Colombia, 75–76
Congo Basin, development of, 141–43

DDT, 22, 30
Development, agricultural. *See* LDCs, agricultural development
Development, rural
  central regulated markets, 87–89
  change, xxv, 35
  enlarge rural system, 50–51
  and government, xxiii

181

Development, rural *(continued)*
  and implementation, 72–75
  and inequities, xii
  integrated regional approach, 89–91
  interaction of problems, 37
  and international trade, 110–12
  junior-grade ministry, xxi, 65, 72–73, 75
  obstacles, man-made, xii–xiii, xx, xxv
  and planning, 71–72
  production transcends village, 89
  quality of personnel attracted, 68–69
  and rural-urban continuum, 86–87
  significance, 58–59
  traditional planning, 86–87
  and unemployment, 89, 107
  and urban-industrial sector, 63–64
  and urbanization, 92–93
Diet, deficiency in LDCs, 3–4, 41–42
Diversification, agrarian, 112

East Caribbean Common Market, 120
ECA (Economic Commission for Africa), 124–27, 143
ECAFE (Economic Commission for Asia and Far East), 120
  and Asian regional integration, 122–23
    Lower Mekong studies (1952, 1957), 134
ECLA (Economic Commission for Latin America), 120–22
Ecosystem
  protection costs to LDCs, 55
  and wastes, 7
  and water, 19
Energy
  cost of desalting water, 157, 158, 159, 160, 161, 162
  fossil fuels, 150–51, 162–64
  future world prospects, 150, 162–64
  and LDC agriculture, 144–45, 150–51
  LDCs and conventional energy systems, 146–47
  and Mekong project, 137
  present situation and Third World, 162–63
  and rice production, 156–57
  small-scale efficiency, 147–48
  solar, 8, 151
  and water management, 154
Energy, nuclear
  hypothetical desalting plant, Mexico, 159
  lower Colorado River Basin desalting plant, 158
  Oak Ridge National Laboratory studies, 159–62

Environment
  cost of expanding production, xiv, xvi
  "closed" to "open" system, 55–56
  effects of Green Revolution, xvii–xviii, 32–33
  and food and fiber needs, xi
  interacting components in, xvi–xvii
  junior-grade ministry, xxi, 65
  quality of personnel attracted, 68–69
  and "social property," 130, 132
  and technology, xvii, 54–56
Ethiopia
  and foreign assistance/investment, 77
  land reform, 76, 77
  population distribution, 36
  second Five-Year Plan, 73
  Selassie, Haile, 76
European Common Market, xxvi, 46, 112

FAO (UN Food and Agriculture Organization), 34, 68, 94
FAO Indicative World Plan. *See* IWP
Farming
  development of technology, 22–23
  institutional reforms, 52
  interaction of factors, 3, 9–10, 14–15
  junior-grade ministry, xxi, xxii, 65
  quality of personnel attracted, 68–69
  and soils, 8
  system of, 28
Fertilizers
  chemical, improved, 23
  "miracle" seed response to, 27–28
  and pollution, 29
  and water and high-yielding grains, 45
Food
  carrying capacity, limit of system, 6–7
  critical problem of Third World, xi, 3–6
  price policies, environmental costs, 56–57
  supplies, xx, 4–5
  world problem, 4–5, 24–25, 164
France, 96

Gap between rich and poor, xix, 40, 129
  and ecosystem protection, 55
  exploitation of, 48–49
  and government policy, 108
  and land reform, 52
  LDCs and energy, 144
  and rural unemployment, 107–8
Gaps between rich and poor countries, xii, xiii, 4, 118

INDEX

GATT (General Agreement on Tariffs and Trade), 112
   and LDC export trade, 128
   and trade concessions, 116
GDP. *See* LDCs
Germany, Federal Republic of, 96
GNP. *See* LDCs
Government services, inappropriate separation of, xxi–xxii, 19, 67–68
Grain, high-yielding varieties
   development of, 25–27
   impact on rural system, xix–xx, 26
   and U.S. foundations, 94
   variation of growing conditions, 15–16
Green Revolution
   economic and social impact, xviii–xix, 24, 26–27, 48–50, 111
   and economic equilibrium, 45–46, 51
   environmental effects, 45–46, 51
   financial cost to LDC farmers, 25
   genetic innovation, 27, 45
   and institutional change, 26, 51, 52
   irreversible change, xvii, 57
   and irrigation, 47
   and land tenure system, 49
   long-range effects, 27, 47, 57
   model of production-increasing technique, 47
   short-range effects, xx, 27, 45
   technological impact, xvii–xviii, 23, 26, 52
   timing, 65

Hydrology, 152

ILO (UN International Labor Organization), 68, 96
India
   agricultural policy, 78
   Congress Party, 78, 80
   Gandhi, Indira, 78, 81
   gap between rich and poor, 35, 50
   and Green Revolution, 45, 49–50, 80
   integrated regional trade, 119
   land reform, 78–81
   New Congress Party, 81
   population distribution, 36
   public regulated markets, 88
   third Five-Year Plan, 71
Indus Basin, xvii, xxviii, 17, 18, 45, 64
Infrastructure
   inadequate in LDCs, 47, 85
   lack, Africa, 125
   lack, LDC critical impediment, 88
   missing, LDC potential markets, 117
   regulated markets, 88–89
Innovation
   consequences of, 53–54
   in farming and land reform, 52
   planning and management, 53
   profit motivation, 44
   socioeconomic reform, 149–50
Institutions, development-fostering and -inhibiting, 92
Interactions
   and new farm technology, 44, 154
   principle of, 9–10, 14
Inter-American Development Bank, 120
International Maize and Wheat Improvement Center, 27
International Rice Research Institute, 26, 27, 156
International Tea and Coffee Agreements, 116
Iron Curtain countries, 96
Irrigation
   and chemical fertilizers, arid regions, 13
   development planning, 14–19
   drainage problems, 17, 56
   and engineering technology, xxii, 10–11
   and Mekong project, 137
   and new technology, 153–54
   principle of interactions, 14–15
   pumped groundwater, 16–17, 18–19, 47, 153–54
   and salinity, 17–18, 56, 64
Israel
   desalted water, costs, 157
   energy resources, costs, 157–58
   rural light-industry centers, 89
IWP (FAO Indicative World Plan)
   energy needs, LDCs, 150–51
   food projections and needs, xv–xvi, 24–25
   irrigation and farming, 14

Jackson, Sir Robert, Jackson report, xxiv
Japan
   contributor to LDCs, 96
   land reform, 104
   and LDC grain exports, 46
   population distribution, 36
Japanese Land Reform Program, 70
Java, "agricultural involution," 149

LAFTA (Latin American Free Trade Association), 120, 122
Lake Nasser, 64
Land reform, 75–77
   Africa, 76–77
   Asia, 122
   Ethiopia, 76, 77
   failure to try, xxiii

Land reform *(continued)*
  India, 78–81
  Latin America, 75
  necessity of, 52, 104
  and regional banks, xxv
  successful, xxv, 104
  and USAID, 104
  Venezuela, 75
  and Viet Cong, 105
Land tenure, inequitable
  development-inhibiting, 92
  Freeman, Orville, 105
  Latin America, 75, 104
  LDCs, xix, 40, 49
  and political leadership, 63–64
  South Vietnam, 104–6
    Freeman, Orville, 105
    MacArthur, General Douglas, 106
    McGovern, Senator George, 106
    Thieu, President Nguyen Van, 106
Latin America
  ECLA, 120–22
  and Green Revolution, 50
  land reform, 75
  regional economic integration, xxvii–xxviii, 121
  regional trade development, 120–22
  rural political power, lack, 58–59
Latin American Institute for Economic and Social Planning, 120
LDCs
  agricultural development
    and energy, 144–45, 150–51, 162–63
    grant funds, 100
    inadequacies, 42
    models, 146–47
    output, 83–84
    principal overseas contributors, 97–98
    self-financed, 95
  agriculture
    and exports, 34
    increase production of, xv–xvi
    inferior official rank, xxi–xxii, 65
    percentages engaged in, 34
    potentially arable land, xiv, 12, 154
  agro-rural systems, 34–37
  demands, xiv
  development assistance, 97–98, 99
    effective, 102
    and foreign trade, xxv–xxvii, 113, 114
    and human energy, 37–38
  dietary deficiency, 3–4, 41–42
  economic needs, 46
  exports
    agricultural, xxvi, 46, 127
    barriers, European Common Market, xxvi, 46, 111–12
    markets, price shifts, 119
  farmers, xiii, xviii–xix, 39
  farming
    and new technology, 50
    subsistence to commercial, 38–39, 83
  GDP (Gross Domestic Product), 34, 40
  GNP (Gross National Product), 83, 107
  governments
    central political power, 60–61
    leadership, political, xxii, 63–65
    participation, political, 61–62
    and rural people, 60
    services, inappropriate separation of, xxi–xxii, 19, 67–68
    structure, 59
  population, xii, xiii, 3, 40–41
  rurality, 34, 82–84
    complex system, xviii–xix
    variety, 35–37
Lower Mekong Basin, development of, xxviii, 133–38

Markets
  central regulated, 87
  government regulation of, 88, 110
  price shifts, LDC exports, 119
  public regulated, infrastructure, 88–89
  and rural unemployment, 109–10
Mekong Basin, development cost, 47
Mekong Committee, 134, 135, 137
Ministries, junior-grade, 65
  staff, 66, 68–69
Multiple-cropping
  Green Revolution, 47
  irrigation, 13
  in modern farming, 32
  and rice, 155
  solar energy, 151

Nile Valley (lower), 36
Nitrogen, 20–21
Northern Colorado Water Conservancy District, 132–33

Oak Ridge National Laboratory studies, 159–62
OAS (Organization of American States)
  regional economic integration, 127
  regional trade, 120–21
OECD (Organization for Economic Co-operation and Development), 71, 72, 127
OPEC (Organization of Petroleum Exporting Countries), 150, 160
Organization of African Unity, 127, 143

INDEX

Pakistan
  Green Revolution, 27, 45
  pumped groundwater irrigation, 18–19
Pa Mong project, 136–37
Participation
  constraints in development, 42–43
  denied to rural unemployed, 107
  institutions lacking, 69
Pearson, Lester, Pearson report, xxiv, 103
Pesticides and herbicides, 23, 30–31, 56
Peterson, Rudolph, Peterson report, xxiv
Population/land resource ratios, 154–55
Production
  agricultural, xii, 24–25
  and ecosystem, 5–6
  profit incentive, 45
  and resources and unemployment, 108
Puerto Rico, 89

Reform
  of inequities, 103–4
  institutional, 52
  land. *See* Land reform
  and traditional rural system, xx
Regions
  development
    authorities, 131–32
    delineation of valid regions, 90–91
    integrated, 133
    and larger perspective, 90
    rural, xxi
    strategy, 91
    and subregional interests, 90
    traditional approach, 84–87
  planning and population control, 117
Regions, economic integration of, xi, xxvii–xxviii, 116, 127–29
  and environmental protection, 117
  government policy for agriculture, 129
  and land reform, 129
  obstacles, xxvii–xxviii
Research
  importance, 31–32
  inadequate in LDCs, 42
  public-supported, 50
  rice, 43–44
  wheat, 26
Resources
  allocation and rural development, 71
  natural
    administration of, 65
    administration personnel, 68–69
    development of regions, 130–33
    junior-grade ministry, xxi, xxii, 65
    management of, xi
Rice, 27, 43, 155–57
Rockefeller Foundation, 27, 45

Rural-urban continuum
  and development strategy, 92
  integrated rural development, 82, 84
  rural development planning, 86–87
  urbanization of rurality, xxi, 84

SEATO (Southeast Asia Treaty Organization), 123
"Social property," 130–32
Soils, 8–12
South Korea, xxv, 104
South Vietnam, 104–6
Soviet Union, 64, 94, 146
Stanford Research Institute, 106

Taiwan, xxv, 104
Tanganyika, groundnut fiasco, 11
Tanzania
  distribution of population, 36
  first Five-Year Plan, 74
  and land reform, 77–78
  Nyerere, Julius, 77, 78
  regional economic integration, xxvii
  TANU, 77, 77 n
  Ujamaa village principle, 77–78
Technology
  change and sociopolitical systems, 57
  consequences in United States, 56
  and environmental repercussions, 54–57
  impact on rural system, 43
  move from "closed" to "open" system, 55–56
  new genetics, 25–27
  and pollution, 29
  and population problem, 149
  problems in rural areas, 145–46
  and pumped water irrigation, 153–54
Third World
  definition, xi
  human conditions of, xii–xiii, xviii–xix, xx, 41–42, 54, 83, 106–7
Tocqueville, Alexis de, 61–62
  pattern, 70
Trade
  African intracontinental, 124–25
  ASA, 123
  Asian regional, 118
  assistance, LDCs, 110–12
  Charter of Altagrácias, 116–17
  competition between LDCs, 115
  concessions, xxvi–xxvii, 115–17
  and European Common Market countries, xxvi, 46, 112
  integrated regional, 115, 116
  Latin American regional, 120–22
  and LDC economy, xxv–xxvii, 113–15
  and LDC exports, 111–12
  LDCs and GATT, 128

Trade *(continued)*
  LDCs, new requirements, 114
  MAPHLINDO, 123
  regional units, nationalism, 117–18
  reorientation, obstacles, 117–19
  World Bank, xxvi, 112, 127

UNCTAD (UN Conference on Trade and Development), 112, 116, 128
UN Development Programme, xxiv, 100–101, 120
UN Office of Legal Affairs, 135
USAID (United States Agency for International Development), 94
  amounts reflect orientation, 97
  assistance to LDCs, 96
  criticisms of, 103
  and land reform, 104
  largest binational development agency, 98
  and long-range assistance, India, 71
  and OAS, 120
  and rural development, xxiv
U.S. Bureau of Reclamation, 19, 134
Ujamaa village principle, 77–78
Unemployment, 41, 89, 106–10
Urbanization of rurality
  integrated rural development, xxi, 84
  and rural unemployment, 110

Water
  and agriculture, 152
  and chemical fertilizers, 45
  and electricity and agriculture, 157–62
  and energy, 152–53
  and farming, 12
  groundwater
    aquifers, 153–54
    pumped for irrigation, 16–17, 18–19, 47, 153–54
  tube wells, 45
  and rice, 155–57
Water, control
  for agricultural purposes, 152
  drainage, 13–14
  and farming, 13–14
Water, desalting
  Colorado River Basin plant, 158
  costs, 157, 158, 159, 160, 161, 162
  energy requirements, 157
  hypothetical Mexico plant, 159
  and nuclear energy, 157, 158, 159, 160, 161, 162
  Oak Ridge National Laboratory studies, 159–62
  proposals for agriculture, 157
  technology requirement, 160
Water, development, 19–20
  and environment, 54–55
Wheeler Mission, 134, 141
White Mission, 135, 141
World Bank, 120
  assistance to LDCs, 96
  and land tenure, xxv
  and regional banks, xxvi
  and regional economic integration, 127
  river basin development, 94
  and rural development, xxiii-xxiv
  and trade, 112
World Development Authority, 131

Yugoslavia, 89

Zaire, 141, 143
Zamindar, system, 79